Modern European History

A Garland Series of Outstanding Dissertations

General Editor
William H. McNeill
University of Chicago

Associate Editors

Eastern Europe
Charles Jelavich
Indiana University

Great Britain
Peter Stansky
Stanford University

France
David H. Pinkney
University of Washington

Russia
Barbara Jelavich
Indiana University

Germany
Enno E. Kraehe
University of Virginia

MODERN EUROPEAN HISTORY

Millenarian Bolshevism, 1900 to 1920

David G. Rowley

Garland Publishing, Inc.
New York and London 1987

Library of Congress Cataloging-in-Publication Data

Rowley, David G., 1949–
    Millenarian bolshevism, 1900 to 1920.

    (Modern European history)
    Thesis (Ph.D.)—University of Michigan, 1982.
    Bibliography: p.
    1. Communism—Soviet Union—History—20th
century.   2. Philosophy, Marxist—Soviet Union—
History—20th century.   3. Communism and re-
ligion—History—20th century.   4. Millennialism—
Soviet Union—History—20th century.   I. Title.
II. Series.
HX313.R59 1987   335.43'0947   87-25808
ISBN 0-8240-8061-0 (alk. paper)

All volumes in this series are printed on acid-
free, 250-year-life paper.

Printed in the United States of America

MILLENARIAN BOLSHEVISM:

EMPIRIOMONISM, GOD-BUILDING, PROLETARIAN CULTURE

by
David Graeme Rowley

A dissertation submitted in partial fulfillment
of the requirements for the degree of
Doctor of Philosophy
(History)
in The University of Michigan
1982

Doctoral Committee:

Professor Arthur P. Mendel, Chairman
Professor William G. Rosenberg
Assistant Professor Mark E. Suino
Professor Stephen J. Tonsor

ABSTRACT

MILLENARIAN BOLSHEVISM:
EMPIRIOMONISM, GOD-BUILDING, PROLETARIAN CULTURE

by

David Graeme Rowley

Chairman: Arthur P. Mendel

There existed within the Russian Social-Democratic
Labor Party during the first two decades of the twentieth
century a group of philosophically oriented revolutionaries
who conceived of socialist revolution in religious and millenarian terms. Constituting a left wing of the Bolshevik
faction, these radical philosophers believed that the socialist movement embodied the most sacred ideals of humankind,
that the proletariat possessed all the attributes of God,
that the evil world of capitalism must be destroyed, and that
an ideal socialist paradise would spontaneously arise after
that apocalypse.

A. Bogdanov was the seminal thinker who elaborated
the philosophy upon which millenarian Bolshevism was based.
In attempting to support Marx's sociology upon positivist
epistemology, Bogdanov ultimately created a voluntarist,
idealist philosophy which held that collective humankind
could master the elemental universe.

This work follows the development of millenarian
Bolshevism by studying the careers of A. Bogdanov and A. V.
Lunacharsky and analyzing their relations with V. I. Lenin,

A. M. Gorky, and various left Bolsheviks. Millenarian Bolshevism had its origins in a debate between positivist and
idealist Marxists (principally Bogdanov versus N. Berdiaev)
at the turn of the century. The first full statement of the
millenarians' world-view appeared in the God-building works
of Gorky and Lunacharsky. These left Bolsheviks' millenialism was ultimately manifested in early Soviet society through
the nationwide organization of the Proletkult.

It is the thesis of this work that the millenarian
Bolsheviks were not religious deviants on the radical fringe
of the Social-Democratic movement but were rather at its
intellectual center. They differed from other Bolsheviks
only by being more introspective and philosophically fearless.
In examining their relationship with Lenin, it is seen that
the millenarian Bolsheviks gave explicit expression to the
voluntarist, idealist, and chiliastic spirit that was inherent in the program and organization of Bolshevism and
that provided the philosophy of Soviet socialist idealism.

TABLE OF CONTENTS

INTRODUCTION

It is not a new idea to consider Russian Marxism in religious terms. The parallels between Marxism and religion are obvious. Like a religion Marxism claims absolute, universal validity. Like a religion Marxism offers explanations of the origins, history, and future of human life and explains the causes of evil and misery. And like a religion Marxism promises the ultimate realization of a peaceful and joyous existence for all humankind.

Furthermore, the Marxian vision of revolution is patently analagous to religious millenarianism: the transition from an evil world to a perfect paradise will be an immediate, total transformation; all evil will be destroyed in a universal cataclysm, and goodness will spontaneously arise. Neither Marxism nor religious chiliasm offer a blueprint for the construction of the future perfect world. That world will arise from non-human forces--either divine power or the logic of history.

There is, however, a completely understandable dearth of Marxist revolutionaries who are willing to explicitly admit that they are committed to revolution because of religious motivations. According to Marx, religion and morality are no more than by-products of economic relations; they are instruments of class domination. Furthermore, the

1

Marxist understands revolution to be an inevitable event:
the idea of "good" or "evil" is alien to historical materialism. Thus the entire edifice of Marxism rests upon a
foundation of materialism and determinism that explicitly
denies the objective validity of any mystical sense of holiness, transcendent moral idealism, or divine purpose. In
the very process of understanding and accepting Marxism,
the revolutionary must logically deny that moral or religious
commitment could have played a role in his acceptance.

A search for religious elements in Russian Marxism
is further discouraged by an historiographical emphasis upon
the appeal of Marxism's "inevitability" to Russia's disil-
lusioned populists. The populists supposedly embraced Marxism because it gave them new hope for social betterment; Marx
proved to them that the socialist revolution was historically
inevitable.

However, it seems obvious that a literal interpretation of this Marxian "inevitability" would tend to produce
passive social observers rather than impatient revolutionary
activists. After all, there is nothing in Marxism that logically entails the active participation of Marxists in the
making of the proletarian revolution. Whether any one particular individual views the revolution from an armchair or
from the barricades is irrelevant to the inexorable progress
of history.

Indeed, those Russians who were most attracted by
the purely scientific, determinist elements of Marxism were

also the first to renounce it. Struve, Kistiakovsky, and Tugan-Baranovsky, for example, followed their scholarly pre-occupation with economic and social theory from orthodox Marxism to revisionism and finally to economic liberalism.

The motivation to act--to actively promote the soc-ialist revolution--is a motivation that must have its source outside Marxism. The individual chooses to participate in the revolutionary movement not because of the principles he preaches but because of the subjective feelings that impel him to do the preaching. Those Russians who were active in the Social-Democratic movement did not become revolution-aries because they had read Marx. Rather, they welcomed Marxism because they already had revolutionary inclinations. Consequently, it is in this commitment to social activity that the idealistic, religious nature of Russian Marxism is most clearly revealed.

In a letter to Georgii Plekhanov, Pavel Axelrod ad-mitted that his own commitment to the revolutionary movement arose from a spirit of religious conviction. (Indeed, in this statement Axelrod actually anticipated the program of God-building.)

> The inner motivation of my idealism, of all my social activity, has been and is the concept of infinite progress of human nature . . . And strange to say: the more insignificant present-day human nature appears, the more passionately I dream of its perfection in the future--in a thousand years . . . And yet, this infinitely far-off perspective with its "supermen" is for me the impulse, the source, or you might say the inspiration . . . I think the psychological root of this strangeness . . . lies in a kind of re-ligious feeling, which I do not know how to

> characterize otherwise than in the words: wor-
> ship of wisdom; consciousness of spirit reaches
> in me the stage of fanaticism or enthusiasm . . .
> If there is no God who had created the universe
> --and glory be to him there is none--then we
> are preparing for the appearance upon earth of
> divine men, possessed of the essence of all-
> powerful reason and will . . . capable through
> wisdom of changing the world and directing
> it . . .¹

In theory, Marxism avoids the question of idealism:
the ideal socialist future that Marxism promises is nothing
more than a supposed prediction of fact. The "ideals" that
will be realized are nothing more than the real desires of
a particular class of people--the proletariat. These
"ideals" are no more than a description of what must inevitably be realized in the material world as a result of the
operation of universal laws. In theory, then, the individual
Marxist revolutionary is not serving his own subjective ideals
but rather the objective needs and desires of the working
class.

In practice, however, the problem of individual,
subjective idealism can become enormously important. As
long as the revolutionary can perceive no difference between
his own inner desires and the apparent strivings of the
working class, then there will be no conflict between the
real world and the revolutionary's ideal world. But if the
proletariat begins to show tendencies that do not meet (or
even contradict) the beliefs of the revolutionary, then he
will be forced to make a choice. He must either stifle his
own sense of what is right and follow the lead of the work-

ing class, or he must affirm his personal, subjective values
by attempting to convert the working class movement to his
own way of thinking.

Thus, the crisis of Economism and Revisionism in the
Russian Social-Democratic Labor Party at the turn of the
twentieth century was fundamentally a crisis of idealism.
When it became apparent that the spontaneous working class
movement was oriented toward gradualism, compromise, and
economic self-interest, the members of the "workers' party"
had to choose between faith in the proletariat as the historical source of the ideal and faith in their own personal
ideals.

Axelrod's statement of religious commitment to the
socialist movement (quoted above) was written in reaction
to Eduard Bernstein's revision of Marxism. In it Axelrod
did not contradict Bernstein's description of the working
class movement. He did not challenge Bernstein's marshalling
of the factual data; he abhorred his lack of revolutionary
spirit. Axelrod was appalled because a realistic acceptance
of the trade union movement implied the abandonment of socialist idealism.[2]

Few Marxist revolutionaries in Russia made the same
explicit confession of idealism as Axelrod did. Yet the
fact was that they believed that their own ideal values were
more valid as a basis for the proletarian revolutionary
movement than were the real desires of the working class.
Their subjective idealism was manifested in the creation of

a highly organized revolutionary party whose object was to resist "trade-union consciousness" and instill in the working class the ideals of socialism.

Furthermore, the difficulty in discovering such moral and idealistic sources of Russian Marxism does not arise only from the limitations that Marx's conceptual framework place upon the individual Marxist. The active revolutionaries simply did not spend much time in introspection--or at least in writing about it. Questions of ethics, metaphysics, and certainly religion were insignificant to the activists compared with questions of party organization, program, strategy, and tactics. They sought not to analyze their Marxism in philosophical terms but to interpret Marxism in practical terms. Indeed, there was a tendency for those who did concern themselves with philosophical problems to drop out of the revolutionary movement and for those who were concerned with the practical side of the revolutionary movement to ignore questions of philosophy.

There was, however, a significant exception to the split between the revolutionary activists and the scholarly philosophers. At the extreme left of the RSDRP there coalesced a small group of Marxists who were committed to actively organizing and leading the working class toward socialist revolution and at the same time committed to elaborating a consistent Marxist world-view that solved the dilemmas presented by the crisis over idealism.

By refusing to shrink from facing the contradiction

between subjective idealism and scientific socialism, these revolutionaries made explicit the religious idealism and millenarianism which were implicit in the revolutionary organization and program of their Bolshevik comrades. The nature of their world-view and their ties with Lenin is the subject of this study.

NOTES TO THE INTRODUCTION

[1]Quoted in Samuel H. Baron, Plekhanov, The Father of Russian Marxism (Stanford: Stanford University Press, 1963), p. 173.

[2]Ibid., pp. 172-3.

CHAPTER I

THE BEGINNINGS OF MILLENARIAN MARXISM

The Tsar's police first brought together the four
young Marxist revolutionaries whose interaction produced
the agenda for Bolshevik millenarianism. Nikolai Berdiaev,
Anatoly Vasilevich Lunacharsky, A. Bogdanov (Aleksandr Alek-
sandrovich Malinovsky), and V. A. Bazarov (Vladimir Alekse-
evich Rudnev) had all been arrested at different times and
places and for different activities, but all four found
themselves exiled together in Vologda in 1899. Berdiaev
and Lunacharsky had grown up in Kiev, and both Bogdanov and
Bazarov were from Tula. But it was only in Vologda that
all four were introduced to one another for the first time.
Their association was not an agreeable one: Berdiaev argued
strenuously with the other three Marxists over the problems
of idealism. From this very disagreement, however, was to
be created a religious Marxism.

Bogdanov and Bazarov

Both A. Bogdanov and V. A. Bazarov were born in Tula
(Bogdanov in 1873, Bazarov in 1874) and both had attended
the Tula gymnasium.[1] They may have known one another socially, as well, since their families were of the same social
status: Bazarov's father was a doctor, and Bogdanov's

9

father was a teacher and later a school administrator.
Upon graduation from the gymnasium in the early 1890s, both
young men enrolled in the division of natural sciences at
the University of Moscow. Bogdanov studied physics and mathematics; Bazarov took up chemistry.

It was while attending the University that the two
students began their revolutionary activity. They were at
first populists following the traditions of "The People's
Will." Like other young activist populists of the decade,
they seem to have been converted to Marxism through the exigencies of their revolutionary activities: oriented toward
the peasantry at first, Bogdanov had, by 1895, formed a workers' circle in Kaluga and enlisted the aid of Bazarov to
help lead the group. It was "in the course of involvement
with the workers that [Bogdanov] became, at the beginning of
1896, a Social-Democrat."[2]

Bogdanov's experience in that workers' circle had a
decisive influence upon his future intellectual development
and upon his conception of the role of the intelligentsia
in the proletarian revolution. As he recounted his experiences of that Kaluga circle many years later, Bogdanov must
surely have distorted the truth. As he depicted it, the
real originator of the group was a young worker, Ivan Saveliev, who had gathered together a group of fellow workers
to form a revolutionary study circle. Realizing their own
lack of education, these workers searched for members of the
intelligentsia to guide them in their pursuit of knowledge.[3]

In Bogdanov's subsequent telling of the story, it was as a servant and not a master that he entered the group and brought with him his friends, Bazarov and Skvortsov-Stepanov. The young Marxist revolutionaries thought of themselves simply as sources of information; they had to do nothing to stimulate the workers' desire to learn, to raise their class-consciousness, or to make them commit themselves to socialist revolution.

When Bogdanov and Bazarov began to arrange courses of study for the workers' circle, they realized how imperfectly they themselves understood science, economics, and scientific socialism. At first they tried to prepare their students for the theory of Marxism by teaching the fundamentals of economics from basic bourgeois textbooks. They found this to be unsatisfactory. The solution was Bogdanov's first book, A Short Course of Economic Science, in which he succinctly outlined Marxism in a simple, popular manner.[4]

Nevertheless, this simple exposition of Marxism was not enough to satisfy the workers' demands for knowledge for very long. The circle lasted for four and one-half years--an unusual longevity in those days of police vigilance and revolutionary carelessness. Consequently the leaders of the group had time to elaborate upon scientific socialism at much greater length than was usually possible. They soon exhausted the material in Bogdanov's Short Course.

> And then the demands of the listeners went
> further and further and encompassed the most
> complicated themes of science and philosophy;

the lecturers were themselves forced to study
many things that they had previously thought
required only a superficial knowledge.[5]

Bogdanov's attempt to answer all these questions--
or at least to provide the students with the tools for answering the questions by themselves-- set the principal
theme for his own future intellectual development: to discover and elaborate the basic principles or laws of nature
by which all aspects of reality could be explained. Bogdanov strove to create a "universal science" which a student
could apply to any realm of intellectual endeavor.

It was completely impossible in a short
time to give to the listeners factual material
in all the areas that excited their interest.
This made the lecturers revise their tasks,
to use their principal energy to teach the
students how to learn, to point out to them
the path and the methods of independent work.
It was necessary to focus their attention on
the methods of those sciences of which it was
necessary to impart an understanding . . . We
ran up against a kind of innate striving toward
monism; they demanded from us--not always with
success, of course--monistic answers to all
possible questions, complex and simple. We
were forced to direct our activity and thinking in this direction; for me personally this
predetermined to a considerable extent the
character of all my subsequent scientific and
philosophical work.[6]

One may believe that Bogdanov's experience in the
Saveliev circle was of great importance to his intellectual
development without accepting his story as it was later told.
Bogdanov's assertion that he and his comrades were simply
passive sources of information to the young, impatient,
active workers is hardly credible. This ideal image fits
too well into Bogdanov's theories of Proletarian Culture to

be taken at face value. His story was part of a polemic.
Nevertheless, it does reveal a basic faith in the revolutionary socialist character of the proletariat that Bogdanov
never relinquished.

What also has a ring of truth to it is Bogdanov's
account of how his interests were necessarily broadened as
his work in the study circle was prolonged. Neither can
there be a doubt of Bogdanov's desire to unify all the sciences into a monistic world-view. It is easily understandable that the long life of the Saveliev circle contributed
to that desire.

Most revolutionary activists of the 1890s had only
brief contacts with the workers. They barely had time to
explain the general principles of socialism before their
circles were liquidated by the police. Their revolutionary
activity was therefore limited principally to questions of
organization and agitation and to the search for immediate
issues and events that could be exploited for short-term
revolutionary purposes. Immediate, practical, conspiratorial concerns held their attention; theory was not a daily
preoccupation.

Quite the contrary of such typical experience, Bogdanov's long association with the Saveliev circle made philosophy the primary concern. The Marxist leaders of the
group were not simply trying to inspire the workers of the
circle to immediate revolutionary activity, they were trying
to develop in the workers a consistent world-view so that

they could respond to changing social situations as consistent scientific socialists. Bogdanov's description of how his own interests widened is entirely believable.

This desire for a universal world-view is also substantiated by the evidence of Bogdanov's subsequent work. Beginning with The Foundations of an Historical View of Nature (published in 1899) and concluding with the final, revised edition of Tektology: Universal Organizational Science (published in the mid-1920s), Bogdanov dedicated his life to the creation of a systematic, monistic, universal system of knowledge.[7]

Bogdanov thus felt himself obligated to systematize Marx's thought so that it could be applied to all aspects of reality. In doing so he was forced to deal with fundamental philosophical problems that would never have occurred to the average Marxist revolutionary organizer. Bogdanov spent the next decade creating an original revision of Marxism.

The Saveliev circle was to have another, although indirect, influence upon Bogdanov's life. Early in 1899 Bogdanov and his circle of now politically conscious worker-revolutionaries travelled to Moscow to begin systematic propaganda among the workers there. The Moscow police were more vigilant than those in the provincial Kaluga where the circle had flourished for almost five years. The newcomers to Moscow were arrested immediately.

Bogdanov was exiled to Vologda where he met Luna-

charsky and Berdiaev for the first time. Their association
in Vologda was to have incalculable consequences for the
future intellectual development of Russian Marxism.

A. V. Lunacharsky

Anatoly Lunacharsky had grown up in quite a different environment from that of Bogdanov's youth. Bogdanov
was one of the raznochintsy; Lunacharsky's father was a
gentry bureaucrat. Born in Poltava in 1875, Lunacharsky
grew up in the cultured atmosphere of Kievan society.[8]
Also contrary to Bogdanov's experience, Lunacharsky accepted
Marxism before he became an active social revolutionary.
Bogdanov had turned to Marxism only after he had begun to
agitate among the workers. Lunacharsky began to organize
actively only after he had become a Marxist.

Lunacharsky attended the Kiev Gymnasium, and it was
there in the early 1890s that he first read Kapital and
joined Kiev's Marxist circle--one of the first Marxist study
groups to arise in Russia. During his last years in the
gymnasium, Lunacharsky became involved in some propagandis-
tic activities among local artisans and railroad workers,
but political activity was not his primary interest.[9]

As he would continually reveal in the course of his
life, Lunacharsky was a thinker and not a doer. He was
attracted not so much to revolution as to the philosophy
of revolution.

> It must be said, however, that, along with
> revolutionary practice, I was personally inter-
> ested not so much in political economy or even

> Marxist sociology, as by its philosophy. And
> here my ideas were not absolutely orthodox.
> In my last years at the gymnasium I was great-
> ly attracted to Spencer and I tried to create
> a synthesis of Spencer and Marx. This, of
> course, did not satisfy me much, but I felt
> it was necessary to lay a serious positivist
> foundation beneath Marx's teachings.[10]

Like Bogdanov, Lunacharsky began his intellectual
development with a desire to revise Marxism. But unlike
Bogdanov, Lunacharsky's motivation did not arise from practical revolutionary activity. Lunacharsky's revision was
a purely intellectual excercise; he wanted to create a systematic world-view more for personal satisfaction than as
a guide for the revolutionary movement.

After graduating from the gymnasium, Lunacharsky
decided (against his family's wishes) not to enter the university immediately. Instead, he set off for Zurich to better acquaint himself with both Marxism and positivism.
His Marxist friends gave Lunacharsky a letter of introduction to Pavel Axelrod--a leading Russian representative of
orthodox Marxism. An instructor from the Gymnasium gave
him a letter of introduction to Richard Avenarius--one of
the two founders of neo-positivist epistemology, "empiriocriticism."[11]

Lunacharsky found courses at the University of Zurich (where Avenarius lectured) tedious, but he did much
extra-curricular reading in the university libraries. He
sat in on lectures in the faculties of law, natural sciences,
and philosophy. Through Axelrod, Lunacharsky gained access
to the dynamic community of Russian and Polish revolution-

aries who were at that time congregated in Zurich. Axelrod contributed as much to Lunacharsky's understanding of Marxism as Avenarius contributed to his grasp of positivist philosophy. In 1896, at the age of 21, Lunacharsky returned to Russia still determined to unite Marxism and positivism.[12]

In 1897 Lunacharsky travelled to Moscow to help ressurect a Marxist revolutionary organization that had been liquidated by the police during the previous year. Bazarov had been a member of that organization and had just been arrested, so Lunacharsky just missed meeting him for the first time. Their introduction was not postponed for very long, however, since the second incarnation of the organization was also promptly dissolved by the police. Lunacharsky found himself under arrest and on the way to exile and the making of important new acquaintances.

At first sentenced to solitary confinement for eight months, Lunacharsky found his prison term an excellent opportunity for reading "whole libraries of books" and for working out "the final development of [his] philosophical views."[13] Following this period of (involuntarily) intensive study and introspection, Lunacharsky embarked on a journey that greatly influenced the future course of his revolutionary and philosophical career. His first town of exile was Kaluga. There he met Bogdanov and Bazarov for the first time and became not only their revolutionary comrade but their personal friend as well. He and Bogdanov were subsequently exiled to Vologda where Lunacharsky renewed his youthful acquaintance with Berdiaev.

"My being in Kaluga," said Lunacharsky years later, "played a very important role in my personal life and also in my life as a Social-Democrat."[14] In particular, Bogdanov and Lunacharsky found their personalities to be mutually sympathetic. From that time forth they were not simply literary allies or party comrades but close personal friends. For the remainder of their careers, the two were inseparable. They remained loyal to one another throughout all the organizational and ideological squabbles that beset Russian Marxism. Even when Lunacharsky was Commissar of Education under the new Soviet regime and "Bogdanovism" was officially condemned by the Bolshevik party, Lunacharsky did all in his power to further the policies of his friend. In 1900 their personal ties became family ties; Lunacharsky married Anna Aleksandrovna Malinovskaia, Bogdanov's sister.

Bogdanov, Bazarov, and Lunacharsky also found their philosophical concerns to be complementary.

> I think that there were not many towns in Russia at that time where one could find such a circle of Marxist forces. Above all we were united by a certain original tendency. We were all deeply interested in the philosophical side of Marxism and because of this we desired to strengthen the epistemological, ethical, and esthetic aspects of Marxism--independent of Kantianism, on one hand, toward which a tendency had already begun . . . (Berdiaev, Bulgakov), and not yielding, on the other hand, to that narrow, French-Encyclopedistic orthodoxy upon which Plekhanov was attempting to base all Marxism.[15]

Perhaps even more important than Bogdanov's and

Lunacharsky's similarities, however, were their differences. Despite their common predisposition to the philosophical revision of Marxism, they had quite dissimilar backgrounds and attitudes toward the Russian revolutionary movement. It was the attraction of these opposites and their synthesis that made their collaboration so fruitful.

Lunacharsky was typical of the idealistic Russian intelligentsia who had been attracted to Marxism while studying at the gymnasium or university and who was more interested in its original world-view and the ideal future that it promised than in its applicability to the actual revolutionary movement in Russia. Bogdanov, on the contrary, had begun as a revolutionary activist preaching the principles of populism, and who had only gradually become committed to Marxism while organizing and teaching the working class.

Had the two not met and found their ways of thinking supplementary, they might well have directed their lives in quite different directions. Instead of affirming his faith in the historical role of the proletariat and committing himself to a Marxist social orientation, Lunacharsky might well have joined Berdiaev and Bulgakov in their religious seeking. As an organizer, Bogdanov could easily have become completely immersed in the practical, organizational affairs of the RSDRP without feeling the need to undertake a fundamental reconstruction of Marxism.

Lunacharsky brought to Bogdanov not only a clearly

expressed feeling for the intelligentsia's ethical motivation for progressive social change, but he also reinforced
Bogdanov's search for a total, systematic world-view. In
material terms, Lunacharsky introduced Mach's and Avenarius'
positivist philosophy to Bogdanov. It was this "empiriocriticism" that would supply Bogdanov with the theories of
ontology, epistemology, and causality that would make up
the foundation of his ultimate theoretical construction.

For his part, Bogdanov strove to reaffirm Lunacharsky's commitment to practical revolutionary activity. Over
the next fifteen years it was always Bogdanov who kept encouraging Lunacharsky to participate in the activity of the
Russian Social-Democratic movement. Lunacharsky followed
Bogdanov into the Bolshevik faction in 1903, out of that
faction in 1908, and into the "Vpered Group" in 1909. After
the October Revolution, Lunacharsky was an enthusiastic
supporter of Bogdanov's "Proletarian Culture" movement.

Furthermore, despite being more of a political activist, Bogdanov was also Lunacharsky's superior in technical philosophy. Ultimately, it was Bogdanov's synthesis
of historical materialism and neo-positivism that provided
the philosophical foundation for Lunacharsky's theories of
esthetics, ethics, and religion of socialism.

In the course of their friendship, Bogdanov and
Lunacharsky collaborated to produce a synthesis of the two
great currents in Russian intellectual life of the early
twentieth century: the search for a new religious conscious-

ness and the revolutionary quest for socialism.

Encounter with Berdiaev and Idealism

No less important for Bogdanov's and Lunacharsky's intellectual development was the intellectual milieu into which they were exiled in 1899. Kaluga was only a temporary place of exile. In 1900 both men were transferred to Vologda to serve the remainder of their sentences. Vologda at that time was a major center of political exile. By chance it occurred that the prevailing mood among the Social-Democrats in Vologda was philosophically and not organizationally inclined. Among the exiles were Berdiaev, Kistiakovsky, and Remizov.

It was at this time that controversies of crucial importance for the organizational development of the RSDRP were raging among emigre Social-Democratic groups. At the same time that Bogdanov was settling down in Vologda, Lenin was making his way to Zurich. By the end of the year, _Iskra_ would already have been formed and would be battling with _Rabochaia Mysl_ and _Rabochee Delo_ over the program, tactics, and organization of the infant RSDRP.

In Vologda, however, the Marxist exiles heard only "confused rumors" of those emigre debates.[16] The burning issues of the day for Social-Democrats in Vologda were philosophical. At that time Nikolai Berdiaev was in the process of transition from Marxism to Neo-Kantian idealism. Berdiaev's dominating personality and polemical powers had attracted to his position a large circle of followers from among Vologda's revolutionary exiles.

Lunacharsky and Bogdanov were quick to establish a rival circle. Though the two newcomers shared with Berdiaev a common concern for the philosophical foundations of the socialist revolutionary movement, their point of view in regard to social activism was quite different. Berdiaev was committed to philosophical truth above all else. His involvement in the revolutionary movement had only been a corollary to his early Marxist orientation. He was fully prepared to leave the revolutionary struggle if his philosophical speculations look him beyond Marxism.

With Lunacharsky and Bogdanov quite the opposite was true. They were socialists and revolutionaries above all. Their concern in the realm of philosophy was not as much to arrive at an abstract system of "truth" as it was to establish a consistent foundation and a justification for their revolutionary impulses. Despite the fact that they ultimately transformed Marxism, their initial and continuing objective was to defend it.

Temperamentally, Lunacharsky appeared to have much in common with Berdiaev and the other Marxist idealists. Berdiaev even exerted considerable influence upon Lunacharsky's thought. Yet the similarites concealed an important difference: Berdiaev's search for truth was open-ended, while for Lunacharsky the truth before which everything else was subservient was socialist revolution.

Both Berdiaev and Lunacharsky had arisen out of

much the same environment. Berdiaev, too, was a scion of
minor Kievan nobility, and he received an upbringing and
education typical of his class. Born in 1874, Berdiaev
was just a year older than Lunacharsky, and the two became
acquainted as schoolmates at the Kiev Gymnasium. They probably met more often in Marxist circles than in school, for
it was a close friend of Lunacharsky who first introduced
Berdiaev to Marxism.[17]

It was not until later (1894, Berdiaev's first year
at the University of Kiev), however, that Berdiaev really
began to study Marxism and to accept it as his own world-
view. Also like Lunacharsky, when Berdiaev finally did become a Marxist, he was not particularly attracted by the
prospect of an economic or social revolution. Berdiaev was
intrigued with the idea of the transformation of the human
spirit much more than he was attracted by the idea of change
in the ownership of the means of production. In his autobiography he admitted that in Marxism "What struck me above
all was the prospect of a spiritual revolution: a rising
of the spirit, of freedom and meaning, against the deadly
weight, the slavery, and the meaninglessness of the world."[18]

What most distinguished between Berdiaev and Lunacharsky was perhaps Berdiaev's clearer introspection. Berdiaev saw his desire for the ideal as a clearly personal
matter; Lunacharsky's idealism was concealed behind his expressions of social concern.

Lunacharsky began his autiobiographical sketch, "I

became a revolutionary so early that I can't even remember
when I was not one."[19] He went on to note that he was
brought up in a liberal intelligentsia family where anti-
religious and anti-monarchist feelings were combined with a
concern for the well-being of Russia's peasantry. Lunacharsky was ultimately never able to separate his idealistic
desires for goodness, truth, and beauty from his inbred desire to improve the lot of Russia's poverty-stricken laboring classes. It was this identification of the struggle
for social change with the realization of his own subjective idealism that kept Lunacharsky within the revolutionary
movement.

Berdiaev made no such confusion between the realm
of his own ideals and the realm of objective social existence. From the very beginning he realized that his Marxist
persuasion was related to his own personal desire for free-
dom--quite separate from any larger social significance.

> The revolutionary impulse sprang from an in-
> nate inability to acquiesce in the world-order
> and to submit to its exigencies. It had,
> therefore, primarily a personal, not a social
> significance. I was concerned with the rev-
> olution of the human person rather than of
> the people or the masses.[20]

Berdiaev also understood Marxism more as a religion
than a science.

> Marxism represents the clearest vision of
> the theory or the religion of progress, since
> it inspires in its adherents faith in the im-
> manent, though causally conditioned, emergence
> of the perfect social system... Its strength,
> therefore, is derived not from its scientific
> but from its utopian elements; not from its
> faith.[21]

Nor did Berdiaev feel any particular need to preserve, support, or enshrine Marxism as a universal, final
formulation of scientific socialism. Instead, he took Marxism as a starting point only. Berdiaev looked forward to
the elaboration of a world-view superior to Marxism.

> The theoretical elaboration and further devel-
> opment of Marxism ought to lead to the creation
> of an independent, higher ideology, which would
> give a philosophical-ethical basis to those
> idealistic calls for truth and progress, for
> justice and humanity, which so often accom-
> pany the practical activity of those who are
> fighting for this world-view.[22]

This statement underlines the fundamental difference between Berdiaev and Lunacharsky. Lunacharsky only
wanted to create a new "philosophical foundation for Marxist
knowledge," certainly not "an independent, higher ideology."
Lunacharsky could conceive of nothing higher than Marxism
and his purpose was to develop that world-view and not to
go beyond it. Lunacharsky's belief in Marxism was manifested
in a life-long commitment to socialist revolution. For
Berdiaev Marxism was only an early stage in the development
of his personal philosophy.

Marxism was not a world-view that Berdiaev quickly
abandoned, however. As he made clear in his autobiography,
Berdiaev was strongly attracted to Marxism. It appeared
to him to be a fresh and convincing world-view that promised
to resolve the crisis in Western culture that was felt by
many post-Nietzsche, post-Dostoevsky European intellectuals.[23]
Berdiaev continued to think of himself as a Marxist (although

a "critical" one) long after his former Marxist comrades considered him to be an idealist renegade from their movement. As late as 1903, Berdiaev still professed to be a Marxist.

It is understandable why Berdiaev should have clung to Marxism even while he was philosophically rejecting it. What had attracted him to Marxism in the first place was precisely that element of his personality that made it impossible for him to wholeheartedly believe in it. Berdiaev's primary concern was with ethics. For him, socialist revolution was associated with a "definite social ideal, with the most sacred aspirations of contemporary man."[24] Thus Berdiaev's desire for socialism was an expression of ethical value.

Marxism, however, is fundamentally incapable of accepting an ethical justification. Ethics implies free will, for it involves a choice between good and bad, and choice is possible only by a freely thinking and acting individual. But if individuals are capable of choice, then the determinism that stands at the very heart of Marxism is insupportable, and Marxism loses those characteristics of materialism, science, and determinism that distinguish it from "utopian socialism". Furthermore, ethical choice is explicitly ruled out by the determinist, materialist dictum that "existence determines consciousness."

Such determinism, however, was incompatible with Berdiaev's aristocratic, egocentric personality. He could

not reconcile himself with the idea of a future "ideal"
that he, himself, did not choose of his own free will.
Berdiaev's first major work, Individualism and Subjectivism
in Social Philosophy, (written during his exile in Vologda)
was an attempt to reconcile the free will of the revolutionary socialist with the supposed inevitability of socialist
revolution. Berdiaev wanted to have his cake and eat it,
too: he granted that socialism was materially, historically inevitable, yet at the same time he insisted that the
ideals manifest in socialism should be consistent with his
own personal sense of ethical good.

Following Marx, Berdiaev believed that ". . . there
must be some objective standard which would enable us to set
one subjective ideal above others and would show us the
obligatory truth-justice which exists in the realm of morality."[25] And in demonstrating "how social materialism
grounds its ideal," Berdiaev also echoed Marx. He asserted
that socialism was both historically inevitable and desired
by a particular class.

> First, this social ideal is objectively
> necessary, the tendencies of social develop-
> ment are such that the social order which we
> regard as ideal is bound to come; it will be
> the inevitable result of the immanent confor-
> mity to the law of the historical process.
> Thus the ideal receives an objectively logical,
> scientific sanction . . .[26]
>
> Second, social materialism gives the ideal
> a subjective psychological ground: the ideal
> of social life does not simply conform to sci-
> entific prediction, it is also something sub-
> jectively desirable for a given class, and
> this class is fighting for its actualization.[27]

However, Berdiaev's third justification for the idealism of the revolutionary socialist movement was not only <u>not</u> to be found within Marxism, it actually <u>contradicted</u> the essential principles of Marxism.

> A third foundation is necessary, one which we would call <u>objectively</u> ethical. It is necessary to show that our social ideals . . . are objectively moral and objectively just, that its actualization will be progress in the sense of improvement; in a word, that it is binding on all, has unconditional value, is something obligatory . . .[28]

Not only did Berdiaev's search for absolute ethical principles violate the spirit of Marx in and of itself, but Berdiaev also sought those principles in a contradictory philosophical school. Berdiaev turned to Kant and Idealism.

> As a theory of knowledge, ethics must take Kant's critical philosophy as its starting point. The formal difference between good and evil or between the moral and the immoral precedes every sense of experience; the category of justice is given a priori to our transcendental consciousness, and this ethical a priori is what makes moral experience and moral life possible.[29]

In fact, not only did Berdiaev rely upon Kant to provide a justification for socialist idealism, he actually gave Kant preeminence over all other philosophers, including Marx.

> Man's consciousness has never risen above Kant's thought of man (or mankind) as an end in himself, an end which gives moral sanction to everything else and itself needs no sanction. Kant is the real founder of the religion of man.[30]

By accepting Kant's conception of a priori ethical judgement, Berdiaev affirmed his personal ethical values and his own moral responsibility for his actions even while participating in the "historically inevitable" progress toward socialism. Yet in this third justification for socialist idealism, he contradicted his previous two arguments about the inevitability of socialism. Absolute individual free will and absolute moral values are fundamentally incompatible with Marxism.

Nevertheless, no matter how untenable and contradictory Berdiaev's position was, it was entirely immune from attack from an orthodox Marxist standpoint. In a clever piece of sophistry, Berdiaev demonstrated that any attack upon Kant's idealism would be equally devastating to Marx's materialist determinism. He argued that "Empirically it is just as impossible to arrive at the objective ethical norm that man is an end in himself as it is to arrive at the idea of the universal applicability of the principle of causality."[31]

Berdiaev pointed out that notions of time, space, and causality are given a priori just as are moral judgements. One cannot deny the "objective truth" of any of these concepts without denying the objectivity of them all. Thus a Marxist could not reject the concept of objective morality without also rejecting some of the basic a priori concepts that underlie the scientific, materialist foundation of Marxism.

For example, Marxism cannot stand without the principle of causality. Determinism is a central element of

Marx's system. He devoted his life to proving the imminence of socialism as determined by the universal, objective laws of the natural world. There could be no such thing as chance or even statistical probabilities; every phenomenon must have a material cause if determinism is to be valid.

Furthermore, materialist monism is inseparably bound up with the concept of determinism: if the universe is presumed to operate only according to certain laws of cause and effect, then it must contain only forms of existence which obey those laws. Any force that is independent of cause and effect (human free will, for example) would make the final outcome something other than scientifically predictable and hence not inevitable.

Thus Marxism depends upon at least two a priori concepts: causality and objective, material reality. Paradoxically, it was just such a set of contentions that Kant, himself, was attempting to justify. Kant's theory of knowledge and of existence was a reaction to the empirical, sceptical philosophy of Hume who had argued that the human mind had no access to knowledge of "reality-in-itself." Hume insisted that concepts of space, time, causation, and external existence were no more than psychological traits of the human mind.

Kant, of course, followed Hume's psychological approach to ontology in his assertion that objective reality is known only to the extent that it conforms to the essential structure of the human mind. But by analyzing the "categories of thought" in terms of which the human mind interprets reality, Kant sought to establish an objective structure that would allow scientists to treat the natural world as if it were an objective, absolute existence. And although Kant held that metaphysical questions could not logically be speculated upon, he nevertheless justified belief in freedom, God, immortality, and reality-in-itself as the necessary prerequisites to moral behavior.

Consequently, if a Marxist were to make an empirical critique of Kant's notion of a priori moral judgements, he would necessarily also be undermining those other a priori categories of thought (space, time, and causality) upon which the logic of historical materialism depends. Berdiaev did not belabor the point, but he had clearly established his immunity from orthodox Marxist rebuttal. His philosophical antagonists had first to revise the epistemological and ontological basis of scientific socialism before they could attempt to refute Berdiaev's assertion that socialism represented a transcendent ethical good.

After publishing Individualism and Subjectivism in Social Philosophy, Berdiaev abandoned the futile task of reconciling Kant with Marx. Instead of attempting to systematically and logically develop such a synthesis, Berdiaev resorted to broad subjective appeals to Russia's Marxist revolutionaries to recognize their own ethical motivations.

For instance, in an essay, "The Struggle for

Idealism," Berdiaev's principal appeal for an idealistic
socialist philosophy was simply that Marxism provided no
realm for ideas of heroism, romanticism, or idealism.[32]
He argued that Marx's goal (and Bernstein's, as well) was
nothing more than eudemonism. Berdiaev felt that such simple contentment should be the life goal of only swine and
cattle; human beings must strive toward ideals. It is the
pursuit of ideals and not the pursuit of happiness, argued
Berdiaev, that gives meaning to man's existence. "Happiness is the result of the moral life of man, but never his
goal . . ."[33]

Berdiaev did not undertake a formal, logical argument for this position: he simply made a subjective appeal
to other idealists like himself, who, he thought, comprised
the largest part of the Marxist revolutionary movement.

> It is time to admit that religion, regard-
> less of the fluidity of its content, is an
> eternal, transcendent function of conscious-
> ness and that a total world-view and sense of
> relationship with the world must be a religion.
> The sublime uplifting of the spirit and ideal-
> istic enthusiasm is possible only when I feel
> in all my being that, in serving human progress
> in its contemporary historical form, I serve
> eternal truth . . .[34]

In a later essay, "A Criticism of Historical Materialism," Berdiaev continued to press the Marxists to recognize the idealistic nature of their commitment to socialism.

> The passionate desire of the "orthodox" [Marx-
> ists], my opponents, to defend the totality and
> purity of their ideal was always dear to me,
> since I see in that [desire] the ineradicable
> idealism of the human spirit which bursts through
> material limitations. But this idealistic de-
> mand . . . can find its true satisfaction only in

a new "faith" in the creation of which we must now work.[35]

Berdiaev then went on to elaborate on the kind of new faith that he had in mind:

> A synthesis of the realistic sociology of Marx and the idealistic philosophy of history of Fichte and Hegel is necessary. In this way can be decided the problem that Kant stated but did not solve: the relation between ideal norms that exist in the human soul and the objective currents of the historical process . . .
> We bow also to the work of Marx, that relentless materialist and realist, to his idealistic thirst for justice on earth, the reflection of eternal truth. Therefore, regardless of our resolute criticism of certain Marxist positions, we give tribute of respect and awe to one of the greatest people of all times.[36]

Berdiaev continued to think of himself as a Marxist at least until 1903 and he continued to attempt to resolve the "crisis of Marxism" by injecting his ethical concerns into the Social-Democratic movement. But he had only a small audience among Russian Marxists. The crisis of Marxism of which he spoke seemed to have nothing in common with the organizational, programmatic crisis that was agonizing the emigre leaders of the RSDRP. It was understood as a crisis over idealism only by a few intellectuals like Berdiaev who were recognizing the religious elements of their youthful revolutionary commitment and discovering the fundamental incompatibility of Marxist ontology with that idealism.

And yet the crisis that Berdiaev and other idealists reacted to was no different from the crisis experienced in the Russian Marxist movement as a whole. And the real cause

of the crisis was the success of the trade-union movement.
The Social-Democratic party became split over the question
of what direction to take: to follow the actual tendencies
of the working class or to follow their own ideals as to
the proper course for a revolutionary socialist party.
The question was one of idealism: whose ideals were more
"true;" the actual expressions of the working class, or the
inner beliefs of the Marxists. Consequently this controversy over idealism was waged in organizational terms:
should the RSDRP be a party of leaders or of followers?

The choice the activist revolutionaries faced was
clearly between accepting Marxism as an absolute truth (and
so feeling justified in directing the workers toward that
truth) or accepting the actual demands of the working class
as the sole criterion of party objectives. The dilemma
arose from the fact that the characteristics of socialism
(such as freedom, brotherhood, justice, and equality) are
considered by Marx not to be ideals, but simply statements
of fact about what the proletariat wants to create. Thus
the desires of the proletariat constitute the "ideal."

Once the proletariat began to show evidence that
it did not actually have the desires and inclinations that
Marx believed it would, Marxists had to make a choice.
Those who gave in to Economism, revisionism, and gradualism bowed to material objectivity. Those who continued to
pursue the socialist revolution implicitly affirmed their
own subjective idealism.

Berdiaev had explicitly recognized this dilemma early in his career. In fact, his own passage from Marxism to idealism arose out of this conflict between his own idea of the ideal and the apparent desires of the working class. He had devoted considerable effort (in <u>Subjectivism and Individualism in Social Philosophy</u>) to proving that his own personal sense of the ideal was identical with the concrete desires of the "historically advanced class." But when he had to choose between his own subjective values and the reality of the working class movement, the aristocratic Berdiaev had no trouble making the choice.

> Let us imagine a situation of this kind: social development is leading in the most obvious way to results which for me are repulsive . . . Am I then obliged to discard my ideal and embrace the predatory ideal as one that is more viable? Surely not.[37]

Berdiaev expressed both the dilemma and the choice made by that tendency in the RSDRP which maintained the principles of orthodox Marxism in defiance of the ideas actually arising from the trade union movement. When they sought to create a strong, centralized party in order to advance socialist revolution in Russia, Lenin and his Bolshevik comrades were taking the path toward subjective idealism and abandoning the notion that the ideals of socialism were no more than simple facts of working class desire.

<u>Problems of Idealism</u> appeared in 1901.[38] It was a symposium in which Russia's most prominent Marxist philoso-

phers of the preceding decade announced their discovery of
Neo-Kantian idealism. Berdiaev, Bulgakov, Frank, Kistiakovsky, Lappo-Danilevsky, and Trubetskoi all were making
the transition from materialist determinism to idealism.
Problems of Idealism heralded the new religious direction
in which the Russian intelligentsia was headed. For the
next decade, cultured Russians would be concerned with ethical and religious questions rather than social ones. The
intelligentsia finally chose to pursue its own idealism
without seeking to identify it with the needs of the Russian
people.

Just as Marxism had been the dominating intellectual
fashion of the 1890s, so religious search became the principal enthusiasm of the intelligentsia during the first
decade of the twentieth century. Russia's new intellectual
trend-setters would no longer be the social scientists but
the poets. Marxism was to be left in the hands not of philosophers but of revolutionary activists and practical politicians.

To such practical, active, revolutionary Marxists,
there was little point in becoming involved in the controversy over idealism. They did not appreciate--or simply
refused to contemplate--the extent to which their continuing
commitment to Marxism was actually a commitment to their
own subjective idealism. Organizational and programmatic
concerns of the Social-Democratic Party seemed far more
important than philosophical disputes with a group of intel-

lectuals who had already, for all intents and purposes, abandoned the revolutionary movement. The controversy over idealism and Marxism actually had a greater influence in Russian intellectual and cultural circles than it did in the revolutionary community.

Indirectly, however,--through their influence on Bogdanov and Lunacharsky--the idealists exerted a considerable influence upon the Marxist movement. Though the debate over idealism was far from the center of revolutionary Marxism, it was very close to Bogdanov and Lunacharsky. They shared a year of exile with Berdiaev and Kistiakovsky and could not but become involved in the debate. The threat of "Economism" was distant from Vologda, but idealism was in their very midst. The two friends sought to defend their Marxist world-view from the attacks of the idealists.

The influence of Berdiaev and the Vologda experience upon Bogdanov and Lunacharsky can hardly be overestimated. Had Lenin, Martov, Krichevsky, or Martynov been in Vologda at that time, instead of the idealists, Bogdanov and Lunacharsky might never have been forced to undertake so systematic a reevaluation of Marxism as they did. In close association with party activists instead of philosophers, the two would inevitably have worked out the crisis of idealism in terms of the spontaneity of the proletariat and the role and organization of the Social-Democratic party in the revolutionary socialist movement. They might never have had the impetus to carry out to its conclusion the philosophical search they had begun so tentatively earlier in the decade.

In defending Marxian orthodoxy from the idealists' attacks, Bogdanov and Lunacharsky were forced to wage the battle upon the philosophical grounds established by Berdiaev. The principal theoretical works in which Bogdanov and Lunacharsky first laid the foundations of their new version of scientific socialism were actually polemical responses to the idealists. Though they supplied different answers, the two Marxists accepted as valid the questions that the idealists asked.

It was the 1905 Revolution that brought the controversy to an end. By that time the Marxists were too involved in practical affairs to bother arguing with people so obviously lost to the revolutionary movement. For their part, the idealists had moved so far from Marxism that they no longer felt the need to transform it; they simply abandoned it.

Nevertheless, the issues that were raised in the debate were to continue as a tendency within the Russian Social-Democratic movement well into the Soviet era. The idealists had neither converted Bogdanov and Lunacharsky into Neo-Kantian idealism nor forced them into a rigid Marxist orthodoxy. Rather the idealists made explicit the fundamental philosophical issues that the Marxists had to resolve if they were to maintain their sense of idealistic motivation and yet remain within the Social-Democratic movement.

The task that Bogdanov and Lunacharsky took up was
an empirical critique of both Kant and Marx. By relying
upon positivist epistemology, the two Marxists were able to
reject the notion of an independent, absolute moral system,
while at the same time creating a new conception of causation and objective reality that did not rely upon a priori
justification. The consequences for Marxism were to be far-
reaching.

NOTES TO CHAPTER I

[1]The following biographical information on Bogdanov and Bazarov comes from Deiateli revoliutsionnogo dvizheniia v Rossii (Moscow: Izdatel'stvo Vsesoiuznogo Obshchestvo Politicheskikh Katorzhan i Ssyl'no-poselentsev, 1931), Vol. 5, Part I.

[2]Ibid., p. 373.

[3]A. Bogdanov, "Proletarskii universitet," in O proletarskoi kul'ture (Leningrad, Moscow: Izdatel'skoe Tovarishchestvo "Kniga," 1924), p. 239.

[4]A. Bogdanov, Kratkii kurs ekonomicheskoi nauki (Moscow: n.p., 1897).

[5]O proletarskoi kul'ture, p. 240.

[6]Ibid., pp. 240-1.

[7]A. Bogdanov, Osnovy istoricheskago vzgliada na prirodu (St. Petersburg: Izdanie Spb. Aktsionern. Obshchestva Pech. Dela "Izdatel'," 1899), and Tektologiia: vseobshchaia organizatsionnaia nauka, 3 vols. (Moscow-Leningrad: Izdatel'stvo "Kniga," 1925-29).

[8]Bibliographical information on Lunacharsky comes from A. V. Lunacharsky, "Moe partiinoe proshloe," in Velikii perevorot, (Petrograd: Izdatel'stvo Z. I. Grzhebina, 1919).

[9]Ibid., p. 12.

[10]Ibid., p. 13.

[11]Ibid., pp. 13-14.

[12]Ibid., p. 19.

[13]Ibid., p. 21.

[14]Ibid.
    Plekhanov was the bête noire of the Bolshevik idealists. Plekhanov's interpretation of Marxism was already accepted as "orthodoxy" among Russia's revolutionary Marxists by the turn of the century. On theoretical matters Plekhanov was recognized as authoritative by both Bolsheviks and Mensheviks. What Lunacharsky (and Bogdanov, as well) found objectionable in Plekhanov's "French Encyclopedistic orthodoxy," was his scientism. Echoing the spirit of the Enlightenment, Plekhanov attempted to create a consistent scientific world-view emphasizing the material na-

ture of reality and its operation according to universal physical laws of nature. Whereas the effect of the Enlightenment was to deny transcendent religious truth, Plekhanov's purpose was to discredit the ethical idealism of Russian populism.

Furthermore, to prove the inevitability of socialist revolution in Russia, Plekhanov emphasized Marx's materialism and determinism. Bogdanov and Lunacharsky found his materialist ontology to be outdated and untenable. As shall be seen, they attempted to replace Plekhanov's ontological monism with an epistemological monism in which human thought replaced matter as the essence of reality.

[15]Ibid., p. 22.

[16]Ibid., p. 26.

[17]Nicolas Berdiaev, Dream and Reality (New York: MacMillan Company, 1951), p. 116.

[18]Ibid., p. 108.

[19]Velikii perevorot, p. 9.

[20]Dream and Reality, p. 109.

[21]Ibid., p. 116.

[22]N. Berdiaev, "Subjectivism and Objectivism," in Russian Philosophy, ed. J. M. Eadie, J. P. Scanlan, and M. B. Zeldin, 3 vols. (Chicago: Quadrangle Books, 1965), vol. 3, p. 149.

[23]Dream and Reality, p. 117.

[24]Russian Philosophy, p. 150.

[25]Ibid., p. 149.

[26]Ibid., p. 150.

[27]Ibid.

[28]Ibid.

[29]Ibid., p. 153.

[30]Ibid.

[31]Ibid., p. 154.

[32]N. Berdiaev, "Bor'ba za idealizm," in Sub specie aeternitatis: opyty filosofskie, sotsial'nye i literatur-

nye (St. Petersburg: Izdanie M. V. Pirozhkova, 1907), p. 5.

[33]Ibid., p. 15.

[34]Ibid., p. 33.

[35]N. Berdiaev, "Kritika istoricheskago materializma," in Sub specie aeternitatis, p. 102.

[36]Ibid., p. 116.

[37]Russian Philosophy, p. 152.

[38]P. I. Novgorodtsev, ed., Problemy idealizma (Moscow: Izdanie Moskovskago Psikhologicheskago Obshchestva, 1902).

CHAPTER II

THE INITIAL SYNTHESIS OF MARXISM, POSITIVISM, AND IDEALISM

Bogdanov's Positivist Epistemology

The rebuttal of idealism occupied most of Bogdanov's and Lunacharsky's literary energies until the 1905 Revolution. In 1905 Bogdanov published a collection of his polemical essays written against Berdiaev and the other contributors to Problems of Idealism. Bogdanov entitled his collection On the Psychology of Society. In the introduction he justified its publication on the ground that the sudden great influx of Social-Democrats into the revolutionary movement and the great complexity of political questions demanded a clear elaboration of scientific socialism.

Bogdanov singled out two particularly corrupting influences within Marxism in the preceding decade: Economism and idealism. The first tendency, according to Bogdanov, was a form of "bourgeois idolatry;" the second surrendered the hegemony of the democratic revolution to the bourgeoisie.[1] The cause of both heresies was "theoretical indifference by the rank and file of the RSDRP," and it was that indifference that Bogdanov intended his theoretical writing to erase. Though he criticized Economism in no uncertain terms, he left the thorough critique of that doctrine to Marxists who had been closer to the center of the

controversy. As Bogdanov had himself been in the midst of
the debate over idealism, that was the principal subject
of his theoretical writings.

What Bogdanov found most objectionable about the
idealists was not so much the content of their ideas but
the fact that they continued to represent themselves as
Marxists. He was outraged that they sought to corrupt the
active revolutionaries by turning them away from active faith
in their movement toward passive considerations of the morality of their cause. It was as an orthodox Marxist as well
as an activist revolutionary that Bogdanov opposed idealism.

His answer to the idealist criticism of Marxism took
two forms. He first tried to show that the idealists simply
could not believe in Marxism and Kantianism simultaneously,
as Berdiaev had attempted to do. A synthesis of the two
was impossible; one had to choose either the one or the
other. If a revolutionary chose to be an idealist, Bogdanov felt, he should explicitly announce his departure from
Marxism and not try to present his thought as "critical
Marxism."

This aspect of Bogdanov's argument rested solely
upon the authority of Marx. Bogdanov accepted as unques-
tioned truth Marx's assertion that moral truth is relative
to economics and to labor relations. The idealists' notions
of absolute truth and absolute value were thus no more than
bourgeois ideology--a product of capitalism and no more the
"truth" than any other intellectual superstructure.

Such an argument was not really directed against the idealists in the sense that it was intended to refute their ideas. Rather it was an appeal to other scientific socialists who might have been responsive to the ethical appeals of the idealists. Clearly, what Bogdanov feared was that the Kantian emphasis upon the individual might lead revolutionaries away from the concern for the goals of the proletarian class struggle toward personal, introspective ethical and religious concerns. Bogdanov objected not to idealism, in itself, but to the tendency of idealists to drop out of the socialist revolutionary movement.

In an article entitled "What is Idealism?" Bogdanov revealed to what extent he had himself reacted to Berdiaev's "crisis in Marxism" by leaning toward the direction of idealism. In this article, Bogdanov actually defended idealism. He used the term in its popular and not its technical philosophical sense. In fact, Bogdanov appropriated the term "idealism" to his own cause and denied that the idealists were really "idealistic."

True idealism, wrote Bogdanov, was no more than the willingness of the individual to sacrifice himself for the good of society. "Idealism signifies the victorious struggle of the more social elements of the psyche with the less social."[2] (Thus, Bogdanov's idealism was quite the opposite of introversion.)

> Thus the idealist always strives toward a goal
> that is not narrowly personal, but toward a
> social good; and, of course, the attainment

of that good, which he calls his "ideal" seems
to him to be "progress." The idealist might
be mistaken in this--his ideal might in reality be reactionary . . . but subjectively, for the
idealist, himself, the ideal must be progressive, must express a <u>higher</u> than that which is.[3]

Bogdanov explicitly recognized his involvement in
the revolutionary movement as being idealistic, but he
identified his idealism with the interests of the proletariat
(Berdiaev's original position) and not with his own subjective value judgements (the conclusion that Berdiaev ultimately reached).

Furthermore, Bogdanov insisted that idealism must
be concretely related to the realm of material reality.
The idealists were mistaken in attempting to posit any absolute good above the interests of the socially progressive
class. An objective ideal, according to Bogdanov, was ". . .
an abstraction from non-existing experience; it is a word
for which there is no significant meaning."[4] For Bogdanov
idealism meant not thinking great thoughts but creating
great things. "Idealism is in all cases a <u>social-progres-
ive mood</u>; and the ideal is that concrete goal to which this
feeling leads humanity."[5]

In other words, Bogdanov was appealing to all Social-
Democrats who might sense ethical motivations in themselves
to treat them not as invitations to mystical escapism but
as indications that they were part of a progressive social
movement; furthermore, their ideals should be realized and
not dreamt. Bogdanov concluded his polemic as a proponent
of revolutionary idealism: "This is why the struggle for

idealism appears, at the present moment, as the struggle against idolism."[6]

Thus Bogdanov had really made no advance from Berd-iaev's formulations of the objective-subjective ethical justifications of the revolutionary movement (in Subject-ivism and Individualism). Bogdanov continued to repeat the old materialist, determinist explanation that the striving toward ideals is no more than the desire of the proletariat for socialism produced by the class struggle and the material economic forces of capitalism. Bogdanov also obviously shared Berdiaev's feeling that the socialist movement involved the "sacred aspirations of mankind."

The difference between Bogdanov and Berdiaev was their perception of the proletariat. In the face of a conflict between his own ideals and the aspirations expressed by the workers, Berdiaev embraced a philosophical theory that enshrined his personal ideals as as absolute, objective ethical values. Bogdanov, on the other hand, was apparently so dedicated to the revolutionary movement that he was incapable of perceiving any difference between his desires and the desires of the working class. Until the end of his active involvement in the working class movement, Bogdanov continued to believe that proletarian thought was the source of true idealism. He was indefatigably optimistic that the proletariat would indeed produce the socialist paradise that Marx had predicted.

The second form of Bogdanov's rebuttal of Neo-
Kantian idealism lay in the realm of epistemology. He accepted Berdiaev's argument that to make an empirical, sceptical criticism of a priori moral judgements entails the
rejection of those other a priori categories of thought
(time, space, and causality) upon which the logic of Marxism depends. Instead of attempting to preserve the concepts
on cause-and-effect or objective reality while at the same
time denying the notion of objective morality, Bogdanov
espoused a thorough-going positivism. He denied the existence of a priori truth in any sense at all.

In disposing of Kant in this way, Bogdanov had also
pulled the philosophical foundation out from underneath
Marxism. Consequently, Bogdanov was faced with the problem
of recreating scientific socialism upon a new ontological
and epistemological base.

From the very beginning of his philosophical inves-
tigations--even before he first argued with Berdiaev over
idealism--Bogdanov had been concerned with the nature of
human knowledge. Unlike both Kant and Marx, he explicitly
rejected the notion of absolute truth. In the introduction
to his first philosophical work, Bogdanov asserted that,
"Knowledge cannot attain unconditional, absolute truth.
Truth is always relative."[7]

Following the positivist tradition, Bogdanov took
a purely experiential attitude toward human knowledge of
external reality. He abandoned the concept of ontology

entirely. He insisted that "reality-in-itself" was a mean-
ingless concept; personal perceptions were the only things
one could know. One should not act on the basis of absolute
principle but according to working hypotheses which are
being constantly reevaluated. Bogdanov offered the scientific method as the only way to achieve knowledge.

> [Scientific knowledge] first is a simple
> description of the facts . . . an empirical elab-
> oration of the question . . . then an "explanation"
> that proceeds from this description--in other
> words, a unifying and simplifying grouping of
> the facts upon the basis of an established
> scientific view. If such a process of work-
> ing out of experience succeeds in embracing
> all that is repetetive and typical in the phe-
> nomena, without contradictions or important
> exceptions, then a whole scientific under-
> standing has been attained.[8]

Furthermore, the whole point of "truth" is practi-
cability. Knowledge arises only from activity in the real
world. Consequently, action is the only test of truth.

> If my activity proceeds completely logic-
> ally from a set of judgements, but leads to
> something other than what I expected, then
> among the judgements there is at least one
> "false one". . . . People always call truth that
> which does not lead to contradictions in prac-
> tice. [Truth is necessary] . . . in order to have
> direct and reliable bases for activity, i.e.
> in the final analysis for the struggle with
> nature. Truth is the principal and best weapon
> in that struggle.
> In activity is the beginning and end, the
> source and the inner meaning of truth.[9]

So anxious was Bogdanov to avoid the concept of a
priori knowledge that he went on to deny explicitly yet
another fundamental assumption of Marxism--the principle
of cause and effect.

> Upon this basis one rejects not only a mater-
> ialist foundation, and in general the idea of
> "substance" in all its aspects, but also the
> principle of causation. Any relationship in
> experience can be expressed as a functional
> dependence of one piece of data upon another . . .
> The idea of causality is no more than a false
> hypothesis.[10]

Having thus discarded the basic presuppositions upon

which Marx had constructed scientific socialism, Bogdanov

had to rewrite Marxism. In revising that doctrine, however,

Bogdanov attempted to maintain it in as orthodox a form as

possible. The scientific socialism of Bogdanov, like that

of Marx, took economic life to be the arena in which the

essential processes of history occurred, it emphasized the

importance of the class struggle in social change, and it

interpreted the economic processes of modern society as in-

evitably ushering the proletariat toward socialist revolu-

tion. But in basing Marxist sociology upon positivist epis-

temology, Bogdanov faced two problems. Both were related

to the notion of material determinism--the cornerstone of

Marxism's pretension to be science.

First, if the objective world is unknowable and real-

ity is defined only by human perception, then "matter" can

hardly be considered to have an existence independent of

human thought. In other words, existence cannot determine

consciousness, for reality does not exist independently of

consciousness. Consciousness, in fact, must be identical

with existence, as those terms were understood by Bogdanov.

Second, the lack of a concept of material causality

would rob Marxism of its strict determinism and predictability. Since material reality was replaced by human perception in Bogdanov's system, historical development could no longer be considered to be a material process. History became an intellectual development. Maintaining notions of "objectivity" and "inevitability" in such a system was the principal problem that Bogdanov attempted to solve over the next few years.

Bogdanov's first major revision of Marxism appeared in "The Development of Life in Nature and Society" published in Obrazovanie in 1902. He began by affirming the truth of Marxism relative to all other philosophies of history, but he also offered to improve upon it. He announced that his intention to develop scientific socialism into a truly universal system based upon a theory of historical development that would apply not only to human life but to the entire natural world. (Years later, Bogdanov's final system claimed to embrace the very principles according to which the entire universe operated.) He wanted to unite biology, physics, chemistry, and sociology into a single universal science.[11]

Following Darwin, Bogdanov found the lowest common denominator of historical development in the natural world to be adaptation and natural selection. He tried to synthesize natural selection with economic determinism by arguing that ". . . the motive force that creates new adaptations lies in the relation of an organic form with its environment."[12] For humankind the "relation with its environment" was none

other than the process of labor. Bogdanov saw labor--grow-
ing food, building shelter, etc.--as the way in which mankind engages in the struggle for existence.

"Social instinct" played a prominent role in Bogdanov's scheme, for he considered social groups to be the
principal means of human adaptation to the natural world.
Men had to labor cooperatively in order to survive, and
this cooperation demanded a number of "organizing adaptations" which contributed to social harmony.

Humanity's first and foremost organizing adaptation
was speech, since it was the communication of feelings,
perceptions, needs, and desires that made people realize
that other human beings were like themselves. Such empathy
led to feelings of family and group loyalty and to the sense
of cooperation and altruism.[13] It was also through speech
that members of a social group shared their perceptions of
their environment and thus collectively worked out a picture
of reality.

By thus focusing upon adaptation in the struggle
for survival instead of Marx's more limited concept of "labor relations" as the central element of social development,
Bogdanov achieved a much wider view of social cause and
effect. The entire concept of "social consciousness" was,
according to Bogdanov, an adaptation in the struggle for
survival. "Attentively observing the various elements of
the social life of people, we are easily convinced that they
factually represent in themselves adaptations in their

struggle to live and nothing else."[14] Thus, not only are technology and the relations of production adaptations in the struggle for survival but also such things as science, law, morality, and, indeed, human knowledge of reality.

Furthermore, "In their struggle for existence, people cannot unite except by means of consciousness; without consciousness there is no socialization. Therefore, social life in all its manifestations is conscious-psychological."[15] Here Bogdanov made his first far-reaching revision of Marx's dictum that "existence determines consciousness." Bogdanov asserted that "In general, sociality is indivisable from consciousness. Social existence and social consciousness, in the precise meanings of these words, are one and the same thing."[16]

In such a context "ideology" is no mere result of production relations; it is an adaptation in the struggle for survival. Ideology is not part of the superstructure of society but its very foundation. Concrete reality and material economic forces were ignored entirely in Bogdanov's new system.

When Bogdanov later went on to elaborate on sociology and history, he related them not to matter but to human thought. Knowledge was the stuff of which Bogdanov's real world was made; the course of history was determined by the laws governing the ways in which human beings think. Thus Bogdanov replaced Marx's materialist ontology with his own empirical epistemology.

The whole point of Bogdanov's substitution of epistemology for ontology seems to have been to counter the arguments of the idealists (though, as we shall see, he echoed them). He was reformulating Marxism in such a way that he assumed the real philosophical position of the idealists even while ridiculing the terms in which they formulated their position.

> In the collection Problems of Idealism
> Prince E. Trubetskoi tries to criticise his-
> torical materialism from the idea that in the
> social life of people not only "economic" but
> "psychological" factors have significance.
> It is obvious that such criticism is mistaken
> in its very base since it suggests that "econ-
> omic" is something non-psychological. In
> this regard, "economics" is the labor rela-
> tions of people and not the physical relation-
> ships of bodies; people are a psychic essence
> and labor is a conscious-expedient activity.[17]

Bogdanov fully realized that he could not deny the idealists' concept of absolute ideal or spiritual reality and at the same time attempt to maintain the concept of absolute material reality. His strictly sceptical, positivist epistemology was an attempt to reject the concept of absolute objective reality in any sense and to focus instead upon the means by which human beings make sense out of external existence.

> Just such an actively-organizing activity of
> knowledge can, in our opinion, do away with
> dualistic contradictions and lead to a really
> harmonious world-view. This will not be a
> monism of "spirit" or of "reality"--such con-
> tentless concepts cannot satisfy critical-mon-
> ist thought. It will be a monism of type of
> organization according to which experience is
> systematized, a monism of knowing method.[18]

Nevertheless, although Bogdanov claimed to do away with both halves of the spirit-matter dichotomy, the only effective result of his formulation was to deny the absolute, objective basis of historical materialism. In finding reality to consist only of human thought, Bogdanov was in an obvious sense actually espousing a form of idealism. Clearly it was not matter but ideas that made up what Bogdanov thought of as "reality."

Despite this essential idealism, however, Bogdanov denied that his epistemological monism was subject to the same subjectivity and individuality that was associated with the idealism of the Neo-Kantians. He claimed for his philosophy an objectivity and concreteness that equalled Marx's monist system in its historical determinism.

In <u>Empiriomonism</u>, a major collection of his philosophical studies published in three volumes, Bogdanov illustrated how one could have an <u>objective</u> idealism.

> The basis of "objectivity" must lie in the sphere of <u>collective</u> experience.
> We term "objective" those data of experience which have the same living significance for us and for other people--those data on which not only we may order our activity without contradiction, but others also may base [their activity] . . .
> The objective character of the physical world consists in the fact that it exists not for me alone but for everyone, and for everyone has a definite meaning, exactly as it does for me.[19]

Thus the sense of a real external world and the sense of ethical values that exist in a society are not the mere whims of individuals. External reality arises from the shared perceptions of the collective consciousness of social groups.

Continuing his response to Berdiaev's dependence upon Kant's a priori categories of thought, Bogdanov explicitly and emphatically rejected the possibility of a priori truth. He argued that such concepts as space and time are not immutably inherent in the mind of man. They have changed and developed over time and there is nothing objective or absolute about them.[20] Similarly, Bogdanov took scientific "laws" to be no more than tentative means of organizing experience into an understandable whole; such laws are no more than temporary hypotheses and will never achieve a final, absolute form.[21]

Bogdanov dismissed the distinction between the real (material) and ideal (spiritual) worlds:

> The newest positivism has shown the identity of the elements on which devolve the content of both these realms of experience; the interruption led in this way to two principly-different types of relationships between the elements--psychical and physical.
> Our analysis led us to the conclusion that these two types of relationship are not at all fundamentally dissimilar--that they are two consequent phases of the organization of experience--psychic is individually organized experience, physical is socially organized. The second type appears as one of the results of the development of the former.[22]

In taking human thought to be the essence of "reality," Bogdanov had to revise certain Marxian concepts in order to retain Marx's general sociological and historical scheme. Obviously, economic relations--physical possession of material things--could no longer be considered "real" in an ontological sense. Thus, economic relations could not be the motive force in historical development. Bogdanov replaced the concept of "possession of the means of production" with the notion of "possession of the knowledge of production." In Bogdanov's sociology, the class that held power in any particular society did so by virtue of the fact that it possessed the knowledge of the techniques and technology of economic production. History thus became the logical development of human knowledge and human thought.

Bogdanov based his system upon what he called the "technical labor process"--that is, the concepts and techniques that a society develops in the course of its struggle to survive in a hostile environment. Labor was nothing more the struggle for existence. "The basic, immediate struggle with nature exists in the social-technical labor process. This is the source of social progress."[23]

The labor process was also the source of knowledge of reality, for it was in this interaction with the elemental chaos of the natural world (the struggle for existence) that human concepts and hypotheses were formulated, tested in practice, and revised. Furthermore, the ideology that Bogdanov conceived of as regulating the cultural life of a society--that is, speech, religion, philosophy, law, ethics, custom--serve to "unify and coordinate human activity," "systematically organize labor," and "eliminate the contradictions of social life."[24]

In Bogdanov's sociological scheme, the ruling stratum or class in a society was not identified by its ownership

of material property but by its possession of the knowledge
basic to the organization of the labor process and by its
consequent control over the ideology that organized the
society. "Classes arise on the ground of progressive isolation of the organizing and administering functions in
society."[25]

Any particular form of society, argued Bogdanov,
is founded upon a particular labor-technical process. Those
who have mastered the knowledge and therefore possess the
organizational control over that labor process become the
ruling class. The ruling class then uses its possession
of ideology to control the rest of the classes in the society and to manipulate the labor process for its own enrich-
ment.

However, as the ruling class becomes primarily an
administrator of society and no longer an organizer of knowledge, it gradually loses contact with the constantly developing technology of labor and knowledge of reality. Eventually the ideology of the ruling class—based upon now out-
moded and old-fashioned knowledge—is no longer appropriate
to the new forms of labor. This anachronistic ideology and
culture becomes a dead weight holding back social progress.
The ruling class becomes more and more estranged from the
technical labor process and more and more impotent and reactionary.

All the while a new class has been developing in
that society. It is composed of those who took over the

organizing functions of the technical labor process when
those functions had been abandoned by the old ruling class.
This new class is the creator of the newest system of knowledge of reality. These organizers soon replace the old
administrators and a new economic and social system is born.
The new ruling class begins to administer society, creates
a new ideology based on the new technical labor process,
and then gradually loses contact with the labor process.
The ruling class will ultimately become reactionary, and,
like its predecessor, it will eventually be overthrown by
the newly arisen organizational class. The spiral will
then continue.

Bogdanov thus retained Marx's pattern of social evolution: each stage of economic development produces from
within itself its own destroyer. Feudalism gave rise to
capitalism just as capitalism will one day give way to socialism. The process of history follows its own internal
laws of development quite independent of the will of individual man.

On one hand, Bogdanov agreed with the idealists that
Marx had no real, absolute material ground upon which to
stand. Yet neither did he allow the idealists to consider
their own a priori ideas to possess an independent, objective,
or absolute significance. Though his system could be thought
of as "idealist" in the sense that human thought is the only
kind of reality that can be understood, Bogdanov attempted
to endow this reality with the attributes of objectivity.

Bogdanov's was a "collective idealism" and a "collective a priori." The only proof of reality was that a number of human beings agreed about its attributes. Yet, for all the unanimity of opinion, such "knowledge of reality" was still only a product of the human mind.

In one way, Bogdanov's system was simply an ingenious rebuttal to Berdiaev's equally ingenious attempt to synthesize Kant with Marx. Bogdanov preserved all the superficial characteristics of Marxism while basing his system upon an epistemology that contradicted the philosophy of both Kant and Marx. He created a version of scientific socialism that was free of a priori concepts and hence free from criticism by Berdiaev.

Nevertheless, in thus defending Marxism from idealism, Bogdanov paradoxically transformed Marxism into a potentially more far-reaching idealism that the idealists themselves may have found acceptable. By focusing entirely upon human thought as the foundation of reality, Bogdanov really liberated human creativity from the constraints of the material world. If reality is nothing more than "mutually agreed upon, mutually organized" perception, then the human collective can--to the extent that it can control and regulate its own perceptions--actually create reality. Theoretically, if the collective willed paradise, then paradise would exist.

Bogdanov, himself, clung to a strict empiricism. He emphasized that positivism was a method of knowledge;

he stressed the importance of gathering facts, creating
temporary hypotheses, and then testing the validity of
those hypotheses in practice in the natural world. What he
did not stress, however, was the assumption that there actually did exist a reality external to the human mind.
Bogdanov admitted no presuppositions at all about that absolute reality; he did not admit it as a subject about which
anyone could talk. Whenever he did refer to the concept of
external reality, he called it simply "elementalness"
(stikhiinost').

But thus ignoring the question of a material, objective real world, Bogdanov actually tended to produce a rather
grandiose idealism. Bogdanov emphasized not the limitations
that the "elementalness" imposed upon mankind, but rather
the infinite opportunities that were open to humanity in
mastering that "elementalness."

It was indicative of Nikolai Berdiaev's keen insight
into the nature of the crisis of idealism in the Russian
Marxist movement that he had actually prescribed the sort
of synthesis of idealism and Marxism that Bogdanov ultimately created. Bogdanov was undoubtedly unaware how close his
thinking actually came to Berdiaev's, and even Berdiaev
himself may not have realized that Bogdanov was following
his advice. Nevertheless, in many ways Bogdanov does seem
to have created that "synthesis of the realistic sociology
of Marx and the idealistic philosophy of history of Fichte
and Hegel" that Berdiaev had felt was necessary to resolve

the contradiction between historical objectivity and individual idealism.

Bogdanov did create an apparently objective concept
of reality. Though the stuff of which his reality was composed (perception) had its origin in the individual human
mind, the reality that was created (collectively organized
experience) was entirely independent of subjective individual influence. Thus Bogdanov avoided the idealist solipsism. In Bogdanov's system each individual human is caught
up in a universal, monistic determinism. The process of
collective consciousness in its ongoing creation of objective reality was subject only to the laws of its own internal development.

The similarity between Bogdanov's universe and Hegel's
is striking. Hegel's universe began with a chaos of elemental matter alienated from itself. This chaos is gradually
ordered into a whole; it is a process of the "universal
spirit" coming to know itself. Hegel understood the development of this "universal spirit" (its movement toward complete self-knowledge) to be an objective process of the natural universe. Humanity is only an element in this development. The laws governing the development and the motive
force behind it form the essence of a self-generating, self-
directing, self-creating cosmic existence. The concept is
usually denoted by the word "God."

Bogdanov's system appears Hegelian except for the
position of the human race in the universe. For Bogdanov,

humanity is not simply a phenomenon of the natural universe.
The collective consciousness of humankind was <u>identical</u> with
the universe. This sort of social subjectivism made the
collective human mind actually the creator of the universe;
this collective mind replaced Hegel's "universal spirit."

In Bogdanov's system humankind makes order out of
the primordial chaos of individual perceptions and progresses toward the creation of an orderly reality. The socialist
revolution would signify that "Extra-social [natural] and
social spontaneity are both overcome by the purposive, organized force of humanity, and its power over nature grows
without bound."[26]

Bogdanov emphasized the infinite possibilities a-
waiting humanity after the dawn of the new era of socialism.
The contemporary struggle between labor and capital was only
the prelude to a much greater struggle between labor and
"elementalness." "The ideal of practical life in our times
is becoming clearer--it reflects the striving to harmoniously
unite all humanity for the struggle with the elemental world
for the ceaseless development of power."[27]

Bogdanov's "collective idealism" laid the foundations for the future theories of God-building.

Lunacharsky's Positivist Esthetics

Though not nearly as profound a thinker as Bogdanov,
Lunacharsky was only slightly less prolific a writer. Beginning with his exile in Vologda and continuing through
the 1905 Revolution, he contributed a steady stream of pole-

mics and essays feeding the fires of the debate between the
Marxists and the idealists. It was indicative of his own
temperamental closeness to the idealist intelligentsia that
Lunacharsky did not cease literary sparring with the idealists in 1905 as so many of his Marxist comrades did. Other
Social-Democrats were anxious to abandon such a seemingly
pointless task as debating philosophical questions when a
real social revolution provided them with very practical
tasks to perform. Throughout his life Lunacharsky almost
always put intellectual pursuits before practical activities.

In the years immediately before the 1905 Revolution,
Lunacharsky maintained a running battle with the idealists
in the pages of the leading scholarly Marxist journals of
the time: Pravda, Osvobozhdenie, and Mir Bozhii. His most
important articles were collected and published in book form
as Polemical and Critical Studies and Comments on Life.
Lunacharsky also contributed to Outlines of a Realistic
World-view—a symposium of anti-idealist Marxists that Bogdanov edited and published in 1903 as a rebuttal to the
idealist symposium, Problems of Idealism.

Lunacharsky was not as systematic a thinker as was
Bogdanov. Though he did reveal in his writings a definite
world-view, Lunacharsky did not take care to develop that
world-view consistently and rigorously. In his works he
attempted to combine the positivist epistemology that he
had imbibed in Zurich with both the scientific socialism
of his revolutionary party and the essentially idealistic

and romantic nature of his personality. The synthesis of
these three elements produced a passionate, visionary, revolutionary voluntarism.

Lunacharsky had more of the poet than the scientist
in his personality. (He was, in fact, a prolific--if med-
iocre--poet and playwright.) The purpose of his philosophical writings was more to create enthusiasm for his ideas
than to support them with logic or factual data. Indeed,
Lunacharsky's arguments frequently degenerate into a purple
prose in which little is apparent aside from an almost mystical enthusiasm for the proletarian revolutionary movement.

In Lunacharsky's works during the period before the
1905 Revolution, the actual world-view that underlay his
thought is rather to be inferred than directly understood.
Where Lunacharsky dealt with positivism and particularly
with positivist epistemology, he limited himself for the
most part to a straightforward, elementary exposition of
the philosophy of his former teacher, Richard Avenarius.

As to the revision of Marxism, Lunacharsky was silent; he left that work entirely to Bogdanov. In the preface to Comments on Life, he explicitly deferred to Bogdanov, praising him as the authoritative thinker in establishing the "scientific underpinnings" of Marxism.

> We are convinced that the future of Marxist
> epistemology and psychology lies in the dir-
> ection in which comrade Bogdanov has been
> searching, i.e., the direction of organic as-
> similation and transformation of empirical
> scientific philosophy into the flesh and blood
> of scientific socialism.[28]

When he, himself, referred to Marxism, Lunacharsky did not concern himself with either its science or its philosophy. He said nothing to suggest that the Marxism to which he was referring was in any way different from the Marxism espoused by the orthodox revolutionary activists of the Social-Democratic party. For the most part Lunacharsky was content to contribute to the Marxist-idealist debate essays of purely polemical intent. Rather than presenting his argument systematically and logically, Lunacharsky tended to exhort his readers with inspirational sermonizing.

The fact that Lunacharsky's vision of the world was at times diametrically opposed to the usual views of scientific socialism was a contradiction that Lunacharsky left to his readers to resolve. Lunacharsky presented his synthetic world-view to the public only after the 1905 Revolution.

In his arguments with the idealists, Lunacharsky followed Bogdanov's lead and attempted to combine Marxism with positivism. He denied the existence of transcendent ethical ideals as being outside the realm of experience and hence unknowable. He asserted that the ideals of socialism were not absolute values but simple empirical statements of fact. That is, the principles of socialism were no more than the concrete needs and desires of the working class. Lunacharsky also followed Bogdanov's epistemology closely.

Nevertheless, there was a significant difference of emphasis between Lunacharsky and Bogdanov. Although he

actually proved the opposite, Bogdanov's principal interest
seemed to have been protecting Marxism's spirit of objective
determinism and preventing revolutionary Marxists from being seduced by idealism into passive introspection. Bogdanov revised Marxism in such a way as to maintain that sense
of strict scientific objectivity and monistic determinism
that distinguished scientific from utopian socialism. As
a result of this interest, Bogdanov's main concern was to
elaborate upon the nature of reality--or rather the nature
of human knowledge of reality--and to establish his own conception of objectivity and causality that would be immune
from the attacks of the idealists.

Lunacharsky, on the other hand, did not seem nearly
as interested in preventing the scientific socialists from
deserting the revolutionary movement as he was concerned
with summoning the idealists back into the Social-Democratic
camp. Lunacharsky did pay lip service to the objectivity
of Marxism and the inevitability of the proletarian revolutionary movement, but he did not insist that there was anything wrong with the ideals of the idealists. Instead of
arguing that those ideals had no objective foundation, Lunacharsky simply insisted that the only way in which the ideals
could be realized was through social activity.

Whereas Bogdanov began his system with the primacy
of human perception, Lunacharsky took human desire and will
as his principal themes. His purpose was to demonstrate
that ideals were of purely social origin and could not be

realized except in the realm of social existence. Not sur-
prisingly, Lunacharsky discovered the foundations of his
world-view in the realm of esthetics.

The Foundations of a Positive Esthetics was Lunacharsky's principal theoretical work of the pre-revolution-
ary period. He began by observing that,

> . . . the deeper we went into questions of esthet-
> ics, the clearer became for us the tremendous
> significance of the laws [of esthetics] for
> the related realms of ethics and epistemology.
> The basic laws of esthetics, properly under-
> stood, throw a clear light on all of psycho-
> logy and can serve as a basis for a total
> world-view.[29]

Lunacharsky denied that ethics was a viable philosophical concern since a positivist could only make descrip-
tive, empirical statements about the external world. Nothing, to a positivist, can be good or bad in any absolute
sense--it simply exists. The only area in which value
judgements can be made in the real world, according to Lunacharsky's analysis, was in the direct relationship of the
individual animal to its environment. He argued that an
animal has no real basis upon which to conceive of something
as good or bad except in the personal sensations of "agreeable" or "disagreeable." Such evaluations seemed to Lunacharsky to be more akin to esthetic than to ethical judgements.

> All that supports life--truth, goodness, and
> beauty--is something that is in general posi-
> tive, good, attractive; all that destroys or
> lowers life--false, evil, and ugly--is some-
> thing that is in general negative, bad, and
> repulsive.[30]

> . . . the ideal [of life] is life itself;
> full, complete, flourishing, victorious, cre-
> ative life. . . . From the point of view of
> his ideal--that is, his desires (in the form
> of the most immediate everyday needs or in
> the form of elaborate and finished notions
> of truth, beauty, and justice)--man judges
> all phenomena. Esthetics is the science of
> value; the theory of knowledge and of ethics
> are only ramifications--having, of course,
> their own particular characteristics.[31]

Lunacharsky's conception of positivist esthetics was to reduce all questions of value to purely animal terms. Like Bogdanov, Lunacharsky sought a systematic formulation that would apply not only to man but to the entire natural world as well. His system of esthetics was based on purely behavioral, mechanistic concepts that seemed to lend themselves to scientific observation and measurement.

> The ideal of life appears to the organism as
> that life in which it experiences the maximum
> pleasure . . . when the organism is abundantly
> nourished and is expending its energy freely,
> subject only to its own internal laws. . .
> Therefore, the ideal of life is the most power-
> ful and free life, life in which the organs
> are rhythmical, harmonious, fluent, and pleas-
> ant, in which the very instincts of growth and
> creativity are luxuriantly satisfied . . .[32]

The ultimate point toward which Lunacharsky directed the argument of his treatise was to prove that human ideals were of natural origin and would be realized in the objective world of human experience. He concluded his work by asserting that,

> The people thirst for a better future; the
> people have been idealists from time immemorial.
> But their ideals have become more realistic
> to the extent that they are more conscious of
> their powers. [The people] are more and more
> willing to abandon thought of achieving the
> heavens and to live an earthly life--

> broadening and uplifting life endlessly. To
> promote the growth of the faith of the people
> in their own powers and in a better future,
> to search for a rational path to that future:
> this is the task of man.[33]

Thus Lunacharsky used esthetic judgement in the
same way that Bogdanov had used sense perception: as a
natural, objective, positivist, relative basis upon which
to rest Marx's theory that socialist revolution was historically inevitable. But whereas Bogdanov had taken considerable pains to elaborate upon the ways in which positivist
epistemology affected the sociological and philosophical
underpinnings of Marxism, Lunacharsky apparently thought
the subject was better left undiscussed. He simply suggested ways in which his positivist esthetics might contribute
to the objectivity and scientific nature of the Social-Democratic movement.

However, quite the contrary of his intent, the very
terms in which Lunacharsky tried to make esthetics into a
natural science produced, in the end, an almost mystical
vision of social transformation. In his concern with esthetics, he came to substitute esthetic sensibility for material economic relationships and art for historical materialism. In Lunacharsky's conception, art became the means
by which socialist revolutionaries could raise up the working class and transform the world.

In Lunacharsky's esthetic system, art performed
three functions: to describe the present evil condition
of the world, to depict the struggle of humankind in over-

coming that evil, and to give glimpses of the ideal world toward which humanity is striving.[34]

> These kinds of art can be called <u>realistic</u> idealism because they all lead to the ideal; striving toward [the ideal] is the essence [of art]. But this ideal applies to the world. In all its aspects, in all the paths along which it moves toward [the ideal], it does not cross the boundaries of the real.[35]

Art performed precisely the same function in Lunacharsky's esthetics as knowledge did in Bogdanov's empiriomonism. Both are means by which humanity liberates itself from the realm of causality (that is, from the limitations imposed upon man by the hostile natural world or from bondage to oppressive ruling classes) and by which humanity asserts its mastery over the chaos of the elemental universe. Throughout <u>The Foundations of a Positive Esthetics</u>, Lunacharsky continually drew parallels between humankind and Prometheus; the theme of the book is, in fact, mankind's taking possession of the domain of the gods.

In his conclusion, after stressing that humanity would realize its ideals in the here and now, Lunacharsky suggested how it would be done:

> To beautify as strongly as possible the life of the people, to depict the radiant pictures of the happiness and the perfection of the future; and at the same time to show all the repulsive evil of the past, to develop a feeling of tragedy, the love of struggle and victory, Promethean striving, stubborn pride, uncompromising courage, to unite hearts in a general sense of ascent toward the superman --here is the task of the artist.[36]

It was thus in 1903 that the foundations of "Socialist Realism" were laid. Lunacharsky's definition of art became the formula for that Soviet genre. Lunacharsky's positivist esthetics also provided the theoretical justification of Maksim Gorky's God-building novels--the actual prototypes of Socialist Realism.

In "What is Idealism?" Bogdanov had attempted to portray the Social-Democratic revolutionaries as the true idealists because they were actively trying to realize their ideals on earth while the idealists were merely passive dreamers. This idea was the inspiration for nearly everything that Lunacharsky wrote in his polemics with the idealists. He objected to the idealists not because there was anything wrong with their ideals but because they relegated their ideals to the realm of dreams or to some transcendent existence: "The more clearly the idealist tries to illuminate the reign of heaven, the more tragic gloom he casts upon the earth."[37]

In "On 'Problems of Idealism'" Lunacharsky admitted that he sympathized with the idealists because they believed in lofty moral ideals and longed for spiritual and social perfection. He objected to their position because they made no effort to realize their ideals in the physical world. For Lunacharsky, ideals were inseparable from the social existence of all humanity. Goodness, truth, and beauty would be real only when they were actually experienced by mankind on earth.

Novgorodtsev, one of the contributors to Problems of Idealism, had accused the positivists of apathy; Lunacharsky quoted him as saying that the positivist personality cannot deal with the highest concepts of thought--moral consciousness, philosophical curiosity, and human creativity. Novgorodtsev argued that positivists were capable only of observing and recording sterile, lifeless facts.

Lunacharsky, however, pointed to the positivist Populists of the 1860s and 1870s as people who both possessed lofty ideals and actively sought to realize them in the material world.[38] Lunacharsky argued that it was not the positivists but the idealists who were apathetic dreamers: they hoped that if they "believed" in something that would make it come true.[39]

> The idealists do not have the courage to look truth in the eye, to state that we cannot relate sceptically to the human mission in the world; [they] do not have the courage to clearly see that the future is not definite and man must depend only on his own power to attain what he desires.[40]

By this point in the argument, however, Lunacharsky's logic had taken a paradoxical twist. He was actually berating the idealists for possessing the very trait that the idealists found so objectionable in Marxism--that is, belief in determinism. Though he never admitted it in so many words, Lunacharsky clearly conceived of the "scientific socialist" movement as an act of voluntarism on the part of an organization of idealists and not as a materially determined social upheaval.

In his preface to Comments on Life, Lunacharsky did pay lip service to the scientific basis of Marxism. But he

discovered in the concept of "existence determines consciousness" a relationship between material existence and human
thought that destroyed the concept of determinism completely.
Lunacharsky asserted that only vulgar Marxism ". . . denies
the tremendous complexity of the process of psychological
adaptation of the individual and the mass to the forces and
impulses of social environment."[41]   He added,

> The human psyche--both of the individual
> and the collective--is an exceedingly compli-
> cated and subtle mechanism. How to determine
> precisely the material ground of the birth,
> growth, and death of this or that idea, how
> enthusiasm flares up in the heart or is exting-
> uished in cold apathy, by what path collective
> goals are transformed into individual ideals
> that are so powerful that it can silence all
> egoistic instincts including even the instinct
> of self-preservation--these are a few of the
> tasks which psychology presents.[42]

In "Idealists and Positivists as Psychological Types,"
Lunacharsky argued that the principal difference between
the idealists and the positivists was a matter of personality. Both types of people shared precisely the same feelings of social obligations, duties, and ideals, according
to Lunacharsky. But whereas the idealist "anthropomorphizes"
nature and imagines that such feelings on the part of the
individual are objectively valid in a metaphysical or ethical sense, Lunacharsky asserted that those feelings have a
natural source in the real world and have no transcendent
ethical value.

> We think that a human is always led by in-
> terest and feeling, and that this interest,
> this feeling, grows along with the growth of
> culture, becomes more complicated and elevated.
> The human works at his own ideal, heeding the

voice of his needs, and due to the growth of
social feeling, this ideal attains a social
or cultural character. The realist does not
want to anthropomorphize nature; he accepts
it as it is, from the point of view of human,
full indefiniteness and is boundlessly happy
that it presents such marvelous material for
the transformation of [the real] into the
ideal. The ideal will appear when nature has
become the arena for the most powerful life,
the most powerful human species.[43]

But once again, just as he had done in the Preface

to Comments on Life, under the pretense of defending mater-

ial determinism, Lunacharsky actually argued from the point

of view of voluntaristic idealism. He apparently took for

granted a material, deterministic universe, but he empha-

sized the fact that individual human beings must believe

themselves to have free will and to act as if they do. Lun-

acharsky distinguished between the concept of determinism

and the sense of fatalism.

Fatalism contradicts freedom, it supposes a
consciousness outside us . . . determinism
does not in the least contradict freedom. It
only analyzes the fact of my freedom, and
finds that it is my freedom, i.e., determined
by my organism in its turn found in the chain
of events.[44]

This is not an uncommon form of justification of

the sense of individual free will by people who believe in

universal determinism. Nevertheless, when Lunacharsky talk-

ed about "the human mission in the world" he certainly im-

plied that human will lay outside the realm of material

cause and effect. Furthermore, even when he spoke of de-

terminism, he emphasized that determinism was a tool for

mankind to use and not a constraint upon it. He said that,

"The same determinism teaches that no action can pass without an effect, and that we, depending upon definite laws,
can always count on the result we want from the appropriate
action on the environment."[45]

Thus it was not by any logical argument, but simply
by repetition and emphasis, that Lunacharsky insisted upon
human free will. Echoing Bogdanov's conclusions, if not
his reasoning, Lunacharsky asserted that human beings can
excercise control over nature by learning about the real
world and understanding the laws according to which the universe operates.

> Knowledge is that terrific power which sets
> [mankind] off against nature. The more objec-
> tive knowledge, the less empty fantasy it con-
> tains, the more precise its correspondence with
> reality, the easier it is to be armed with it
> and to subjugate the elemental world and master
> it.[46]

What really separated Lunacharsky from the idealists was his epistemology; he called himself a "positivist
idealist."[47] Like the idealists, Lunacharsky believed in
certain social ideals such as love, brotherhood, equality,
justice, etc. But whereas the idealists tended to expect
those ideals to exist only on some transcendent plane and
unrealizable in the real world, Lunacharsky believed them
to be attainable through social action.

Nevertheless, Lunacharsky found nothing contradictory between S. Frank's idea that human beings can have
"desires of the mind" with his own purely naturalist interpretation of human values. He quoted with complete appro-

bation Frank's statement that, "The Faustian striving of humanity is infinitely higher than animals because it insures the endless growth of the spiritual power of humankind."[48]

In an essay entitled "Philosophy and Life," Lunacharsky gave his clearest expression of the way in which he understood Marxism to be related to life. He began by asserting that philosophy is alien to the practical affairs of life and hence is a useless field of thought. Philosophy and life appear to be mutually contradictory, and the question that Lunacharsky set for himself was, "A philosophy of life, a philosophy of concrete reality--Is it possible?"[49]

> After all, in the first place, philosophy is
> always based on generalization; in the second
> place, in what way could such a philosophy
> help mankind? Philosophy which does not gen-
> eralize can have no value as a science. A
> philosophy which does not console can have
> no moral value.[50]

Lunacharsky then announced that "the realistic philosophy, created by the ideologues of the proletariat does, to a great extent, possess both those values."[51] He asserted that, first of all, Marxism was based upon generalizations from the factual data of human experience in the real world. Lunacharsky considered that Marxism was in fact a relative and not absolute description of the world. It was, indeed, a positivist science.

> It [Marxism] generalizes, but does not scorn-
> fully disregard time, does not try to imagine
> motion in an integral, eternal formula. [Marx-
> ism] simply finds laws of this concrete histori-
> cal movement, and deduces the leading principles

for predicting the future from an analysis of
past and present reality. . . . Here there is
no place for general laws for all times--here
all leads to the investigation of constantly
changing reality, the calculation of the full
tendencies of life in the development of society.[52]

Secondly, Lunacharsky also discovered a moral value

to be present in Marxism. He said that "Marxist historical

philosophy gives meaning to that chaos of life which fright-

ens the alienated individual."[53] Lunacharsky did not spell

out the precise nature or origin of that "meaning to life."

But it is apparent that the meaning--the ideals and morals

that "console" the individual--of Marxism is identical with

the needs and desires of the proletariat:

This philosophy does not set against the
horror of reality dreams of "order" that exists
somewhere, it does not seek to escape from life
into the realm of dreams, it does not form various laws which, with the help of "the heavenly
spirit" can sometime be realized in our world.
No, the proletariat does not need to run away
from life: no matter how heavy it is, [the
proletariat] is not afraid, it will overcome
it and does not wait for the help of "the a-
bove" to realize its ideals, and therefore does
not need to believe that God himself and his
angels approve of their program.[54]

Here, in "Philosophy and Life," Lunacharsky once

again transformed Marxism--by implication rather than ex-

plicit revision--into a form of positivist idealism. His

presentation of "generalization of laws from reality" was

obviously identical with the epistemological positivism of

Bogdanov and Avenarius. And while his conception of ideal-

ism supposedly had its origins in the actual desires of the

proletariat, it is clear that the ideals that Lunacharsky

was really talking about were the subjective ideals of himself and of the class to which he belonged.

Once again, Lunacharsky was not directing his appeals
toward those who were already active in the revolutionary
movement. Rather he tried to show the idealists that they
should bring their idealistic desires into the social struggle. He offered Marxism not as an inflexible prediction
of the future, but as a (positivist) method of understanding
reality and acting in the real world in order to realize
social perfection. Marxism, from Lunacharsky's positivist
perspective, became a guide to practical action and not a
universal, absolute system. It was no more than a means
by which ideals could be made real.

Lunacharsky's overwhelming desire to reconcile his
romantic, idealist personality with his commitment to the
socialist revolutionary movement and to the theories of scientific socialism is well illustrated in an essay entitled
"Cathedral or Workshop?" published in Obrazovanie in 1906.
His objective was to justify the presence of subjective,
individual ideals in the revolutionary socialist movement.
For the text of his sermon, Lunacharsky took a statement
that Bazarov makes in Fathers and Sons: "The world is not
a cathedral but a workshop."

Lunacharsky began by recognizing the good that had
been done by the realism, materialism, and scientism of the
Enlightenment, yet he regretted the fact that realism ignored the significance of ideals and the human spirit.

"Militant bourgeois realism dispersed much fog, destroyed many stifling laws, but not all free hearts welcomed without reservation the destructive work of Enlightenment ideas."[55]

Lunacharsky said that he was not thinking about religious people who wanted to continue to believe in angels, but rather about idealistic yet scientific people such as Goethe: "Young Goethe, having read Holbach's System of Nature, eloquently described that heavy spiritual condition into which he was plunged by his acquaintance with the materialist view of the world."[56]

According to Lunacharsky, the confusion under which thinkers such as Goethe labored was the belief that spiritual ideals could exist only if they were transcendent--embodied in an idealist metaphysics. Lunacharsky solved the problem by asserting that ideals are not to be believed to exist in any abstract way but rather actively created--made to exist in the real world.

Once again, the only difference between an idealist and Lunacharsky's conception of a positivist is personality. The idealist loses himself in solipsism and imaginative escapism from the real world, while the positivist strives to actively live his idealism and make his ideals real.

In his concluding answer to the question "Cathedral or Workshop?," Lunacharsky refused to think of the world as a workshop. That was too pessimistic a view: "A nasty, capitalist workshop, full of pointless noise, elemental hatred, forced labor, and parasitism . . . And from the

workshop everyone plods wearily to the grave."[57] Lunacharsky
announced that he preferred to think of the world as a cathedral, but he insisted that his attitude did not imply a
belief in the existence of God. "Strong and brave man
proudly raises his head and lifts up his strong hands, [and
says] 'God is not, now I must become God.'"[58]

Anticipating the millenarian theme of his later
works, Lunacharsky portrayed the proletarian revolutionary
movement as the heir of idealism by asserting that the proletariat will take the place of God and create a heaven
upon the earth.

> In the world there is a place for enthusiasm,
> for creativity, for colossal construction, for
> limitless love that masters time and space. And
> you still find that it is insufficiently poet-
> ical, Messrs. Romantics? Poor dry hearts!
> The world is an evil workshop, but, through
> the power of its sufferers, that workshop be-
> comes the arena of the greatest world-wide
> struggle and is transformed into a cathedral.
> Yes, transformed into a cathedral in which the
> God will be man himself.[59]

Thus, paradoxically, Lunacharsky had begun by defending scientific socialism from idealism and ended up with a
more optimistic idealism that the idealists themselves espoused. The origin of this development is to be found in
the debate with Berdiaev over the question of objectivity.
Berdiaev had demonstrated that a Marxist had no logical
ground on which to attack Kant's absolute idealism without
also discrediting Marx's absolute materialism.

Both the objective ideal and the objective real are
outside human experience. Kant tried to accept the exis-

tence of both; Marx and his followers wanted to accept only the concept of absolute material reality. However, the conception of absolute objectivity depends upon a priori categories of thought. Consequently, when Bogdanov and Lunacharsky used positivist epistemology to criticise the idealists, they inevitably also undermined the materialism and determinism of scientific socialism.

They adopted the positivist point of view because it seemed to provide the objectivity and predictability that are the attributes of science. However, in restricting their analysis of reality solely to human perception and ignoring questions of ontology entirely, the "empiriomonists" gradually began to portray the human mind as the source of reality--not simply in the sense of interpreting but actually creating the real world. Thus the ultimate idealism (the identification of the proletariat with the all-knowing, all-creating God) that would soon be elaborated upon in God-building and Proletarian Culture had its origins in the attempt of two young Marxist revolutionaries to prevent Marxists from straying into idealism.

NOTES TO CHAPTER II

[1]A. Bogdanov, Iz psikhologii ovshchestva, 2nd ed. (St. Petersburg: Elektropechatnia tovarishchestva "Delo," 1906), p. iii.

[2]A. Bogdanov, "Chto takoe idealizma," in Iz psikhologii obshchestva, p. 14.

[3]Ibid., p. 21.

[4]Ibid., p. 31.

[5]Ibid., p. 22.

[6]Ibid., p. 37.

[7]A. Bogdanov, Osnovy istoricheskago vzgliada na prirodu (St. Petersburg: Izdanie Spb. Aktsionern. Obshchestva Pech. Dela "Izdatel'," 1899), p. 9.

[8]Ibid.

[9]Ibid., p. 3.

[10]Ibid., p. 17.

[11]A. Bogdanov, "Razvitie zhizni v prirode i obshchestve," in Iz psikhologii obshchestva, p. 41.

[12]Ibid., p. 48.

[13]Ibid., p. 72.

[14]Ibid., p. 52.

[15]Ibid., p. 57.

[16]Ibid., p. 51.

[17]Ibid., p. 57.

[18]Ibid., p. 54.

[19]A. Bogdanov, Empiriomonism, 3 vols., 2nd ed. (Moscow: S. Dorovatovskago i A. Charushnikova, 1905), vol. 1, p. 25.

[20]Ibid., p. 31.

[21]Ibid., p. 40.

[22]Ibid., p. 41.

[23]Empiriomonism, vol 3., p. 34.

[24]Ibid., pp. 41-2.

[25]Ibid., pp. 139-40.

[26]Ibid., p. 53.

[27]Ibid., p. 59.

[28]A. V. Lunacharsky, Otkliki zhizni (St. Petersburg: Izdatel'stvo O. N. Popovoi, 1906), p. vi.

[29]A. V. Lunacharsky, "Osnovy pozitivnoi estetiki," in Ocherki realisticheskago mirovozreniia, 2nd ed. (St. Petersburg: S. Dorovatovskago i A. Charushnikova, 1905), p. 114.

[30]Ibid., p. 67.

[31]Ibid., p. 131.

[32]Ibid., p. 66.

[33]Ibid., p. 180.

[34]Ibid., p. 172.

[35]Ibid., p. 71.

[36]Ibid., p. 180.

[37]Ibid., p. 131.

[38]A. V. Lunacharsky, "O 'problemakh idealizma,'" in Etiudy kriticheskie i polemicheskie (Moscow: Izdanie zhurnala "Pravda," 1905), p. 215.

[39]Ibid.

[40]Ibid., pp. 215-16.

[41]Otkliki zhizni, p. iii.

[42]Ibid., p. iv.

[43]A. V. Lunacharsky, "Idealist i pozitivist kak psikhologicheskie tipy," in Etiudy polemicheskie i kriticheskie, p. 273.

[44]"O 'Problemakh idealizma,'" pp. 236-7.

[45]Ibid., p. 237.

[46]Ibid., p. 235.

[47]Ibid.

[48]Ibid.

[49]A. V. Lunacharsky, "Filosofiia i zhizn'," in Ot-kliki zhizni, p. 178.

[50]Ibid., pp. 178-9.

[51]Ibid., p. 179.

[52]Ibid.

[53]Ibid.

[54]Ibid., p. 180.

[55]A. V. Lunacharsky, "Khram ili masterskaia?" in Otkliki zhizni, p. 181.

[56]Ibid., p. 182.

[57]Ibid., p. 185.

[58]Ibid., p. 187.

[59]Ibid., p. 189.

CHAPTER III

BOLSHEVISM AND IDEALISM

Lenin's Politics: Idealism in Organizational Form

The first decade of Russian Marxism had been intellectually lively but organizationally diffuse. There had
been too many different kinds of Marxists to allow any unity
in the movement. Though uniformity was never to be a characteristic of the RSDRP and ideological and programmatic
squabbles were to rage in the party for the next three decades, nevertheless, soon after the turn of the twentieth
century certain important issues had been resolved.

First of all, Marxism was no longer fashionable in
intellectual circles. The sociologists, economists, philosophers, and religious searchers had dropped out of the
movement to pursue their interests in non-revolutionary directions. Secondly, Marxism lost from its ranks its moderate
and gradualist political activists. The successes of the
workers' movement of the 1890s encouraged some labor organizers to place their hope for progress in the hands of the
workers. Labor unions and democratic processes would gradually transform Russian society for the better. Thus the
defection of the academics left Marxism in the hands of the
political activists, and the defection of the moderates left
it in the hands of the revolutionaries.

Marxism had been represented in Russia during the 1890s in innumerable small study circles and propaganda circles with tremendous variation in kind and degree of revolutionary commitment. The loss of the non-revolutionary Marxists from these circles was the prerequisite to the consolidation of such groups into a single, unified Social-Democratic party. The term "Marxist" soon became synonomous with membership in the RSDRP; the only Russians who remained Marxists were those whose primary commitment was to promoting socialist revolution.

Those Russians who remained convinced Marxists after 1900 had sought in Marx's theories not answers to philosophical questions but a justification for their revolutionary commitment. They devoted their lives to practical political activity. They had neither the intellectual need nor the inclination to question the fundamental philosophical foundation of Marxism. They accepted Marx's descriptions, analyses, and predictions as statements of scientific fact. True to Marx, they strove to promote proletarian revolution, but they had no interest in intellectually resolving any contradiction between their practical tactics or programs and the philosophy of Marxism. They sought to prove Marx's predictions not by logic but by concrete demonstration.

It was natural that Lenin should have risen to prominence in the RSDRP at this time since political organization and not philosophy was his particular genius. Lenin was the first Russian Social-Democratic revolutionary to

realize just how a unified, politically effective, nation-
wide revolutionary party could be formed. While still in
exile in 1899, Lenin foresaw the organizational, central-
izing significance of a single, central party journal that
could develop and propagate a consistent party viewpoint.

The isolation of local party circles from one another,
the constant surveillance of the police, and the consequent
impossibility of direct communication among those groups
made a cohesive national organization almost inconceivable.
An effective, coordinated political party could hardly be
built upon a representative system in which elected regional and national assemblies could democratically discuss
issues and formulate policies.

The solution that Lenin proposed involved the publication of a single theoretical journal that could be made
available to all party members and would present a party
program for all to follow. The central organ would--ideal-
ly--represent a consensus of party opinion. An indirect
system of representation, and the presence of agents of the
organ at the local level, would bring ideas from the lowest
levels to the top. Nevertheless, if the party was to be
capable of united action, then the program of the central
organ had to be obligatory upon all members. It was only
by following the party line of such an organ that all Social-
Democrats, no matter where in Russia they found themselves,
could feel confident that they were participating in a united,
nation-wide movement.

Soon after arriving in Switzerland in 1900 after
his exile was over, Lenin convinced the emigre leaders of
revolutionary Marxism of the significance of such a central
journal. Iskra was begun before the year ended, and the
unification of the RSDRP began in earnest. Or, rather,
the unification of an RSDRP began. Iskra spoke only for
the Marxists who were social revolutionaries. It expressed
faith in the coming socialist revolution and championed the
idea of a tightly knit party of political activists who
would lead the proletariat in making that revolution.

The process of creating a Social-Democratic revolutionary party in Russia had very little to do with the scientific interpretation of Russia in terms of orthodox Marxism. Both the "Economists" and the "Iskrists" believed
themselves to be Marxists; they buttressed their arguments
with and founded their programs upon the authority of Marx.
What occurred as Iskra sent its agents--along with its news-
paper--out into Russia to organize a national party was the
separation of the impatient Marxist revolutionaries from
the moderate Marxist gradualists.

It was, perhaps, natural that the revolutionary
activists came to dominate the RSDRP. The idea of a tightly
organized, centralized party was alien to the political convictions of the moderates. They expected the working class
to make its revolution spontaneously; it would not need an
elite leadership. The Economists therefore did not fight
hard for either the creation or the content of a strong

party center. As the Iskra-ists consolidated and centralized the party, the moderates found themselves excluded from
it. There was no room in Iskra's RSDRP for their political
convictions.

The distinguishing characteristic of the RSDRP as
it arose was that it wanted to actively promote proletarian
revolution. It was not composed of passive social observers
but of activists who wanted to hasten the process of history.
The purpose of a nation-wide organization, a network of
agents, and a centralized policy-making organ was to create
an efficient political party capable of organizing the working class, instilling in them the proper Social-Democratic
consciousness, and leading them in the revolution.

Thus, the entire reason for the existence of the
RSDRP was a result of the very "crisis of idealism" that
Berdiaev had identified within Russian Marxism. That crisis
involved the choice between having faith in the ideals of
the working class (as revealed in the concrete demands of
the actual labor movement) or having faith in the individual
Marxist's own conception of the ideals of socialism. Those
who accepted the values of the trade-union movement had no
need of a separate, underground, centralized party. But
such a party was absolutely essential to those who saw that
their own personal ideals were at variance with the goals
of the working class and who wanted to direct the labor
movement according to those ideals.

At first Lenin's organizational views were praised

universally by the revolutionary Marxists, but in a short
time temperamental differences began to emerge even among
the revolutionaries. Lenin himself became the organizer of
one of the two major tendencies. His Bolshevik faction of
the RSDRP took an extreme position in organizational as well
as programmatic terms. They were in favor of the most highly centralized and responsible form of party organization.
The reason why they so strongly favored a centralized party
organization, of course, was because the Bolsheviks were
most impatient for the commencement of working class revolution and most apprehensive that the workers would be unable
to manage their revolution without the help of professional
revolutionaries.

The Bolsheviks were thus the most idealistic of the
Marxists. They were the most confident that their own subjective ideals were the proper goals for the proletarian
revolutionary movement. In his theoretical writings, Lenin
revealed the fundamental idealism that was typical of the
members of the Bolshevik faction.

Lenin was not a philosopher by nature. Had he been,
he might have agreed with Bogdanov that a philosophical or
scientific revision of Marxism was necessary in order to
adapt it to his own idealist, voluntarist revolutionary disposition. As it was, Lenin found Marxism convincing simply
because its attitudes toward revolution were agreeable to
him. As a practical social activist, Lenin simply did not
find it necessary to develop Marxism in a theoretical and

certainly not a philosophical sense.

Lenin argued almost exclusively by reference to the "revolutionary-ness" of any particular doctrine. One was true to Marxism, in Lenin's understanding of it, if one was dedicated to the promotion of socialist revolution. Conversely, one was a renegade from Marxism if one proposed that violent revolution could be delayed, ameliorated, or avoided. Similarly, Lenin chose not to concern himself about the possibility that certain of his organizational principles or programmatic demands might violate any of Marx's theories. The standard by which Lenin judged his program was purely political; he considered that the proper strategy for a Marxist was that strategy that hastened the coming of proletarian revolution.

For the most part the expression of Lenin's true world-view is to be found not in his theoretical pronouncements (which were purely polemical, anyway) but rather in the inferences which can be drawn from his political principles. Lenin did not preach idealism, he acted it.

For instance, on the entire question of idealism—the relation of ideas to material existence and the role of individual will in historical development—Lenin was extremely close to the views of the Millenarian Bolsheviks. Though he argued in print against Bogdanov's rejection of Marx's dictum, "existence determines consciousness," Lenin revealed in his political programs and strategies that he really did live by Bogdanov's views and not Marx's.

What is to be Done? presented an organizational expression of the notion that existence does not determine
consciousness. Lenin's whole point in writing that work
was based on the assumption that socialist consciousness
could not arise among the working class simply as a result
of their existence as wage laborers. Consciousness had to
be brought to them by another class.

Not being a theorist by nature, Lenin did not try
to compose his own philosophical justification of his revision of Marxism. Neither did he quote from Bogdanov, though
he could easily have borrowed one of Bogdanov's notions
about the primacy of human thought over the data of physical
existence (or experience, as Bogdanov would have said).

Instead, Lenin relied on the arguments of Karl Kautsky. Kautsky, like Bogdanov, seems to have envisioned knowledge and ideology as a development parallel with economic
development and not a product of it. Consciousness was independent of existence; ideology could influence economics.
Lenin quoted Kautsky:

> Many of our revisionist critics believe
> that Marx asserted that economic development
> and the class struggle create not only the
> conditions for socialist production, but also,
> and directly, the consciousness (K. K.'s ital-
> ics) of its necessity. . . . In this conncec-
> tion socialist consciousness appears to be a
> necessary and direct result of the proletarian
> class struggle. But this is absolutely untrue.
> Of course, socialism, as a doctrine, has its
> roots in modern economic relationships just
> as the class struggle of the proletariat has,
> and, like the latter, emerges from the strug-
> gle against the capitalist-created poverty and
> misery of the masses. But socialism and the
> class struggle arise side by side and not one

> out of the other; each arises under different
> conditions. [My italics.] Modern socialist
> consciousness can arise only on the basis of
> profound scientific knowledge. Indeed, modern
> economic science is as much a condition for
> socialist production as, say, modern technology,
> and the proletariat can create neither the one
> nor the other . . . The vehicle of science
> is not the proletariat, but the bourgeois in-
> telligentsia (K. K.'s italics): It was in the
> minds of individuals of this stratum that mod-
> ern socialism originated, and it was they who
> communicated it to the more intellectually de-
> veloped proletarians . . . Thus socialist con-
> sciousness is something introduced into the
> proletarian class struggle from without and
> not something that arose within it spontan-
> eously.[1]

The intention of Kautsky, Lenin, and Bogdanov is

clearly the same. They did not wish to bow to the imperson-

al, inevitable forces of history. They were not fatalists;

they did not believe that their individual efforts were use-

less in hastening the arrival of socialism. Indeed, their

voluntarism inevitably drew them toward idealism.

Like Bogdanov, in his article "What is Idealism?,"

Lenin was anxious to appropriate idealism to his own cause.

He wanted Social-Democratic revolutionaries not to be sober

social scientists and mechanical organizers; he wanted them

to dream. In What is to be Done?, Lenin spoke of the neces-

sity of dreaming. In mock shame that a Marxist would con-

sider dreaming, Lenin said that he would "hide behind the

back of Pisarev," and he quoted the latter:

> "The rift between dreams and reality causes
> no harm if only the person dreaming believes
> seriously in his dream, if he attentively ob-
> serves life, compares his observations with
> his castles in the air, and if, generally speak-
> ing, he works conscientiously for the achieve-
> ment of his fantasies. If there is some connec-

> tion between dreams and life then all is well."
>   Of this kind of dreaming there is unfortunate-
> ly too little in our movement. And the people
> most responsible for this are those who boast
> of their sober views, their "closeness" to the
> "concrete," the representatives of legal crit-
> icism and of illegal "tailism."[2]

One of Lenin's objections to Plekhanov's "Second
Draft Program" for the Second Congress of the RSDRP had to
do with just this issue of emotional involvement of the revolutionaries in the task of accelerating the historical
process. Once again, Lenin's attitude reinforces the idea
that the positions of various Russian revolutionaries had
little to do with Marxism and much to do with individual
temperament. Lenin and Plekhanov were both avowed Marxists,
but each interpreted Marx in a different way. Lenin was an
activist revolutionary, and he consequently emphasized all
the elements of Marxism that tended to support fervent revolutionary activity. Plekhanov (in his mature years, at any
rate) was a scholar of society, history, and philosophy.
He was a writer and not an organizer. Plekhanov therefore
emphasized the scientific, passive, deterministic elements
of Marxism.

In criticizing Plekhanov's draft program, Lenin said
that "The entire character of the programme is, in my opinion, the most general and basic defect of this draft . . .
Specifically, it is not the program of a party engaged in
a practical struggle . . . it is rather a program for students . . ."[3]

Lenin further objected to Plekhanov's program because

his style of writing was unacceptable.

> This is not the language of a revolutionary
> party but the language of Russkie Vedomosti.
> This is the terminology not of socialist prop-
> aganda but of a statistical abstract. These
> words seem, as it were, deliberately chosen
> with a view to giving the reader the impression
> that the process described is a mild one, cul-
> minating in nothing definite, a painless pro-
> cess. Since in reality the reverse is true,
> these words are to that extent quite wrong.
> We cannot and should not choose the most ab-
> stract formulations, for what we are writing
> is not an article directed against the critics,
> but the programme of a militant party, which
> makes its appeal to the masses of handicrafts-
> men and peasants.[4]

Lenin wanted to emphasize the emotion of the revo-

lutionary movement and not the scientific inevitability of

socialism. He wanted not to logically prove that what he

wanted to happen would actually occur, but rather to moti-

vate people to participate in the event and cause it to

happen. Contrary to his subsequent polemic against Bogdanov

in 1908 (Materialism and Empiriocriticism), Lenin showed in

his writings that he really did believe that ideas are in-

fluential over the course of material events. Much later,

on the eve of the October Revolution, Lenin asserted that:

> Ideas become a power when they grip the people.
> And precisely at the present time the Bolshe-
> viks, i.e., the representatives of revolution-
> ary proletarian internationalism, have embodied
> in their policy the idea that is motivating
> countless working people all over the world.[5]

Lenin also expressed his revolutionary voluntarism

in Two Tactics of Social-Democracy in the Democratic Revolu-

tion. The proper function of the revolutionary party, as

Lenin described it, was as much an inspiring as an organiz-

ing force. A major role of the party was to imbue the working class with revolutionary spirit. In the concluding
chapter, "Dare We Win?," Lenin scolded the Mensheviks for
discouraging the working class movement because ". . . it
curtails the revolutionary energy of the democratic revolution and dampens revolutionary ardor because it is afraid
to win . . ."[6]

Lenin went on to wax eloquent on the spiritual power
of the masses--once aroused--and on the significance of the
party in spiritually arousing them.

> Revolutions are festivals of the oppressed
> and the exploited. At no other time are the
> mass of the people in a position to come for-
> ward so actively as creators of a new social
> order, as at a time of revolution. At such
> times the people are capable of performing
> miracles, if judged by the limited yardstick
> of gradualist progress.[7]

Not to slight the importance of the organized vanguard of the proletariat, Lenin added:

> But it is essential that leaders of the rev-
> olutionary parties, too, should advance their
> aims more comprehensively and boldly at such
> a time, so that their slogans shall always be
> in advance of the revolutionary initiative of
> the masses, serve as a beacon, reveal to them
> our democratic and socialist ideal in all its
> magnitude and splendour, and show them the
> shortest and most direct route to complete,
> absolute, and decisive victory.[8]

In Two Tactics Lenin referred hardly at all to the
material conditions or to the practical organizational details of leading a working class revolution. He seemed to
be most interested in providing an ideal for the movement
and in nurturing the revolutionary fervor that would inspire

the struggle toward that ideal.

In the pages of Two Tactics Lenin was clearly at odds with the more scientific Social-Democrats who used Marxism to interpret Russia's present situation and to predict what would happen next. Lenin did not want to predict the future but to shape it. With his emphasis upon spirit over matter, Lenin attempted not to rely passively on the prophecy of Marxism but to make Marx's prophecy self-fulfilling.

> Every "serious revolutionary situation" confronts the party of the proletariat with the task of giving purposive leadership to the uprising, of organizing the revolution, of centralizing all the revolutionary forces, of boldly launching a military offensive, and of making the most energetic use of the revolutionary governmental power.[9]

Lenin's final conception was of a partnership between the ideals and will of the active revolutionaries and the material conditions of social reality. Individuals can have an important impact upon history because if they do not act when the time is ripe then certain historical possibilities may not be achieved.

> Undoubtedly, the revolution will teach us and will teach the masses of the people. But the question that now confronts a militant political party is: shall we be able to teach the revolution anything? Shall we be able to make use of the correctness of our Social-Democratic doctrine, of our bond with the only thoroughly revolutionary class, the proletariat, to put a proletarian imprint on the revolution, to carry the revolution to a real and decisive victory, not in word but in deed, and to paralyse the instability, half-heartedness, and treachery of the democratic bourgeoisie?[10]

Thus Lenin and his Bolshevik comrades did not conceive of Marxism as a social science but as an ideal des-

cription of the world. They did not follow the progress of
the working class as scientific observers would have. Rather,
they devoted their lives to attempting to make the proletariat fit into the ideal scheme that Marx had drawn up.

Lenin was a revolutionary before all other considerations. The socialist revolution was his highest ideal.
Consequently, when he argued in support of Marxism, he was
interested not in logic or empirical data but simply in the
ways in which Marxist theory contributed to the socialist
revolutionary movement. For Lenin, the standard for gauging
the Marxian orthodoxy of any particular position was whether
or not that position was a revolutionary one.

Indeed, Lenin believed that Marxism was essential
to the revolutionary socialist movement not because it was
necessarily true but because it was _revolutionary_. In _What
is to be Done?_, Lenin defended orthodox Marxism from revisionism not on the basis of scientific proof but because of
the need of a revolutionary doctrine. He said that "There
can be no strong socialist party without a revolutionary
theory which unites all socialists, from which they draw
all their convictions, and which they apply in their methods
of struggle and means of action."[11]

Not only _What is to be Done?_ but Lenin's entire work
of this period consists of variations on the theme: "Without a revolutionary theory there can be no revolutionary
movement . . . This idea cannot be insisted upon too strongly."[12]

Lenin's objections to Bernstein had nothing to do with the validity or falsity of Bernstein's revision of Marxism in any technical scientific or philosophical sense. For Lenin the appeal of Marxism was not its scientific or philosophical foundation but rather the fact that it promised socialist revolution. Lenin believed that he had only to show that Bernstein denied the necessity of revolution in order to prove that Bernstein's arguments were wrong.

Similarly, Lenin seemed to feel that no other rebuttal against any of the other tendencies in Russian Social-Democracy was necessary except to demonstrate that they did not stress violent revolution as the first and foremost goal of the party. This, of course, was Lenin's famous objection to "Economism":

> We have said that there could not have been Social-Democratic consciousness among the workers. It would have to be brought to them from without. The history of all countries shows that the working class, exclusively by its own effort, is able to develop only trade-union consciousness . . .[13]

Lenin pointed out that socialist theory rose as a natural and inevitable historical process, but it arose among the bourgeois intelligentsia and not among the workers. The "revolutionary socialist intelligentsia" is thus obligated to resist the trade-union mentality of the actual proletariat, to work to raise the consciousness of the working class, and to further the socialist revolution.

The premise upon which Lenin was working in these arguments was that the Marxian correctness of any proposal

was to be gauged by whether or not it promoted revolution.
The necessity of participation of the bourgeois intelligentsia in leading the proletarian revolution is not to be found
in any of Marx's writings but in the reality of the moment.
Lenin saw that the only way the revolution could be brought
about was through the leadership of the revolutionary bourgeois intelligentsia. In short, Lenin's commitment to Marxism took a distant second to his commitment to revolution.

It was as a corollary to this that Lenin's organizational proposals follow. The Social-Democratic party was
not an organization for proletarians or even people sympathetic to the movement; it must consist "first and foremost
of people who make revolutionary activity their profession."[14]
And to facilitate this activity, Lenin proposed the creation
of a party newspaper--a central organ that would contribute
to party unity, cohesiveness, and organizational coordina-
tion by presenting a consistently revolutionary viewpoint.
The agents of this proposed newspaper, in fact, were also
intended to be collaborators capable of "preparing for, ap-
pointing the time for, and carrying out the nationwide armed
uprising."[15]

The voluntarism so clearly expressed in the closing
pages of What is to be Done?--and indeed implicit throughout
the work--was the direct result of Lenin's impatient revolutionary disposition. Furthermore, this voluntarism was the
necessary result of idealism. When Lenin (like Berdiaev and
Lunacharsky and, indeed, most Marxist revolutionaries) de-

cided that his own conception of the ideal social development
was true and the values expressed by the working class were
false, he was justifying the necessity of excercising his
own individual free will in attempting to steer historical
development according to his own vision.

If the proletariat has not developed socialist consciousness and cannot develop it alone, then existence cannot determine consciousness. And if existence does not determine consciousness, then the entire material determinism
of scientific socialism dissolves. Those revolutionaries
who do possess that socialist consciousness have no source
for it other than their subjective ethical choice. In attempting to instill their own values in the working class
movement, these revolutionaries are not serving the laws of
history but excercising their free will. The creation of
socialism thus becomes a moral imperative.

In the face of Berdiaev's "crisis of idealism," Lenin
refused to bow to objective reality and instead reaffirmed
his own subjective idealism. Like Bogdanov and Lunacharsky,
he did not follow this idealism into passive introspection;
Lenin remained dedicated to the revolutionary movement. But
unlike the positivist Marxist idealists, Lenin did not feel
it necessary to justify his idealism in scientific or philo-
sophic terms. Instead, he embodied his idealism in the principles of party organization. Just as Marxism was true because "a revolutionary movement needs a revolutionary theory,"
similarly an organized party of conscious revolutionaries was

necessary because the proletariat could not produce the socialist revolution by itself. The Bolshevik faction was Marxist idealism in organizational form. It was entirely natural that when the positivists completed their terms of exile,
they would gravitate toward Lenin and the Bolshevik faction
of the RSDRP.

The Politics of Idealism

During the period of their exile in Vologda, Bogdanov and Lunacharsky had come to grips with the philosophical problems they had found in Marxism and had arrived at
solutions which only strengthened and reaffirmed their commitment to socialist revolution. It was only natural that
they, like Russia's other activist revolutionary Marxists,
should begin to work toward the consolidation of a national
revolutionary organization. From their scattered points of
exile (Bogdanov from Vologda, Lunacharsky from Tot'ma, and
Bazarov from Siberia), they slowly made their ways toward
the centers of Russian Social-Democratic organizational activity: Moscow, St. Petersburg, and finally Zurich.

As long as they had been involved in purely theoretical discussions, Bogdanov and his friends had not revealed
their attitudes toward the practical concerns of promoting
socialist revolution in Russia. They had expressed no opinions on the crucial questions that divided the moderate from
the extremist Russian Social-Democrats: questions of the
spontaneity of the working class movement, the degree of capitalist dominance of the Russian economy, or the role of the

proletariat in the democratic revolution.

Over the next few years, however, it became clear
that Bogdanov and his close friends were among the most impatient and extreme of Russia's revolutionary Marxists.
They were no doubt attracted to Lenin at the very outset
because he was clearly the most radical and uncompromising
leader among those who were undertaking the centralized
organization of the RSDRP. The positivists were not organizers or administrators; they lacked the temperament and
skill to create an organizational center within the RSDRP
for their own particular political point of view. Hence
they had to choose among the centers that already existed.
They unhesitatingly gravitated toward Lenin's Bolshevik faction.

Lunacharsky became a Bolshevik because, "My whole
world-view, just as my whole character, did not for one instant dispose me to a half-and-half position, to compromise
or to cool the sharp, maximalistic stance of pure revolutionary Marxism."[16]

But it was Bogdanov who first became a Bolshevik;
as in philosophy so in politics, Bogdanov led the way for
the positivist idealists. After concluding his exile in
Vologda in 1901, Bogdanov returned to Tver' where he resumed
the local party work in which he had been engaged prior to
his arrest. It must not have taken him long to realize that
local circle work was no longer the focal point of revolutionary activity as it had been in the 1890s. He must have

welcomed the formation of a unified Social-Democratic party
for he soon began to move toward higher levels of party organization where the formation of a revolutionary party was
being undertaken. Bogdanov's first step was to Moscow.

Bogdanov was serving on the editorial board of Pravda during the time of the Second Party Congress--the scene
of the schism among the Iskrists. Adhering strongly to
Lenin's position in that controversy, Bogdanov travelled to
Switzerland in the spring of 1904 to join Lenin in his polemical and organizational battle with the Mensheviks. He soon
summoned his old comrades--Lunacharsky and Bazarov in par-
ticular--to join him in the Bolshevik camp. Lenin welcomed
them all with open arms.

The positivists gravitated toward the Bolsheviks because they were Marxist polemicists without an organization.
Lenin, on the other hand, welcomed Bogdanov, Lunacharsky,
and Bazarov into his organization because he badly needed
allies who possessed literary skills. At this point in his
career, Lenin needed all the help he could get.

He had had early success in the RSDRP due principally
to his original proposals for organizing a nation-wide party.
But although his organizational ideas were accepted, Lenin's
political program was not. The brilliance of his organizational plan had won over Plekhanov (and the other emigre
leaders) to his side at first, but it was not long before
tensions developed between the two.

Lenin differed from Plekhanov in several practical

respects. Whereas Plekhanov expressed (in the 1902 party program) that "capitalism is becoming more and more dominant," Lenin countered with the assertion that "capitalism has already become dominant." This difference in interpretation of Russia's stage of economic development led to important tactical differences between the two men.

Because capitalism had not yet matured, Plekhanov reasoned that the first goal of Social-Democracy should be to ally with the bourgeoisie in a democratic revolution against the autocracy. Lenin, on the other hand, though in 1902 he did not yet advocate substituting socialist for democratic revolution, nevertheless believed that the proletariat could not ally itself with the bourgeoisie but should fight against autocracy and capitalism simultaneously.

The primacy of personality over ideology is illustrated by the different attitudes of the various Russian Marxists toward the Revolution of 1905. No less than did Lenin, Plekhanov, Martov, and Axelrod all believed Marxism to be true, and they all believed themselves to be orthodox Marxists. Yet when one compares their views on the revolutionary situation in Russia in 1905 and their opinions on the proper tasks of the RSDRP with Lenin's views on these subjects, one must conclude that there was no single "proper" Marxist attitude.

Each practising Marxist interpreted the situation not simply in terms of Marx's theory of historical determinism but according to his own personal temperament. They all used Marxist terminology, and no doubt really believed that they were representing Marx's own views, but what they all were talking about was simply their own personalities. And Lenin's temperament in 1905--as at all other times--was consistently more impatiently, insistently, and intransigently revolutionary than most other Russian Social-Democrats.

In Two Tactics of Social-Democracy in the Democratic Revolution, Lenin wrote furiously against those Marxists who were urging restraint upon the working class movement. These more moderate Marxists argued--in good Marxist fashion --that Russia was undergoing a bourgeois-democratic revolution. These moderates feared that too much radicalism and extremism on the part of the left revolutionary parties might frighten the bourgeoisie into alliance with the autocracy, prevent the full development of the democratic revolution, and thus stifle Russia's development through capitalism toward socialism.

Such timidity was outrageous to Lenin. He did admit that "In its social and economic essence, the democratic revolution in Russia is a bourgeois revolution." But he went on to say that "It is, however, not enough to repeat this correct Marxist proposition."[18] Lenin refused to allow the bourgeoisie to enjoy their own revolution because he did not trust them to complete it.

> We must not forget that there is not, nor
> can there be at the present time, any other
> means of bringing socialism nearer, than com-
> plete political liberty, than a democratic
> republic, than the revolutionary-democratic
> dictatorship of the proletariat and the peas-

> antry. As representatives of the advanced and
> the only revolutionary class, revolutionary
> without any reservations, doubts, or looking
> back, we must confront the whole of the people
> with the tasks of the democratic revolution
> as extensively and boldly as possible and with
> the utmost initiative. To disparage these
> tasks means making a travesty of theoretical
> Marxism, distorting it in a philistine fash-
> ion . . .[19]

The only way in which Lenin was capable of interpret-

ing Marxism was as an intransigently revolutionary doctrine.

To find in it any justification for a policy of moderation

was, for Lenin, not to interpret Marxism but to distort it.

Clearly, in his impatience to achieve his apocalyptic revo-

lution, it was Lenin himself who was distorting Marxism.

In his impetuous insistence upon a popular revolution

above all other considerations, Lenin was revising Marx to

match his own mood. It is hard, for instance, to find a

place in Marx's conception of the bourgeois revolution for

a "revolutionary-democratic dictatorship of the proletariat

and the peasantry." Indeed, in the concluding paragraph of

Two Tactics, Lenin even mentioned socialism (and not merely

a fully-realized bourgeois-democratic revolution) as the

goal of the revolutionary proletariat.[20] He so emphatically

stated the importance of worker leadership in the democratic

revolution and the necessity of the dictatorship of the

proletariat and the peasantry that, throughout the work, the

reader cannot be sure where the democratic revolution will

end and the socialist revolution begin.

In his urgent need for revolution, Lenin apparently

forgot that superstructures arise upon definite material

economic relations and that the logic of dialectical materialism, and not human will, defines which class is the
ruling class.

> At a certain stage of development, the use-
> lessness of the old superstructure becomes ob-
> vious to all: the revolution is recognized by
> all. The task is now to define which classes
> must build the new superstructure and how they
> are to build it. . . . This slogan ["the revo-
> lutionary-democratic dictatorship of the pro-
> letariat and the peasantry"] defines the classes
> upon which the new "builders" of the new super-
> structure can and must rely, the character of
> the new superstructure (a "democratic" as dis-
> tinct from a socialist dictatorship), and how
> it is to be built (dictatorship, i.e., the
> forcible suppression of resistence by force
> and the arming of the revolutionary classes of
> the people).[21]

According to Lenin's scheme of historical development, the builders of the next social and economic stage are
not the bourgeoisie (as Marx predicted) but the working
class. Feudalism will not be replaced by capitalism, and
capitalism will not ultimately give way to socialism. Instead, the transition from autocracy to socialism would be
one continuous and rapid process in which the working class
presided over both the democratic and the socialist revolutions.

> The complete victory of the present revo-
> lution will mark the end of the democratic
> revolution and the beginning of a determined
> struggle for a socialist revolution . . .
> The more complete the democratic revolution,
> the sooner, the more widespread, the cleaner,
> and the more determined will the development
> of this new struggle be. . . . When not only
> the revolution but the complete victory of the
> revolution becomes an accomplished fact, we
> shall "change" . . . the slogan of the demo-
> cratic dictatorship to the slogan of a social-
> ist dictatorship of the proletariat, i.e.,

of a full socialist revolution.[22]

Leon Trotsky is usually given the credit for the origination of the notion of "permanent revolution," but the same concept was here fully expounded by Lenin in Two Tactics. Indeed, by October, 1905, Lenin was also using the expression "uninterrupted revolution" to express the idea.[23]

Though Lenin succeeded in gaining the approval of the Second Congress in 1902 for his own particular proposals, in doing so he alienated himself from the editorial board of Iskra--the very Central Organ he himself had worked so hard to create. The latent conflicts between Lenin and Plekhanov broke out into open hostility, and Lenin gradually lost his influence upon both Iskra and the new Central Committee that Lenin had engineered at the Second Congress. Plekhanov threatened to resign from the editorial board of Iskra if Lenin did not allow him the right of cooptation. Lenin resigned instead, and Plekhanov coopted the entire former editorial board as it had existed before Lenin reorganized it at the Second Congress.

Lenin also became embroiled in a conflict with the Central Committee in which his supporters had originally constituted a majority. By 1904 the Central Committee had proven itself no longer subject to Lenin's authority and was making conciliatory gestures to Plekhanov, Iskra, and the Emigre League.

Thus on the eve of the 1905 Revolution, Lenin was alienated from the party and from the central organs of the

party that he had done so much to create. He had lost his
membership on both the Central Organ and the Central Committee, and he had no influence upon those members who remained
on them.

And so it mattered not at all how many supporters
Lenin had at local levels of the RSDRP in Russia in 1904.
Without a means of communicating with them he would lose
them. In searching for a unifying program, local Social-
Democrats could only choose from among the points of view
expressed in journals smuggled in from abroad. This, indeed,
was precisely the idea which lay behind Lenin's original
suggestion of a central party organ. If Lenin's ideas could
not be disseminated by means of such an organ, Lenin would
not be able to maintain a following of Bolsheviks within
Russia.

Lenin's only recourse was to begin all over again,
to establish another journal which could serve as an organizational center for his own position within the party. It
would provide the nucleus for a new faction of the party just
as Iskra had been a nucleus for party centralization among
Russia's Social-Democratic circles only two years earlier.
The problem that Lenin faced in establishing such a central
journal was a personnel problem. He did not have among his
supporters people with the necessary literary and editorial
skills.

In 1904 there were a number of influential Menshevik
polemicists: Plekhanov, Axelrod, Zasulich, Martov, Potresev,

and others. But there was only one Bolshevik polemicist--
Lenin.

> The split with Plekhanov affected Vladimir
> Ilich; for he valued him very highly. The
> main thing that bothered him was the fact that
> among us, his closest co-workers, there were
> no literary forces such as the Mensheviks were
> rich with.[24]

Boris Liadov was the intermediary whom Lenin chose

to send to Russia to recruit from the native Bolsheviks such

literary types as could make up the editorial board of his

future central organ.

> Among the literati, we could at that time count
> upon the following people: Bogdanov, Vorovsky,
> Lunacharsky, Bazarov, and Stepanov-Skvortsov.
> Vorovsky was planning to come [to Geneva]. I
> could contact the others through Bogdanov, who
> was then living in Tver' and was participating
> in local work.[25]

Bogdanov was the central figure in Liadov's and Len-

in's plans.

> Now Bogdanov was already a famous litera-
> teur, but he remained such a convinced revolu-
> tionary that he therefore very quickly grasped
> our emigre situation. He had almost no reser-
> vations about which side to choose. He was al-
> ready preparing to go abroad . . . He was sure
> that Lunacharsky, who was finishing his exile
> and who was also planning to go abroad after
> his exile, would also join us Bolsheviks.[26]

Bogdanov, Lunacharsky, and Bazarov were nothing if

not highly literate intellectuals who thrived on theoretical

debate. They had gained considerable recognition among

Social-Democrats from their publication in the leading Marx-

ist theoretical journals. They were fervent revolutionaries,

besides, and were the only Bolsheviks capable of helping

Lenin to publish the journal that would be essential to the

continued existence of the Bolshevik faction within the
RSDRP.

Lenin was aware that Bogdanov was interested in philosophical issues that did not fit in well with orthodox Marxism. But esoteric philosophical points were insignificant
to Lenin compared with the practical problems of revolutionary organization. Lenin wrote to Gorky concerning philosophy and the Bolshevik faction:

> In the summer and autumn of 1904, Bogdanov and
> I reached a complete agreement, as <u>Bolsheviks</u>,
> and formed the tacit bloc, which <u>tacitly ruled</u>
> out philosophy as a neutral field, that existed
> all through the revolution and enabled us in
> that revolution to carry out together the tac-
> tics of revolutionary Social-Democracy (= Bol-
> shevism), which, I am profoundly convinced,
> were the only correct tactics.[27]

And, as Lunacharsky reported the alliance from his
point of view:

> My philosophy of revolution was later to earn
> from Lenin his famous disapproval, and our
> work--I speak of the group of Bogdanov, Bazar-
> ov, Suvorov, and I, and several others--he
> really disliked. However, he felt that our
> group, though it went far from the Plekhanov-
> ite orthodoxy in philosophy that was dear to
> him at that time, still stood with both feet
> planted on a really uncompromising and clearly
> distinguishable position in politics. The union
> which had occurred between him and Bogdanov
> was also cemented with me.[28]

Bogdanov did just as Liadov had asked him. Shortly
before he set off for Geneva, he wrote to Lunacharsky and
importuned him to go abroad immediately to meet Lenin personally and to enter the editorial board of the new Bolshevik Central Organ, <u>Vpered</u>.[29] Lunacharsky was indeed convinced by his brother-in-law to go.

> That was the difficult time of complete
> schism between Bolsheviks and Mensheviks.
> I more or less stood for the Bolshevik posi-
> tion, though not all sides of the discord were
> clear to me. The deciding point for me was
> not nearly so much a detailed familiarity with
> the disagreement as the fact that A. A. Malin-
> ovsky-Bogdanov wholeheartedly entered the Bol-
> shevik movement and became the main represen-
> tative in Russia for Lenin and his group.[30]

Lunacharsky did go abroad, but apparently his mind

was not yet entirely made up for he went to Paris instead

of Geneva. Finally Lenin himself travelled to Paris and

managed to convince Lunacharsky of the necessity of the

split in the party and the correctness of the Bolshevik pos-

ition.[31] Lunacharsky returned with Lenin to Geneva and en-

tered the editorial board of Vpered. He was never an active

editor, however. Instead, Lunacharsky spent most of his time

as a Bolshevik propagandist among emigre Russian circles; he

travelled around Europe presenting the Bolshevik standpoint

to the various Russian Social-Democratic groups.

In the meantime, in the fall of 1904, just as Luna-

charsky was travelling to Europe for the first time to join

the emigre Bolsheviks, Bogdanov was already on his way back

to Russia. He was returning to line up financial support

and literary contributions for Vpered and to help organize

the selection of delegates to the Third Party Congress.

Bogdanov's center of operations in Russia was St.

Petersburg where he acted as representative of the Bureau

of the Committees of the Majority in the St. Petersburg Com-

mittee of the RSDRP. It was in St. Petersburg that Bogdanov

once more came into contact with his old friend, Bazarov,

whom he had not seen since their temporary exile in Kaluga five years previously. Bazarov had not returned from his exile in Siberia until 1904 from where he went directly to St. Petersburg. It was no doubt under Bogdanov's influence that Bazarov was coopted into the St. Petersburg Committee of the party in the winter of 1905. For three months he was the leader of its literary section. Unluckily, Bazarov was arrested in May and spent the most turbulent months of the 1905 Revolution in prison; he was released at the time of the October Amnesty.

Bogdanov had apparently already convinced Bazarov to use his polemical talents in support of the Bolshevik faction. After he was again released from prison in October, Bazarov was brought up to membership in the Bolshevik Center and became a member of the editorial board of <u>Proletarii</u>, the successor to <u>Vpered</u>. Bazarov also served on the editorial boards of all St. Petersburg Bolshevik legal publications.[32]

At first Bogdanov's, Lunacharsky's, and Bazarov's roles in the Bolshevik faction were simply supportive. They filled essential organizational positions, edited journals, and wrote articles defending Lenin's policies and programs. Beginning with the Third Party Congress, however, this began to change. Bogdanov began to play an important administrative role as well, and the three men began to exert an influence upon Bolshevik policy.

After Lenin's loss of <u>Iskra</u> in 1903 and his resignanation from the Central Committee in 1904, it became evident that his only way back into influence in the party was to arrange the convention of a new Congress which could establish a new Central Organ, Central Committee, and a new party program. A congress would give the Bolshevik faction another opportunity to take organzational control of the RSDRP.

Bogdanov lost no time in establishing himself as a leading organizer of the Bolsheviks and played a central role in carrying out Lenin's strategy. He participated in the August (1904) Conference of Twenty-Two--a convention of Bolsheviks who gathered at Lenin's behest to call for a third congress. Bogdanov was the principal organizer for the congress and was the most prominent Bolshevik inside Russia at the time.

> Bogdanov was the main organizer of the [Third] Congress in Russia. Standing at the head of the "Organizational Bureau of the Committee of Bolsheviks," Bogdanov travelled all over Russia and secured for the congress a significant influx of important workers from the localities.[33]

The congress was convened in London in April and May, 1905, and ended up as a purely Bolshevik affair. The Mensheviks, already in full control of the party's central institutions, had felt no need for a new party congress (particularly one organized and controlled by Bolsheviks) and so boycotted it and refused to recognize its legitimacy.

Nevertheless, the congress provided a sense of legitimacy for the Bolshevik faction. Before the congress the journal Vpered and the Bureau of Committees of the Majority had been unofficial institutions. The convening of the Third

Congress was an attempt to legitimize those Bolshevik organs
as the official Central Organ and Central Committee of the
entire RSDRP.

It was also at this time that Bogdanov's first major
Bolshevik polemic appeared, and that Lenin's recruitment
of the positivist Marxist literati into his faction began to
pay off.

> After Lenin's "One Step Forward, Two Steps
> back," the first Bolshevik attack was "Our
> Differences" by Galyorka and Riadovoi [Bogdan-
> of] in September, 1904. It caused a great
> sensation both in Russia and abroad. It show-
> ed that Lenin was not alone--that the Bolshe-
> viks had plenty of literary intellectuals and
> could start a journal of their own.[34]

Our Differences was a collection of articles by Bogdanov and Galyorka (a Menshevik) to popularize the differences of opinion between the two factions of the RSDRP.
Bogdanov took the position of an unwavering supporter of
Lenin and the Bolshevik position. Writing under the pen
name "Riadovoi," Bogdanov took a very straightforward, prosaic approach. There was no hint in his writings in Our
Differences that Riadovoi might ever have engaged in philosophical speculation. Bogdanov used Marxism as a polemical
tool in precisely the way that Lenin always used it. He
implicitly accepted without reservation that Marx's writings
were scientific truth, he quoted from Marx at length to justify his positions, and he seemed oblivious to the possibility
that any of his positions might actually contradict Marxism.

In the first article by Bogdanov printed in Our Dif-
erences, he undertook the justification of the various points

that separated the Bolsheviks from the Mensheviks. He emphasized the significance of Lenin's Paragraph One of the party
charter as keeping the revolutionary standards of the party
high. He objected to Plekhanov's cooptation of Mensheviks
onto the editorial board of Iskra. And in general Bogdanov
argued in favor of greater party centralization.[35]

It was this last issue of centralization--the re-
sponsiveness of local groups to the direction of the central
party policy-making apparatus--that most clearly separated
the two factions of the RSDRP. As we have seen, the emphasis upon party centralization was a result of idealism: the
more the revolutionary stressed the primacy of his own ideal
conception of the direction the working class movement should
take, the greater he felt the need for a centralized party
to efficiently advance those ideals.

Such a centralized party contradicts Marx's idea
that "existence determines consciousness" because it is the
party and not economic conditions that will determine the
social consciousness of the working class. Paradoxically,
Bogdanov chose just this theme of "existence determines consciousness" (which he was himself at that time explicitly
denying in his philosophical writings) to argue in favor of
greater party centralization. In "Rosa Luxemburg against
Karl Marx," Bogdanov scoffed at Luxemburg's objections to
the Bolshevik program as excessive direction of the working
class by an intellectual elite. He quoted passages from
Marx indicating that the workers' movement would be highly

organized. Simple existence in a capitalist economy inevitably determined that a centralized, highly disciplined workers' movement would arise.

> . . . On the basis of concentration of capital, "there develops in continually greater and greater degree the cooperative form of the labor process," and because of it, the working class "is constantly taught, united, and organized by the very methods of the capitalist process of production."[36]

Discipline, according to Bogdanov was not a sin, as Luxemburg had suggested, but was actually a necessary and inevitable element in the revolutionary movement. He concluded his polemic with the following passage printed in italics:

> The developing, conscious avant garde of the Russian proletariat constitutes the organizational basis of Russian Social-Democracy. And the conditions of production and the conditions of the class struggle have given this avant garde sufficient education in the spirit of comradely discipline so that it is possible to set about the creation of a tight organization that is as centralized as possible.[37]

In all his discussions of the subject, Bogdanov seemed oblivious to the fact that he was not talking about a working class movement that was being organized and disciplined by economic conditions. He was clearly advocating that a group of intellectuals, gathered together in the Bolshevik faction, should do the organizing and disciplining. In What is to be Done?, Lenin had explicitly recognized that the workers were incapable of developing socialist consciousness on their own. He thus contradicted the notion that existence determines consciousness and suggested the creation

of a centralized party of intelligentsia revolutionaries as
the necessary means of raising proletarian consciousness.
Bogdanov, on the other hand, did not try to justify centralism and discipline as a conscious tool of the revolutionaries
but as an inevitable product of material economic forces.

Indeed, in the final article in Our Differences,
Bogdanov treated the issue of centralization and discipline
of the RSDRP as a demand of the working class![38] The proletarian revolutionary movement, according to Bogdanov, objectively required a highly organized avant garde. The Menshevik insistence upon autonomy of local organizations and more
open membership policies was a result of "intelligentsia
individualism." Thus Bogdanov polemically turned the tables
on the Menshevik critics of "Bonapartism." He categorized
those who tended to leave the working class to carry out
its historical mission by its own devices as individualists
and elitists while he portrayed those who actively sought to
organize and influence the working class and hasten the process of history as mere agents of proletarian desires.

In his writings before the Third Congress, Bogdanov
thus held a position very supportive of Lenin's policies.
However, beginning with that congress he began to reveal a
distinct independence of thought from Lenin in internal
party affairs as well as beginning to assume an influential
role in formulating party policy in his own right. It was
his leadership that prevented Lenin from having his own way
entirely at the Third Congress.

Lenin had hoped to use the congress to appropriate all party authority to his own faction; he wanted the congress to censure Plekhanov and to expel all the Mensheviks from the RSDRP. The congress did abolish the Menshevik Party Council and established a new Central Committee (composed entirely of Bolsheviks, of course), but it did not go as far as Lenin wished.[39] Despite Bogdanov's extreme position on the party program, he excercised a moderating influence on internal party affairs. While he wholeheartedly supported Lenin's plans for an efficient, disciplined, centrally organized revolutionary party, Bogdanov had no objection to that party containing a number of differing points of view. He wanted to bridge the gap between the Bolsheviks and Mensheviks instead of widening it.[40]

During the three years following the Third Congress, Bogdanov held positions at the highest levels of both the Bolshevik faction and the RSDRP as a whole. At that congress he had been elected to the new Central Committee and to the editorial board of the new Central Organ, _Proletarii_ (which then took the place of _Vpered_). In St. Petersburg in 1905 Bogdanov helped establish the Standing Bureau of the Central Committee and served as a representative of the Central Committee on the St. Petersburg Soviet. At the same time, he served on the editorial board (along with his friends, Lunacharsky, Bazarov, and Gorky) of the legal Bolshevik journal, _Novaia Zhizn'_.

Bogdanov was arrested in the suppression of the

Soviet in the fall of 1905 and suffered a brief exile. Upon his return from exile, he was given a position on the newly formed "United Central Committee." (In the revolutionary upsurge during the fall of 1905, the two factions of the RSDRP had begun to forget their differences and to reunite.) Then in 1906 Bogdanov went to the Fourth Party Congress as a representative of the Central Committee and reported to the congress on behalf of the Bolshevik members of the Central Committee. He was also later a delegate to the Second and Third All-Russian Party Conferences held in 1907.

Meanwhile, both Bogdanov's long-time comrades, Bazarov and Lunacharsky, held similar positions in the party. Both were delegates to the Third and Fourth Party Congresses. And, although neither held important executive or administrative positions in the Bolshevik faction or in the RSDRP, they played significant roles on the editorial boards of the major Bolshevik journals: Vpered, Novaia Zhizn', and Proletarii. This literary service was, of course, just the reason for which Lenin had recruited them into his faction.

It gradually became clear, however, that Bogdanov and his associates were not to be passive literary mouthpieces for Lenin's point of view. In fact, they ultimately became a danger to Lenin's theoretical leadership of the Bolshevik faction for they united with another group of radical Bolsheviks and threatened to lead Bolshevism upon a course of revolutionary adventurism too extreme for even Lenin to accept.

The first signs of revolutionary extremism appeared at the Third Congress of the RSDRP in the spring of 1905. Lunacharsky and Bogdanov reported to the congress on "military-fighting" organizations. Lunacharsky spoke on the theoretical, Bogdanov on the practical aspects of armed uprising. In their presentations, Lunacharsky and Bogdanov argued for immediate and vigorous promotion of armed insurrection among the working class. The terms in which they formulated their position and the arguments they used to support it clearly reveal the extent to which the demand for working class insurrection was a product of idealism and voluntarism.

In orthodox Marxist terms, of course, the proletarian revolution is an elemental social upheaval—determined by the historical logic of economic development. An orthodox materialist determinist could not admit that the proletarian revolution could be led by another class. Lunacharsky opened his address to the congress by bowing in the direction of orthodox Marxism without conceding to it.

> "Revolutions are not made. Revolutions are elemental phenomena, independent of the will of any leader or political party." This phrase has been repeated often, and, of course, it has its truth. However, despite this it could produce as much harm in the near future as it has produced good in the past.[41]

The more moderate, orthodox Social-Democrats were using the term "unleash" (razviaziat') the revolution to signify their conviction that the professional revolutionaries were not attempting to violate the laws of history and

create an insurrection; they believed that they were simply
encouraging the working class to initiate their own elemental
uprising. Lunacharsky accepted the expression but twisted
its meaning.

> We have nothing at all against the term "un-
> leash the revolution," if only that term is
> used with full consciousness. As a matter of
> fact, who is able to unleash the revolution,
> who can promote the conscious transition from
> latent revolutionary energies to open upris-
> ing? Of course this task can be fulfilled
> only by the revolutionist-agitator.[42]

In order to "unleash" the revolutionary forces of
the proletariat, it seemed necessary to Lunacharsky that the
proletariat must be actively organized and led by Social-
Democrats.

> In the current epoch we--in the general opinion
> of all Social-Democrats--cannot refuse to sum-
> mon the proletariat to direct revolt, cannot
> refuse to "unleash" its revolutionary forces.
> From this inevitably proceeds our first obli-
> gation: to organize those forces. [We must]
> organize them for that definite goal which we
> are completely and concretely promoting in our
> current agitation, that is, for revolutionary
> onslaught against the government.[43]

Furthermore, Lunacharsky revealed in his speech the
essential idealism that lay behind his voluntaristic desire
to organize and direct a working class uprising. When he
spoke of the Social-Democratic party, Lunacharsky spoke in
idealistic terms. He stressed the importance of faith and
purity of principle. Lunacharsky scoffed at "realists" and
emphasized the power of will over sheer numbers.

> Lack of faith in its own power would be an
> unforgettable sin for Social-Democracy. . . .
> What is our party? Is it really just certain
> people in a certain organization? No, it is

> a principle. It is an ideological banner a-
> round which--if it goes in the right direction
> --tomorrow will gather millions. In a revolu-
> tionary atmosphere everything matures quickly,
> and if our party is small, like a mustard seed,
> it can still grow with fantastic quickness
> into a huge tree. Those pessimists would be
> very mistaken who would weigh [the party] in
> the metaphysical scales of a "realist.". . .
> At present what is important is not the size
> of our party as much as it is the purity of
> its principles and the consistency of its tac-
> tics.[44]

To justify his voluntarism, Lunacharsky quoted at
length from the famous passage from Marx's <u>Revolution and
Counter-Revolution in Germany</u> that begins, "Revolution is
an art." Here Marx presented a highly voluntarist view of
revolution in which the key to success is not the material
economic situation but the initiative of the revolutionary
leaders.

> . . . Once you have entered upon the insurrec-
> tionary attack, act with the greatest determin-
> ation, and be on the offensive. The defensive
> is the death of every armed rising; it is lost
> before it measures itself against its enemies.
> Surprise your antagonists while their forces
> are scattered . . . keep up the moral superior-
> ity which the first successful uprising has
> given to you . . . force your enemies to re-
> treat before they can collect their strength
> against you; in the words of Danton, the great-
> est master of revolutionary tactics yet known:
> audacity, audacity, and again audacity![45]

By quoting Marx's reference to Danton, Lunacharsky
did not let his audience overlook the fact that Marx was
verging on that heresy of scientific socialism, "Jacobinism."

Immediately following Lunacharsky in addressing the
congress, Bogdanov's task was not to theoretically justify
armed insurrection but to deal with the practical, organiza-

tional tasks in promoting the idea of insurrection among the working class. Like Lunacharsky, Bogdanov conceived of the uprising as an event (though perhaps elemental in origin) that would be planned, organized, and led by the Social-Democratic party. In his address, Bogdanov expressed ". . . the conviction that the tasks of the Social-Democratic party in regard to popular insurrection against the existing order are the thorough, well-planned preparation of the uprising as well as the organized leadership [of the insurrection] in the interests of the proletariat . . ."[46]

Bogdanov went on to elaborate on the crucial "general strike," the need of the immediate support by the workers in basic industries (to cripple the economy), the workers in communication industries (to hamper retaliation by the autocracy), and naturally by the rank and file soldiers in the army. Weapons were to be siezed from factories, arsenals, and obtained from sympathetic troops. Bogdanov also stressed the need for more agitation among the workers to both stimulate their enthusiasm for armed uprising and to teach them the proper insurrectionary tactics.

The congress that listened to Lunacharsky's and Bogdanov's appeals shared their revolutionary voluntarism and idealism and approved their resolutions on armed uprising by unanimous acclamation.

> The Third Congress of the RSDRP recognizes that the task of organizing the proletariat for direct struggle against the autocracy by means of an armed uprising is one of the most important and most urgent tasks of the party at the present time . . .[47]

Therefore, the Congress instructs all party organizations:
a. to explain to the proletariat, through propaganda and agitation, not only the political significance but also the practical, organizational side of the impending armed uprising,
b. to explain in their propaganda and agitation the role of mass political strikes which may be of major significance at the onset and during the actual course of the uprising,
c. to take the most energetic measures to arm the proletariat and also to develop a plan for the armed uprising and for its direct guidance, creating for this purpose special groups of party workers whenever necessary.[48]

Armed uprising was a popular notion among the Bolsheviks in the revolutionary year of 1905. Their attitude toward it was consistently more extreme that the resolutions passed by the Mensheviks. Whereas the Mensheviks preferred to allow the workers to arm themselves and to rise up spontaneously, the Bolsheviks desired to give the workers both arms and leadership. The resolution on armed uprising that was approved by the Menshevik-dominated Fourth Party Congress only one year later was considerably less militant than that of the Bolshevik Third Congress. Indeed, the Mensheviks actually resolved ". . . that the party is obliged to oppose all attempts to involve the proletariat in an armed clash under unfavorable conditions, regardless of the motivation of such attempts."[49]

Lunacharsky and Bogdanov were thus at the very forefront of Social-Democratic radicalism during the 1905 Revolution. They were the first two speakers to read reports to the Third Congress, and their idealist, voluntarist resolution on armed-military organizations was unanimously approved.

The Bolshevik faction was clearly dominated by voluntaristic revolutionaries who were impatient to prod the proletariat into beginning the revolution.

Lunacharsky had admitted his own idealism quite openly. Bogdanov's idealism was embodied in his theoretical works, and Lenin's idealism was manifest in his principles of party organization. That same revolutionary idealism was revealed simply in the practice of the Bolshevik rank and file. They did not act as if they were merely observing an inevitable historical process but as if their ideals could not be realized without a strenuous effort to achieve them.

The most serious and ambitious attempt at instigating an armed insurrection during the 1905 Revolution was staged in Moscow by the Bolshevik Moscow Committee of the RSDRP. The Moscow insurrection--the last major event of the Revolution--began on December 19. Under the influence of its Bolshevik members, the Moscow Soviet declared a general strike. The Bolshevik Committee took advantage of the strike (just as Bogdanov had prescribed at the Third Congress) to lead an armed revolt. Within a week both the strike and the insurrection had been suppressed by the autocracy.

The idealism of the Bolshevik leaders of the Moscow insurrection was revealed not only in their political activities but in their revolutionary, romantic temperaments. V. L. Shantser (who revealingly chose as his party pseudonym the name of the Jacobin, "Marat") after an altercation with the police went about armed with one revolver in his belt and another hidden in a boot. Marat and another leader of the Moscow Bolshevik Committee, Boris Liadov, were prepared for military action at any time and on one occasion exchanged gunfire with a group of Black Hundreds.[50]

These leaders of the Moscow insurrection were soon to join Bogdanov and Lunacharsky as the nucleus of a group among the Bolsheviks that was radical even by Bolshevik standards. The extremism and revolutionary intransigence of Boris Liadov, V. L. Shantser, and Stanislav Volsky (V. A. Rudnev) made them natural allies for Bogdanov and Lunacharsky in their insistence upon an idealistic and voluntarist course for Bolshevism.

Even after the failure of the Moscow insurrection when the revolutionary tide began to ebb, the enthusiasm of these radical Bolsheviks remained high. In June, 1906, the Bolshevik members of the Central Committee (Bogdanov, Krasin, and Desnitsky) called upon it to immediately turn to the workers with a summons to armed uprising. The occasion was the prorogation of the First Duma. The Central Committee declined to follow the Bolshevik suggestion.[51]

In November of the same year, the Menshevik-dominated Central Committee refused to convene a conference to discuss and prepare for armed uprising. In defiance, a number of Bolshevik proponents of immediate insurrection held a conference of their own in Tammerfors, Finland. They called their meeting the "First Conference of Fighting-Military

Organizations." The delegates from eleven militant Social-Democratic organizations attempted to create a centralized military organization. The conference was not opposed by Lenin, but he did not participate in it and the Bolshevik Center did not officially authorize it. Nevertheless, all but one of the delegates were Bolsheviks. Liadov and other Bolsheviks from the Moscow Committee were most prominent at the conference.[52]

But long before the conference was held the revolutionary wave had broken and was rapidly receding. The local RSDRP organizations were disintegrating and the workers were succumbing to the repressive measures taken by the autocracy. Revolutionary extremism was no longer appropriate to the conditions in Russia. Lenin recognized the earliest of all the Bolsheviks that the party had to retrench its forces, begin to organize anew, and to take advantage of whatever means of agitation and propaganda were available--even legal avenues of communication. It was this realization that turned Lenin against the radicals in his own faction. He felt that the Bolsheviks had to suit their programs to the counter-revolutionary tenor of the times and patiently await the next revolutionary resurgence.

Bogdanov and the left Bolsheviks, on the contrary, firmly believed in the continuing revolutionary spirit of the Russian proletariat. They wanted to combat the pall of reaction that had descended over Russia in 1906 by immediately initiating an armed struggle against the autocracy and sum-

moning the proletariat to join them in socialist (and not
simply democratic) revolution.

The disagreement over the proper tactics for Bolshevism
was bitter. Lenin perceived the radicals as engaging in a
course of revolutionary adventurism that could only destroy
the RSDRP. The radicals saw Lenin's position as impermis-
sibly conservative; they felt that Lenin was abandoning the
revolutionary movement and depriving the emotionally ready
working class of the leadership which it required to effect
the revolution.

This division of moderate and radical Bolsheviks had
more to do with political acumen than with revolutionary
principles, however. Lenin had revealed in 1905 and would
later reveal in 1917 that he was as temperamentally idealistic and voluntaristic as any of his Bolshevik comrades.
But between 1906 and 1909, Lenin realized the abyssmal futility of promoting armed insurrection in Russia. His disagreement with the Bolshevik radicals was simply over the tactics
appropriate to the moment.

Yet the bitterness of the dispute was so intense
that it led to an open schism within the Bolshevik faction.
In the heat of the argument over tactics, Lenin began to
assume for himself the standpoint of Plekhanovite Marxian
orthodoxy and to berate his opponents for their irresponsible
revolutionary adventurism and their philosophical idealism.
Of course, he was certainly correct in seeing a direct connection between their voluntarist political tactics and

their idealist philosophy. Ironically, Lenin's criticism of the radicals' idealism could have applied equally well to his own programmatic positions in both 1905 and 1907.

When the final break between Lenin and Bogdanov came, it was fought on two levels: the question of Social-Democratic participation in the Duma and the new development of Marxist idealism. These are the subjects of the next two chapters.

133

NOTES TO CHAPTER III

[1] V. I. Lenin, What is to be Done?, in Collected Works, 45 vols. (Moscow: Progress Publishers, 1960-1970) vol. 5, pp. 383-84.

[2] Ibid., p. 510.

[3] V. I. Lenin, "Notes on Plekhanov's Second Draft Programme," CW, vol. 4, p. 35.

[4] Ibid., pp. 41-42.

[5] V. I. Lenin, "Can the Bolsheviks Retain State Power?" CW, vol. 26, p. 130.

[6] V. I. Lenin, Two Tactics of Social-Democracy in the Democratic Revolution, CW, vol. 9, p. 113.

[7] Ibid.

[8] Ibid.

[9] V. I. Lenin, "On the Provisional Revolutionary Government," CW, vol. 8, p. 481.

[10] Two Tactics, p. 18.

[11] V. I. Lenin, "Our Program," CW, vol. 4, p. 211.

[12] What is to be Done?, p. 369.

[13] Ibid., p. 375.

[14] Ibid., p. 452.

[15] Ibid., p. 515

[16] Velikii perevorot, p. 31.

[17] Two Tactics, p. 111.

[18] Ibid.

[19] Ibid., p. 112.

[20] Ibid., p. 114.

[21] Ibid., pp. 128-29.

[22] Ibid., p. 130.

[23]V. I. Lenin, "The Political Strike and the Street Fighting in Moscow," CW, vol. 9, p. 347.

[24]M. N. Liadov, Iz zhizni partii v 1903-1907 godakh, (Moscow: Gosudarstvennoe Izdatel'stvo Politicheskoi Literatury, 1956), pp. 24-25.

[25]Ibid., p. 27.

[26]Ibid., pp. 34-35.

[27]V. I. Lenin, "A Letter to A. M. Gorky," CW, vol. 13, p. 449.

[28]Velikii perevorot, p. 31.

[29]Ibid.

[30]Ibid., p. 29.

[31]Ibid., p. 30.

[32]Deiateli revoliutsionnogo dvizheniia v Rossii, pp. 191-94.

[33]Liadov, p. 66.

[34]Ibid., p. 64.

[35]Galerka i Riadovoi, Nashi nedorazumeniia (Geneva: Izdanie avtorov, 1904), pp. 33-39.

[36]Ibid., p. 48.

[37]Ibid., pp. 58-59.

[38]Ibid., pp. 60-72.

[39]Ralph Carter Elwood, ed., Resolutions and Decisions of the Communist Party of the Soviet Union (Toronto: University of Toronto Press, 1974), p. 55.

[40]Liadov, p. 166.

[41]Institut Marksizma-Leninizma pri TsK KPSS, Tretii S"ezd RSDRP, Protokoly (Moscow: Gosudarstvennoe Izdatel'-stvo Politicheskoi Literatury, 1959), p. 98.

[42]Ibid., p. 100.

[43]Ibid., p. 101.

[44]Ibid., p. 102.

[45]Ibid., p. 105.

[46]Ibid., pp. 106-7.

[47]Ibid., p. 450.

[48]Ibid., p. 451.

[49]Elwood, p. 98.

[50]Liadov, p. 100.

[51]Institut Marksizma-Leninizma pri TsK KPSS, <u>Istoriia Kommunisticheskoi Partii Sovetskogo Soiuza</u> (Moscow: <u>Izdatel'stvo Politicheskoi Literatury</u>, 1966), p. 204.

[52]Liadov, p. 188.

CHAPTER IV

GOD-BUILDING:

IDEALISM BECOMES MILLENIALISM

The years of Russia's first twentieth century revolutionary upheaval found Bogdanov and Lunacharsky involved
in continuous work for the Bolshevik faction. They edited
journals, wrote polemical and agitational articles, attended
the major party conferences and congresses, and in general
participated in the active, organizational life of the RSDRP.
Yet their involvement in practical revolutionary activity
did not limit their capacity or their enthusiasm for continuing their theoretical work. If anything, the enthusiasm
of the revolutionary period only added fuel to the intellectual fires that had been kindled in Vologda half a decade
before.

Just as their optimism was manifested in extreme revolutionary programs for the RSDRP, so it also appeared in
more extreme formulations of their revolutionary world-view.
In 1905 and 1906 the more radical Bolsheviks were no longer
content to think in terms of a purely democratic revolution
in which the working class would merely aid in making the
bourgeois revolution. Instead, the Bolsheviks impatiently
looked forward to an independent armed uprising of the working class. They longed for the ultimate socialist revolution

and not just its bourgeois-democratic predecessor.

The concrete popular upheaval of the 1905 Revolution not only added to the optimism of their politics, it gave greater immediacy to their theoretical speculations. Bogdanov, Lunacharsky, Bazarov, and their left Bolshevik comrades found themselves facing not simply an abstract historical-social concept but the imminent realization of a new world. The sense of expectation that they expressed was not one of simple change in political or economic institutions but the expectation of the transformation of their entire culture. They looked forward to entirely new relationships between human beings and to humanity's unlimited capacity to create a perfect world. In fact, they produced a form of Marxist millenialism.

Marxism, after all, clearly follows the pattern of religious chiliasm. It assumes the existence of an irremedially evil world whose destruction in a universal cataclysm is followed by the supernatural creation of a heavenly paradise. What disguises Marxism's essential millenarianism is its apparent reliance upon the scientific method: observation of the factual data of material reality, deduction of natural laws, and the prediction of the future based upon those laws of nature.

The Bolshevik idealists, however, had done away with all these supports of scientific socialism. They had denied the primacy of matter and replaced it with a monist ontology based on human thought. They retained the scientific method,

but they emphasized its relativity and subjectivity and
asserted that it could not produce knowledge of absolute
truths. These left Bolsheviks did not envisage socialism
as the end product of a sequence of material causes and ef-
fects; they conceived of it as the culmination of the evolution of human thought. They could conceive of no limitations
upon the coming socialist reality; it would be as ideal as
the human mind could conceive. Thus the left Bolsheviks'
Marxist idealism proceeded naturally into Marxist chiliasm.

As was noted in Chapter II, Bogdanov's positivist
epistemology established the basis for Marxist millenialism.
He specifically asserted that "absolute reality" was a concept with no meaning. He argued that human consciousness
has no direct access to reality; the source of human knowledge of the world is nothing more than subjective human perceptions. It was easy for the reader to lose sight of absolute, material reality and take human thought to be the only
reality. Indeed, though Bogdanov ruled out individual solipsism (because collective human thought arises independently
of individual consciousness), he made possible the conception
of a "collective solipsism." Humanity, in organizing its
perceptions, actually _creates_ the real world.

On the eve of the 1905 Revolution, Bogdanov wrote
a brief summary of his thought, "The Goals and Norms of Life,"
in which he divorced human thought yet further from the
realm of material existence. He actually asserted that human
thought did not merely _reflect_ an external reality, it rather

<u>shaped</u> that reality. Bogdanov argued that the universe
exists in the form of "elemental chaos" and "reality" is
nothing more than the sense that humankind makes out of that
chaos.[1] In its thought, humanity organizes the data of its
perceptions into "knowledge," and in its labor, it organizes
its material surroundings into a man-made "reality." Thus
both physically and mentally humankind organizes its world
out of the elemental chaos.

History, in Bogdanov's understanding of it, was the
development of the human mind as it learned about and organized reality through labor. The source of historical progress was human cooperation in the struggle for survival
(labor), and the goal of its development was human mastery
over nature.

> All this clearly leads to the conclusion that
> the greatest speed and energy of progress,
> its greatest fullness and harmoniousness can
> be attained only in that society whose social
> form will be comradely cooperation and its
> boundaries all humanity. There the forces of
> development will become boundless.[2]

Bogdanov's image of the socialist revolution rose
grandiosely above the vision of simple change in economic,
political, or social relations in Russia. Bogdanov focused
upon the creation of a new world. (In passing, he also emphasized both the voluntarism and the idealism of humanity
in creating the new world.)

> All has changed. Now there is no "fool
> who expects answers" from the waves of the cold,
> lifeless ocean, but a conscious swimmer striving
> to master the waves of the boiling sea of life
> in order to make its terrible power a means
> in moving toward his ideal. And in that process,

a new world is growing up: the reign of har-
monious and whole man, freed from contradictions
and limitations in his practical life and from
fetishism in his consciousness knowledge.[3]

In following this train of thought to its logical
conclusion, one can see no limit to the creative power of
humankind. This progressive "mastery over the waves of the
sea of life" moves inevitably toward that idea of omniscience
and creative power that is usually ascribed to the supernatural. By making the ideals and the will of man dominant
over the chaos of elemental existence, the new world created
by the working class could easily take on the overtones of
transcendent perfection.

Indeed, the rapturous enthusiasm that the left Bolsheviks felt for the revolution closely resembled religious
fervor. As shall be seen in the following pages, it was to
such religious expressions of their revolutionary feelings
that the Marxist idealists turned in the years immediately
following the 1905 Revolution. Though Bogdanov himself
never compared socialism with religion and never used words
with religious connotation to describe the revolutionary
movement, his system of "empiriomonism" unquestionably provided the philosophical foundation for God-building. It
remained only for Gorky, Lunacharsky, and Bazarov to dot
Bogdanov's i's and cross his t's to give concrete expression
to the religious sense that was implicit in Bogdanov's work.
Those three writers explicitly identified the proletariat
with God and socialism with Heaven.

Maksim Gorky among the Bolshevik God-builders

The ultimate assertion that the revolution was a
religious movement, that the working class was God-like, and
that socialism would be the City of God was not made until
after the assimilation of another radical intellectual into
the circle of the left Bolsheviks. That catalyst was Maksim
Gorky.

It was in the late 1890s that Gorky first began to
associate with Social-Democratic revolutionaries. In May,
1898, when the police liquidated a Marxist circle in Tiflis,
Gorky was arrested for his personal associations with members of the group.[4] In the following year, he also seems to
have been quite close to the Marxist revolutionaries in his
home town of Nizhny-Novgorod.[5] In 1901 Gorky had begun to
aid (probably financially) the underground activities of the
Nizhny-Novgorod Social-Democratic organization. In that
year he was once again arrested for suspected collaboration
with social revolutionaries.

Gorky did not profess to Marxism during those years,
and all of his arrests resulted in acquittal due to lack of
evidence. Yet there can be no doubt that he was personally
acquainted with Russian Marxist revolutionaries or that his
own political orientation was becoming increasingly revolutionary. At least by 1902 Gorky considered himself to be a
revolutionary.[6] And his paean to violent revolution, Stormy
Petrel (published in 1898), though far from embodying a scientific socialist analysis of society, certainly expressed a

revolutionary disposition.

At the time when _Iskra_ was undertaking the creation
of a unified and organized RSDRP during the first years of
the twentieth century (when Lenin, Plekhanov, and Martov
were still cooperating with one another), Gorky sided with
Iskra. In early 1902, Gorky met with the Moscow Committee
of the RSDRP and with representatives of _Iskra_. At that
meeting Gorky assured them that he fully supported _Iskra_'s
point of view, that he was ready to aid them in any way he
could, and that he would contribute not less than five thou-
sant rubles annually to their treasury.[7]

By 1902 Gorky was already personally acquainted with
such future Bolsheviks as Veresaev, Desnitsky, and Krasin.
And then, or soon after, he must also have formed a friendship with Bogdanov. Unfortunately, Gorky's relationship
with the latter is difficult to determine; those who have
been in a position to investigate it have apparently not considered it worth their while. No biography of Gorky elabo-
rates on the relationship between Gorky and Bogdanov, and
the nearly exhaustive _Chronicle of the Life and Work of Maksim Gorky_ mentions Bogdanov only at random.

The _Chronicle_ notes that Gorky wrote to E. K. Malinovskaia (Bogdanov's sister or wife?) about his participation
in the revolutionary movement.[8] It was the beginning of a
correspondence that lasted for several years. Unfortunately,
the _Chronicle_ does not print the texts of the letters. In
December, 1906, for example, the _Chronicle_ mentions another

another exchange of letters between the two in which Gorky
thanked Malinovskaia for news of the situation in Russia
and announced his conviction that Russia would play the leading role in the immanent world revolution.[9]

The time, place, and nature of Gorky's first encounter with Bogdanov is not noted in the Chronicle, but it must
have occurred shortly after the turn of the century, and the
two men must have discussed the rift between the Neo-Kantian
Marxists and the Neo-Positivist Marxists. On December, 1903,
Bogdanov wrote to Gorky in regard to the latter's relationship with the Journal for All. That journal had just published an article praising Bulgakov's most recent work, From
Marxism to Idealism. Gorky had been a contributor to Journal for All in the past, and elsewhere in the same issue the
editor claimed that Gorky sympathized with Bulgakov's idealist interpretation of Marxism. Bogdanov was apparently horrified that Gorky should be associated--even so obliquely--
with idealism. In his letter to Gorky, Bogdanov wrote that
he "considered it essential that [Gorky] announce in print
his dissension with the editorial direction of Journal for
All."[10]

One may infer from this not only that Bogdanov and
Gorky were well acquainted but that Bogdanov had reason to
believe that Gorky shared his position in the dispute between positivism and idealism. Such an inference is further
corroborated by a letter written by Gorky to his wife one
month later in January, 1904. In the letter he recommended

that she read Lunacharsky's article, "Idealists and Positivists as Psychological Types," appearing in the first issue
of Pravda.[11] (In that essay, Lunacharsky argued that the
difference between idealists and positivists was simply that
the positivists wanted to achieve their ideals in the real
world.) This suggests that Gorky was following the debate
between the positivist and idealist Marxists, that he read
Marxist journals, and that he agreed with Lunacharsky's position in the debate.

Furthermore, Gorky's thought during the first decade
of the twentieth century had a great affinity with that of
Lunacharsky and Bogdanov in two respects. He shared both
their ethical commitment to socialism and their rejection of
a materialist ontology. (Both, as we have seen, are the
preconditions for revolutionary voluntarism and idealism.)

Gorky actually went far beyond the positivist Marxists in his concern for ethics. He not only explicitly insisted upon the revolution as a moral good (and not simply
an inevitable fact of history), Gorky's entire critique of
Russian society was not economic but moral. As he revealed
later in Mother and Confession, Gorky did not condemn Russian
society because its workers were deprived of the product of
their labor, nor did he welcome revolution as the beginning
of a new system of economic production and distribution of
material goods. Gorky was moved by the hunger, the penury,
the deprivation, but above all by the unhappiness of the
Russian people. He hoped that the revolution would replace

their misery with joy. Gorky felt no need to translate his
ethical judgements and his human compassion into abstract
economic and sociological concepts.

Gorky was also interested in the same philosophical
concerns as were the positivists: what is the nature of
reality, and how can man attain knowledge of it? The difference between Gorky and the positivists was that Bogdanov
had found his answers to these questions in positivist epistemology while Gorky found his answers in Nietzsche. The
fact that this difference remained insignificant at the time
reveals how far beyond the sceptical spirit of scientific
positivism Bogdanov had progressed.

Nietzsche's solution to the problem of how humans
can know reality was to suggest that truth is not to be discovered or reasoned out, but <u>created</u> by human will. Belief
is the source of truth. This, indeed, was precisely Gorky's
conclusion in <u>The Lower Depths</u>. Gorky wrote this play in
1902--at the same time as the positivist Marxists were writing their early philosophical polemics.

<u>The Lower Depths</u> can be considered as a dramatic com-
mentary on positivist epistemology. Gorky's principal theme
was that reality is determined by human consciousness. He
consistently asserted that human beings can be happy in this
world of misery, evil, and cruelty only by lying to themselves. Luka preaches to those people who languish at the
very botton of the social order that they should not accept
the unpleasant facts of their reality and instead believe to

be true whatever would make them happy. Believing a lie
will make it real.

>   Peppel: . . . Listen, old man: does God
>   exist?
>   Luka: If you believe in him he exists.
>   If you don't, he doesn't. Whatever you believe
>   in exists.[12]

>   Luka: Where do you see me lying?
>   Peppel: Everywhere. You say it's fine
>   here and its fine there, but you know you're
>   lying. What for?
>   Luka: Well, take my word for it and go
>   look it over for yourself. What's the good
>   of sticking around here? Anyway, what do you
>   want the truth for?[13]The truth might come down
>   on you like an axe.

>   Peppel: Where are you off to now?
>   Luka: To the Ukrainians. I've heard they
>   have discovered a new faith down there--I must
>   have a look at it. Yes, people keep looking--
>   keep wishing for something better. God give
>   them patience!
>   Peppel: What's your opinion? Will they
>   find it?
>   Luka: Who, people? They'll find it.
>   Look for something--want something with all
>   your heart--you'll find it.[14]

If reality can be identified simply as the collective agreement by humanity as a whole, then to the extent
that humanity can determine its own perceptions or coordinate its beliefs, it can also determine its reality. At the
conclusion of The Lower Depths, Satin praises the God-like
powers of humankind.

>   Satin: Man--that's the truth. What is
>   man? It's not you, nor I, nor they--No, it's
>   you, I, they, the old man, Napoleon, Mohammed
>   --all in one. You understand? It's tremendous!
>   In this are all the beginnings and all the ends.
>   Everything in man, everything for man. Only
>   man exists, the rest is the work of his hands
>   and his brains.[15]

It was in these terms, in 1902, that the first

principles of God-building were established.

Since Gorky and Bogdanov shared both revolutionary temperament and philosophical interests, it is no wonder that Gorky should have followed Bogdanov into the camp of the most radical Russian Social-Democrats. It was late in 1904 that Gorky, like Bogdanov, seems to have become deeply involved in the affairs of the Bolshevik faction. In December of that year, Gorky met with representatives of the Bolshevik Center (including Bogdanov and Desnitsky) to discuss the creation of Lenin's proposed new factional organ. In early January, 1905, Gorky underwrote the publication of Vpered in Moscow.

During the same period, Gorky met in Riga with Boris Liadov, Lenin's personal representative in Russia. This was the same journey mentioned earlier in which Liadov sought the literary support of Lunacharsky, Bazarov, and Bogdanov. Gorky promised that he would "do everything possible" for the Bolshevik faction.[16] He immediately sent (through Bogdanov) a check for three thousand rubles to subsidize the publication of Vpered abroad. By that time Bogdanov was already the chief organizer for Vpered and the Bolshevik Center in Russia.

From this time forth, Gorky was an active supporter of the Bolshevik faction, even though he later said that it was only in the second half of 1905 that he finally became an official member of the RSDRP.[17] Acting as an intermediary between his radical artistic collegues (Minsky, Hippius,

Merezhkovsky, and others) and his Social-Democratic associates (Bogdanov, Bazarov, and Lunacharsky), Gorky played
a central role in the formation of the legal Marxist journal,
New Life, in St. Petersburg in 1905.[18] (This alliance was a
short one, however. As soon as Lenin arrived in St. Petersburg in the summer of 1905, he summoned a meeting of New
Life's editorial board, had the non-party intellectuals re-
moved from it, and transformed the journal into a strictly
Bolshevik organ.)[19]

In October, 1905, Gorky also discussed with Bogdanov and Krasin (by this time they were both members of the
Central Committee of the RSDRP) a plan to establish a special
Social-Democratic section in Gorky's publishing house,
"Znanie." They agreed that the books to be published would
be chosen by a committee of Bolsheviks including Lenin, Bogdanov, Krasin, Lunacharsky, and others. At the same time
Gorky also joined Lenin, Lunacharsky, Shantser, Bogdanov,
and Bazarov on the editorial board of Bor'ba--a Bolshevik
daily newspaper published in Moscow.[20]

It was also in late 1905 that Leonid Krasin, a Bolshevik whose acquaintance with Gorky was more than a decade
old, suggested that Gorky make a speaking tour of America in
order to raise money for the Bolshevik faction. Early the
next year, Gorky set off to the United States to undertake
such a fund-raising campaign.[21] Accompanying him on the
journey was N. E. Burenin, a member of the Bolshevik-dominat-
ed "Military Group of the Central Committee."[22]

Gorky's money-making venture was soon dealt a severe blow when a brush with American morality and politics transformed him from a welcome radical democrat and humanitarian into a social and political pariah. Not only did he offend American moral sensibilities by travelling with a woman who was not his wife, Gorky also offended Americans' bourgeois-democratic complacency by telegraphing a message of support to the IWW's Big Bill Hayward, on trial in Montana for murder.

Having lost his audience, Gorky retired to the Adirondacks to recuperate and to write. The novel that he wrote during his stay in America, Mother, was composed while Gorky was still filled with the elation and enthusiasm of the 1905 Revolution. It also revealed a continuation of his earlier ethical concerns. In it Gorky came one step closer to the creation of a religion of revolution.

The plot of Mother revolves around the involvement of an aging widow and her only son in the revolutionary socialist movement. Her husband had worked--and drunk--himself to death in the factory that looms ominously above their poor cottage. Her son, Pavel, refuses to follow the life of alcoholism and violence that was the lot of the village's working class. Instead Pavel devoted all his spare time to self-education. After much study he becomes a socialist and enters the revolutionary movement.

The local circle of revolutionaries that Pavel forms holds its meetings in his mother's house. These meetings introduce the Mother (a devout Christian) into the milieu of youthful, idealistic, revolutionary socialism. She is bewildered by their expressed atheism for she understands their ideals and goals to be sacred and holy aspirations. Despite their anti-religious disclaimers, the Mother considers the young revolutionaries to be the equivalent of Christian saints and martyrs.

Early in the novel Pavel is arrested for organizing a strike, and he is briefly imprisoned. Shortly after he is released, he organizes a May Day procession to demonstrate working class solidarity. Nearly all the workers in the factory join in the march. The young workers are the first to participate, but before the end of the demonstration the older generation is won over to their point of view. Pavel's second offense against the social order is dealt with more harshly than the first; he is again arrested and this time is exiled to Siberia.

Indeed, for the last two thirds of the novel, Pavel does not participate in the action of the story. His presence exists only in the thoughts of his mother who never forgets her son's martyrdom. The remainder of the book shows Mother's increasing involvement in the revolutionary movement as she takes over the responsibilities left by her son. Despite the tendency of Soviet critics to think of the novel as being "about" Pavel or the revolutionary movement, Mother is, of course, about the Mother. Specifically, it demonstrates from the point of view of an old woman how the socialist revolution can be understood in terms of religion.

The narrative of the novel is related from the Mother's point of view, and the development of the plot focuses upon her transformation from a timid, religious old lady into a passionate socialist revolutionary. Gorky's point in writing Mother was to demonstrate the fundamental identity of religious and socialist motivations and goals. As the Mother becomes a socialist, she does not cast off her religious faith but rather transforms it into a revolution-ary form.

The Mother had been bewildered at first for she saw that the revolutionaries were deeply religious in their ac-tions however much they professed to be atheists.

> "Who will reward you for all this?" asked
> the Mother; and with a sigh she answered the
> question herself. "No one but God! Of course,
> you don't believe in him, either?"
> "No!" said the girl briefly, shaking her
> head.
> "And I don't believe you!" the Mother
> ejaculated in a sudden burst of excitement
> . . . "You don't understand your own faith!
> How could you live the kind of life you are
> living without faith in God?"[23]

Mother's respect for their sacred struggle for social-ism only deepens as the novel progresses. The revolution-aries first seem to her like holy people, then like martyrs and saints, and by the end of the novel the Mother thinks of them as imitators of Christ.

> . . . All of them in the eyes of the Mother
> were identical in the persistent faith that
> characterized them; and although each had his
> own particular cast of countenance, for her
> all their faces blended into one thin, composed,
> resolute face with a profound expression in

its dark eyes, kind yet stern, like the look of Christ's eyes on his way to Emmaus.[24]

Indeed, the revolutionaries represent the resurrected Christ.

By the end of the novel, the Mother's religious devotion becomes transformed into revolutionary activism. Christ had been the central figure in her previous religious experience, and her new revolutionary involvement did not contradict but actually enhanced her understanding of what Christ stood for.

> And it seemed to her that Christ, himself, whom she had always loved with a perplexed love, with a complicated feeling in which fear was closely bound up with hope and joyful emotion with melancholy, now came closer to her and was different from what he had been. His position was loftier, and he was more clearly visible to her. His aspect turned brighter and more cheerful. Now his eyes smiled on her with assurance, and with a live, inward power, as if he had in reality risen to life for mankind, washed and vivified by the hot blood lavishly shed in his name. Yet those who had lost their blood modestly refrained from mentioning the name of the unfortunate friend of the people.[25]

Indeed, the Mother understood the entire revolutionary socialist movement to embody the spirit of Christ's message to the poor and the oppressed of the world.

> Without being aware of it, she prayed less; yet at the same time meditated more and more upon Christ and the people who, without mentioning his name, as though ignorant of him, lived, it seemed to her, according to his will, and like him, regarded the earth as the kingdom of the poor. Her reflections grew in her soul, deepening and embracing everything she saw and heard. They grew and assumed the bright aspect of a prayer, suffusing an even glow over the entire dark world, the whole of life, and all people.[26]

Despite all this religious imagery, however, Mother need not necessarily be interpreted as a frank contradiction of Marxism. After all, it is a portrayal of the rise of class consciousness among the workers at a particular factory. The poverty-striken, brutalized, ignorant workers--who begin by resisting the appeals of the young socialists --ultimately realize the truth and participate first in Pavel's May Day demonstration and then in a strike. The Mother's religious imagery could possibly be explained as the only terms in which a formerly devout old peasant woman could understand the message of scientific socialism. Furthermore, Mother is entirely consistent with the spirit of Lenin's What is to be Done?; it emphasizes the importance of the leadership of the workers' movement by a vanguard of class conscious socialist revolutionaries.

Perhaps it was for such reasons that such a blatantly religious book could have achieved such great popularity among Russia's Marxist revolutionaries. Immediately after its publication it became the most popular novel of the revolutionary movement. Lenin praised it as a "useful book," perhaps because it promoted that spirit of revolutionary dedication and idealism that he himself had called for in What is to be Done?. The assessment of Mother as a work of art has never been particularly high (Gorky himself in later years called it a "really bad book"), but its prestige among revolutionary circles has always been enormous. It is generally hailed in the Soviet Union as the first example of

Socialist Realism.

Nevertheless, the religious themes in <u>Mother</u> are not superficial, nor are they simply a means of describing the revolutionary socialist movement. Gorky presents the movement not "like" a religion but truly and essentially religious. Those Russians who greeted the novel with enthusiasm were surely attracted by this religious aspect and not by such Marxist elements as can be read into the novel. It was the scientific socialism and not the religious enthusiasm that is extraneous to the work.

The Mother's religious perception of the revolutionary cannot simply be explained away as an old form of thinking that remains even after the content of thought has changed. After all, it is not just Mother but the narrator of the novel who speaks from a consistently religious point of view. The very way in which he describes the action of the novel and his figures of speech lend everything in the book a religious significance.

For instance, the narrator says about the passage of time, "The days glided by like the beads on a rosary."[27] In describing the revolutionary songs sung by Pavel's circle, he says, "These they said in an undertone, pensively, and seriously, as church hymns are chanted."[28] Furthermore, Gorky has the May Day demonstration begin in front of a church, and at the end of that march the Mother says, "It's just like a sacred procession."[29]

Furthermore, Gorky does not concern himself with any

of Marxism's social and economic analyses. In describing
the working class he is not nearly so interested in their
social subjugation or economic deprivation as he is in their
cultural and moral degradation. It is not that they are
poor but that they are unhappy and sinful that Gorky pities
them.

In the same spirit, it is not the bodies of the proletariat that Gorky's heroes want to save, it is their souls.
The reader hears very little from the revolutionaries about
a desire for violent revolution, the need to create a strong
revolutionary organization, or about the material promises
and benefits of the coming socialist system. Instead, the
young activists speak continually of rather vague ideals of
"truth, justice, and beauty."

Also, it is not just the Mother but the narrator as
well who sees the revolutionaries as essentially Christian
martyrs. The ideals by which they live are ascetic; they
are joyful in the knowledge that they are sacrificing their
lives for an ideal.

> She wavered between two feelings: pride
> in her son who desired the good of all people,
> had pity for all, and understood the sorrow
> and affliction of life, and the involuntary
> regret for his youth, because he did not speak
> like everybody else, because he resolved to
> enter alone into a fight against the life to
> which all, including herself, were accustomed.[30]

Finally, the Mother is not the only one who is transformed in the course of the novel. The revolutionaries are
influenced by the Mother as much as she is influenced by
them. Those socialists who profess atheism at the beginning

of the novel come to adopt the Mother's religious attitudes
by the end.

> "Comrades!" sang out the Little Russian,
> subduing the noise of the crowd with his mellow
> voice. "Comrades! We have now started a holy
> procession in the name of the new God, the God
> of Truth and Light, the God of Reason and Good-
> ness. We march in this holy procession, com-
> rades, over a long and hard road. Our goal is
> far, far away, and the crown of thorns is near.[31]

Ultimately, it is not the Mother but the young revolutionaries who present Gorky's conception of God-building.
Rybin says:

> "The holy place must not be empty. The
> spot where God dwells is a place of pain; and
> if he drops out from the heart, there will be
> a wound in it, mark my word! It is necessary,
> Pavel, to invent a new faith; it is necessary
> to create a God for all. Not a judge, not a
> warrior, but a God who shall be a friend of
> the people."[32]

And further echoing the massage of The Lower Depths
and anticipating the principal theme of his next novel, The
Confession, Gorky wrote:

> "We shall be victorious, because we are
> with the working people," said Sofia with as-
> surance. "Our power to work, our faith in the
> victory of truth we obtain from you, from the
> people; and the people is the inexhaustible
> source of spiritual and physical strength. In
> the people are vested all possibilities, and
> with them everything is attainable. It's nec-
> essary only to arouse their consciousness,
> their soul . . ."[33]

However, Mother was primarily an evocation of the
religious spirit that pervaded the revolutionary socialist
movement as Gorky understood it. Only at the very end of
the novel did he offer a brief suggestion of the creed of
his religion of revolution. Gorky's most explicit exposition

of that creed appeared two years later in The Confession.

When Gorky returned to Europe from America in late 1906, he made his way to Italy. He settled down in a village on the Isle of Capri that was to be his home for the next six years. Gorky's villa soon became a gathering place for the radical Bolsheviks; from 1906 through 1909 Lunacharsky, Bogdanov, and Bazarov were frequent visitors. Indeed, Capri served as the center for the left Bolsheviks during the schism in the faction that occurred during these years. This was natural since Gorky had become one of the leading intellects of Bolshevik radicalism; his theory of God-building played a significant role in provoking the schism.

The idea that humanity as a whole possesses all the attributes of a God seems to have first occurred to Gorky in 1902. We have already seen in The Lower Depths the idea that human thought creates reality. In a letter to Leonid Andreyev in the same year Gorky said, "We will create a God for ourselves who will be great, splendid, joyous, the protector of life, who loves everyone and everything."[34] Gorky was also the first to use the expression "God-building."

> God is the complex of ideas worked out by tribes nations, mankind, which awaken social feelings and give them organized form with the aim of linking the individual personality to society, and of taming soological individualism . . . God-building is the process of the further development and enlargement of these social feelings in the individual and in society . . .[35]

In philosophy--and particularly in epistemology--Gorky was close to Bogdanov's position; on the question of

religion and socialism he was even closer to Lunacharsky.
Like Gorky, who had been toying with the idea since the turn
of the century, Lunacharsky's identification of religion
with the revolutionary socialist movement was not a recent
idea. Lunacharsky wrote in Religion and Socialism in 1907:

> The present work, in its most essential
> elements, was first conceived about ten years
> ago, in the years of early youth. The basic
> ideas--about the essence of religion in gen-
> eral, about the ties between scientific social-
> ism and the sacred hopes of humankind that are
> expressed in religious myths and dogmas and in
> the metaphysical systems that replaced them,
> and about the central place of "labor" in the
> new world-view--all these ideas had already
> been born quite early in the mind of the author,
> and, not changing them in essence, only widened
> and deepened as a result of a deeper acquaint-
> ance with the history of religion, philosophy,
> and scientific socialism.[36]

Once again, the Chronicle of the Life and Work of
Maxim Gorky seems to slight Gorky's relationship with the
positivist Marxists. The Chronicle states that Gorky "really
met and got close to" Lunacharsky only in late November, 1906,
when they met on the Isle of Capri.[37] Nevertheless, the
Chronicle itself reveals that the two men must have met no
later than the spring of 1905 during the formation of the
journal Novaia Zhizn' on which they both collaborated.[38]
A Soviet scholar of Gorky's life asserts that, though this
initial encounter in 1905 was brief, Gorky and Lunacharsky
began a steady correspondence.[39]

The affinity of Gorky's and Lunacharsky's subsequent
writings certainly suggests that they must have maintained
contact and continued to share ideas with one another.

During 1905, Lunacharsky had begun delivering lectures to
Social-Democratic emigre groups throughout Europe on the
history of religion and its relation to socialism.[40] Lunacharsky was writing Religion and Socialism at the same time
that Gorky was writing Mother. Their collaboration on Capri
in late 1906 was not the beginning but the culmination of
their intellectual cooperation.

The philosophy of God-building seems to have been
developed mutually by the two. The various editions of their
God-building works show the probability of mutual influence.
When, in 1907, Gorky was writing The Confession, he was able
to read Lunacharsky's "The Future of Religion" and Religion
and Socialism. On the other hand, Lunacharsky's "The Future
of Religion" was primarily an elaboration on Gorky's own expressions of God-building. And in later editions of Religion
and Socialism, Lunacharsky quoted the entire last chapter of
The Confession as an example of the new religion of the proletariat.

Whereas in Mother Gorky's concern had been with the
spirit of the revolutionary movement, in The Confession he
focused upon the spirit of Christianity and suggested a revolutionary alternative to it. In Mother Gorky had shown how
the desire to transform society into a world of freedom,
plenty, and happiness was a fundamentally religious desire.
It was, according to Gorky, no less than the desire to imi-
tate the mission and the martyrdom of Christ.

As if he were worried that his readers might think

he was proposing Christianity as the creed for the revolutionary socialist movement, Gorky took great pains in The Confession to prove that Christianity (though not religion as
such) was just what Marx had called it--the opiate of the
masses. Gorky tried to show that the Christianity of the
established Church was a tool used by the ruling class to
oppress the people. His solution was to reject the Christian
religion but not the concept of religion. Since Christianity was incapable of providing inspiration for the revolutionary movement, Gorky drew up the principles of one that
could.

The Confession depicts the religious searchings of
an orphan, Matvei. The first half of the novel deals with
his blissful, unquestioning acceptance of Christianity and
shows how he comes to realize the falsity and evil that it
actually embodies. The second half of The Confession describes Matvei's pilgrimage in search of the true religion
and his ultimate discovery of it among the proletariat.

Matvei begins his life as a most devout Orthodox
Christian. He is pure in mind and body, and he experiences
ecstacies of the soul while praying before the sacred objects
in his church. His whole interest is in the hereafter; the
real world has no meaning for him.

> . . . My heart became filled with the divine
> word. . . . I wept lightly and humbly, without
> thinking and without praying. I had nothing
> to ask of God and I worshipped him with com-
> plete self-forgetfulness.[41]

Gorky rejected this sort of avoidance of reality for

two reasons. First of all, it is wrong because it ignores
the rest of humanity; it is a purely personal, individual
escape from the real world; it lacks social consciousness.

> At times I remained alone in the darkness of
> the temple, but it was light in my heart; for
> my God was there, and there was no place for
> childish troubles, nor for the sufferings which
> surrounded me--that is to say, the human life
> around me. The nearer one comes to God, the
> farther one is from man.[42]

Secondly, Matvei's total immersion in spiritual concerns diverts his attention from the evil that pervades the
real world. Matvei is so complacent in his devotion to religious ritual that he gives no thought to the ethics of his
behavior when he is outside the church. His uncle makes
Matvei his rent collector, and Matvei shamelessly partici-
pates in the extortion of the peasant tenants. Even later,
after he finally comes to realize that he is a tool of the
landlord in oppressing the peasantry, Matvei's Christian conscience does nothing to make him stop.

> . . . I realized . . . that our whole arrange-
> ment was nothing more than theft. The peas-
> ants were over their heads in debt, and worked
> not for themselves but for Titov. I cannot
> say that I was very much surprised at this dis-
> covery. . . . Was it then I who had originated
> this stealing?[43]

Indeed, though he still fervently professed to be a
Christian, Matvei soon became as eager an extorter as his
uncle.

> We began to rob the peasants as if we were
> playing a game. I followed each move he made
> with a bolder one . . . I cheated the peas-
> ants out of every kopeck I could. But I did
> not count the money nor gather in the rubles
> myself.[44]

Matvei gradually realizes that his actions are sinful, and it is this realization that first shakes his faith in the existence of God. If God is both good and all-powerful, they how can he allow Matvei to sin?

> When I thought of God I burned with shame.
> Nevertheless, I threw reproaches at him more than once.
> "Why dost Thou not keep me from falling with thy strong arm? Why dost Thou try me beyond my strength?"[45]

It is not through the church but through nature that Matvei finally receives the moral strength to give up sinful prosperity for honest poverty. Matvei marries, has a child, and seeks his living in the forest. It is in the forest that he again feels at peace with himself and the world.

Yet once again Matvei's spiritual regeneration represents a withdrawal from society. His idyll is brought to a sudden end by the deaths of his wife and son in a house fire. In his new solitude, Matvei proceeds yet further in his religious doubts. Previously his doubts had been personal and selfish. He had not been upset by the fact that the peasantry had been treated badly, he had resented the fact that God had allowed Matvei to commit a sin. This time, however, people whom Matvei had loved had perished for no reason. God had allowed innocent people to suffer.

Matvei begins to look around him, and he can see no evidence of God's beneficence in the human world.

> Why were the children of God sacrificed to misery and hunger? Why were they lowered and dragged to the earth as worms in the mud? Why did God permit it? How could it give him joy to see this degradation of his own work?[46]

It is this question that compels Matvei to begin
his long pilgrimage into Russia. Having experienced the absence of God in his own life, Matvei sets out into the world
to see if others have found Him. His first stop is at a
monastery famous for its austerity and holiness. It is this
experience that conclusively dispels any doubts in Matvei's
mind about the spiritual emptiness of the Christianity of
the established Church.

The monastery turns out to be a purely commercial
enterprise. As a landlord, it exploits its peasant tenants
even more brazenly than secular landlords. It also uses its
religious attractions to extort money from the laity. The
monks live lives of dissipation and debauchery; they rob and
rape visiting pilgrims. Even their famous ascetic who has
walled himself up in a cave is not what he seems. His
Christian brothers are actually starving him to death in
order to create a holy relic to add to the prestige of their
monastery.

By the time Matvei leaves the monastery, he has realized both the falsity of personal, asocial religion and the
falsity of organized religion as well. From the monastery,
he begins a long journey among the people. There, too, at
first, he finds only ugliness and hatred. The people yearn
for God, but they are unable to find Him.

> They fell into mad despair, and, inflamed by
> it, led depraved lives and soiled the earth
> in every way, as if to revenge themselves on
> her that she gave them birth.[47]

Those who seek God are destined to lonely, hopeless,

and endless wandering.

> I saw grey figures with knapsacks on their
> backs and staffs in their hands creeping and
> swaying along the roads and paths, going not
> hurriedly but depressed, white heads bent low,
> walking humbly and thoughtfully, with credu-
> lous, opened hearts.[48]

It is only after six years of wandering among such

God-seekers as these that Matvei finally does discover God.

His religious experience, however, is a revelation of not

the supernatural but the human world. Matvei finally meets

a group of factory laborers who have already abandoned the

hopeless task of seeking for a God and have begun to create

the idea of a God of their own.

> The creators of God are the people. They
> are the great martyrs--greater than the ones
> the church has praised. They are God, the
> creators of miracles--the immortal people! I
> believe in their soul; I have faith in their
> strength. They are the one and certain basis
> of life; they are the father of all gods that
> have been and that will be.[49]

Up to this point Gorky's presentation was little more

than a metaphor for scientific socialism. It is clear that

while the peasantry are scattered in misery and bewilderment,

searching in vain for a transcendent God, the working class

is creating a God of its own. It is also apparent that this

creation of God is identical with the creation of socialism.

It depends first of all upon the unity and cooperation of

all the people.

> Soon the will of the people will awake, and
> that great force, now divided, will unite.
> Many are already seeking the means by which
> all the powers of the earth shall be harmonized
> into one, and from which shall be created the
> holy and beautiful all-embracing God of the earth.[50]

Gorky further insisted that he was speaking not only of an act of spiritual regeneration but also of the violent, physical destruction of the old world.

> But you are not right when you say that we, who are arbitrarily bound in the chains of the terrible misery of our daily toil, can free ourselves from the yoke of greed without destroying the actual prison which surrounds us.[51]

However, despite these more or less material revolutionary and socialist concerns, there can be no doubt that Gorky wrote The Confession from a strong religious feeling. This is no dispassionate expose of the lies and deceits of Christianity. The social perversions of religion did not motivate Gorky politically as much as it offended him morally. He was not just horrified that the myth of God has been used by the ruling class to exploit the people, he is also offended because the myth is a lie.

Matvei's realization that God allows evil and suffering to exist in the world is not just the turning point of the novel, it also reveals the primary motivation of Gorky's own search for a God. It was because of Gorky's outrage at the possibility of human misery that he simply could not discard religion as a hopeless myth. He felt the need for a God that really existed and that was all-powerful, all-knowing, all-compassionate, all-merciful. Such a God could offer the oppressed and downtrodden of the earth the hope of real equality, real justice, and real happiness. Thus when Gorky committed himself to the idea of socialist revolution, he understood it in these religious terms.

Gorky's religious creation is not limited to the last God-building section of The Confession. Matvei's conversion to the new religion actually begins quite early. Matvei's first authentic religious experience (not one of his Christian self-delusions) occurs just after his marriage. Matvei then finds himself at peace only in nature.

> At such times I looked upon the clear sky, the blue space, the woods clothed in golden autumn garments or in silvery winter treasure, and the river, the fields and the hills, the stars and the flowers, and saw them as God. All that was beautiful was of God and all that was of God was related to the soul.[52]

Gorky's precise meaning is not clear though there is a hint of idealism--in that reality is only a reflection of the soul. Most important, however, is the idea that the earth, the natural world, must be a part of the concept of God. Throughout The Confession Gorky waxes eloquent about the beauty of nature and its inspiration for the soul of humankind. Close to the end of the novel, he suggests that the earth represents the feminine principle. Of sleeping in an open field at night Gorky says:

> You lie on her breast and your body grows and you drink the warm, perfumed milk of your dear mother, and you see yourself completely and forever the child of the earth. With gratitude you think of her, "Oh my beloved earth!"[53]

The masculine side of Gorky's God is represented by the people. The people are the "master" of the mother-earth.

> I saw the earth, my mother, in space between the stars and brightly she gazed into the distance and the depths. I saw her like a full bowl of bright red, incessantly seething human blood, and I saw her master, the all-powerful, immortal people.[54]

The proletariat is God.

> Thou art my God, the creator of all gods, which
> thou weavest out of the beauty of thy soul and
> the labor and agony of thy seeking. There
> shall be no God but thou, for thou art the one
> God, the creator of miracles.[55]

The people are strong, creative, active; the earth
is passive and yielding. The earth inspires the people to
create and provides them with the elemental material without
which creation is impossible. Thus Gorky's vision of human
creativity is a poetic form of Bogdanov's empiriomonism.
Reality--or knowledge, which is the same thing in Bogdanov's
conception of it--arises from labor, the interaction between
human beings and the natural world. Human knowledge inevitably progresses toward mastery over nature; humankind is
unlimited in its capacity to create a world that embodies its
ideals. Gorky simply restated this idea in symbolic, religious terms.

The Confession ends with an ecstatic religious experience. The faith of a group of people brings a dead girl
back to life. As part of the resurrecting group, Matvei
feels himself at one with God--both earth and people as one.

> Again I was alone, but now forever and insep-
> arably united with the soul of the people,
> the masters and miracle workers of the earth.
> . . . I have no words to describe the exulta-
> tion of that night, when alone in the darkness,
> I embraced the whole earth with my love and
> stood on the height of my experience and saw
> the world like fiery stream of life-force,
> flowing turbidly to unite into one current,
> the end of which I could not see. I joyfully
> understood that the inaccessibility of the end
> was the source of the infinite growth of my
> soul and the great earthly beauty.[56]

Besides writing The Confession, Gorky made his
theory of God-building explicit in a more reasoned, prosaic
form. In October of 1907, Lunacharsky published an article
in Obrazovanie in which he talked of European attitudes toward "The Future of Religion."[57] The French journal, Mercure de France, had circulated a questionnaire on that topic
to a number of European intellectual leaders. It was the
series of answers published by the Mercure de France that
provided Lunacharsky with the material for his article.
Lunacharsky quoted from most of the respondents' replies but
printed the responses of Plekhanov and Gorky in their entirety. Of the two, Lunacharsky praised Gorky's the more
highly and took it as the standard by which the rest were
measured.

Just as he did in The Confession, Gorky first argued
against belief in religion because it was both a falsehood
and an impediment to progress. In this presentation, however, Gorky objected to religion principally because it was
a limitation upon man's freedom. Religion, he said, taught
that morality was given by divine law, and mankind thus allowed itself to be subjugated to a higher power. "That is why
atheism, to the extent that it denies the existence of a personal God, seems desirable to me: it liberates mankind from
a dangerous delusion."[58]

Having disposed of established religion and the notion of transcendent truth or moral law, Gorky went on to
salvage the spirit of religion. As he had in The Confession,

he recreated religion in a form that he could accept. Gorky
defined his new religion in such a way as to identify it with
the spirit of the socialist revolutionary movement. The
knowledge of the liberated human collective, as Gorky saw it,
gave the collective humanity a God-like power: "I understand the religious sense in these terms: the religious
sense is the joyful and proud feeling of the knowledge of
the harmoniousness of the bonds that unite humankind with
the universe."59

> The path of humanity--no matter what those
> of sick faith say--leads to spiritual perfec-
> tion, and the consciousness of this process in
> each healthy person must summon the faith that
> I call a religious mood, that is, creative and
> complex feelings of faith and power, hope for
> victory, love of life, amazement in the force
> of the subtle harmony that exists between his
> reason and the whole universe.60

Once again, Gorky's message was that collective humanity possessed all the attributes of divinity. Under socialism, the perfect society (heaven) would be realized on earth.
And once again Gorky echoed Bogdanov's emphasis upon the importance of human knowledge--the organization of experience--
in creating reality.

> The mastery of this experience . . . will
> awaken [in man] the consciousness of his own
> worth--the authoritative and proud wish to
> compete in creativity with past generations
> and create forms that are worthy of serving
> the future . . .
> I think that we are witnessing the birth
> of a new psychological type . . .
> For the creation of this, wide and free unity
> among people equal in position is necessary:
> this problem is being resolved by socialism.
> The unification of which I speak will create
> the unity of human experience and the possibil-
> ity of full, mutual understanding; it will

destroy evil, envy, greed; it will permit each
to use the experience of all and by his own
experience to serve all.[61]

When Lunacharsky wrote "The Future of Religion," he

had already published Religion and Socialism, and in that

work he had already expressed the same convictions that

Gorky had revealed in his response to Mercure de France.

Thus the article "The Future of Religion" was a review not

only of Gorky's thought but of Lunacharsky's own thought as

well. Lunacharsky argued that socialism was not only a

religious movement but the highest expression of the relig-

ious development of humankind. He concluded his article by

quoting from his own Religion and Socialism:

> Then what meaning does religion have? It
> means to be able to think of and to feel the
> world in such a way that the contradictions be-
> tween the laws of life and the laws of nature
> are resolved for us. Scientific socialism re-
> solves these contradictions, proposing the idea
> of the victory of life, the defeat of and the
> subjugation of chaos to reason by means of know-
> ledge and labor, science and technology.[62]

Lunacharsky's Religion and Socialism

In Religion and Socialism, Lunacharsky continued to

elaborate upon the desire for an ethical foundation for sci-

entific socialism that he had felt when he first became a

Marxist in the early 1890s. He began by apologizing for Marx

and Engels; he argued that they had written from a scientific

point of view and so their theories of economics and sociology

were expressed in the materialist and determinist terms of

science. Lunacharsky did not take this to mean that the two

founders of scientific socialism had absolutely rejected the

ethical or religious aspect to the proletarian revolution--
only that they had ignored it. Marx and Engels had attempted
to describe the processes of the real world and had tried to
avoid making value judgements on them.

Lunacharsky broke with that objective, scientific
tradition (while claiming that he was not really contradicting the tradition) by insisting that value judgements are
essential.

> But the fullness of human relationships with
> the world is attained only when its processes
> are not only understood but evaluated. A human
> is in essence a knower and an evaluator; only
> from knowledge and valuation can proceed action.[63]

Such a conclusion shows how far from the spirit of
materialism Lunacharsky had strayed. Human action proceeds
from valuation only if one assumes that human beings act with
a will free to choose between alternatives. The individual
must then evaluate those alternatives. If one assumes, however, that human beings are material substances that act
according to the same natural laws as all other matter obeys,
then both choice and evaluation are out of the question. At
the very outset, then, Lunacharsky committed himself to idealism and voluntarism.

The contradictions between Marx's determinism and
Lunacharsky's voluntarism became clear in Lunacharsky's discussion of the ethics of the revolutionary socialist movement. It shows the insight of Berdiaev into the essential
ethical problems of the socialist revolutionary that Lunacharsky reiterated the discussion that Berdiaev had presented

in Subjectivism and Individualism in Social Philosophy nearly
a decade earlier.

Lunacharsky argued that the ideals of the socialist
movement are inevitable because they are not only the desires of the historically most advanced class but because
they are also, in themselves, objectively valid.[64] It is
too narrow, he insisted, to conceive of socialism as an ethical good simply because it is historically inevitable or
simply advantageous to a particular class.[65]

Explicitly contradicting the very idea of material
inevitability, Lunacharsky actually asserted that socialism
is not produced by economic law. After all, the workers'
movement is really led by the intelligentsia and petty bourgeois sympathizers. The commitment of these classes to
socialism is obviously not a product of proletarian class
consciousness caused by material economic conditions. Rather,
the commitment of these intellectual leaders arises from the
objective truth and morality of the workers' cause[66] and
from the "objective loftiness of the socialist idea."[67]

Although outspoken in his apostasy from the materialist philosophy of Marxism, Lunacharsky was really no more
than echoing Lenin's (and Karl Kautsky's) opinions as expressed in What is to be Done?. The workers cannot achieve
socialism by themselves; they must be led by the revolutionaries of another class. By thus stressing the moral choice
of the intelligentsia in leading the revolutionary movement,
Lunacharsky cut the determinist ground from beneath scientific

socialism. For Lunacharsky, the religious essence of socialism consisted in the conscious moral choice by people who
were not the blind agents of the historical process. He
found the source of the religion of socialism to be in Marx's
statement that "past philosophers sought to know the world--
our task is to remake it."[68]

Like Mother, Religion and Socialism was devoted to
demonstrating that socialism is essentially the same as religion. Also like Mother, it was not an attempt to analyze
the essential natures of religion on one hand and of the
socialist revolutionary movement on the other and to demonstrate the identity of the two. Rather, both Gorky and Lunacharsky attempted to make their point by an extended analogy.
Their identification of socialism as religion was intuitive;
their arguments consisted of itemizing the similarities between socialism and religion. As Lunacharsky said, "Now the
matter at hand is not a history of religion but only a more
or less deep investigation into the interrelationship between
religion and socialism; to determine the place of socialism
among other religious systems."[69]

Lunacharsky simply began with his own sense of religious commitment to the ideal of socialism and then went back
through the history of religion to find attitudes, motivations, and desires of various creeds and beliefs that seemed
identical with his own. He ignored all elements of religion
that either contradicted or were not congruent with his own
religious sense; Religion and Socialism was not an investi-

gation into the nature of either religion or socialism but a polemical justification for the tenets of God-building.

Thus, in discussing the religion of the ancient Greeks, Lunacharsky wrote that Hercules should be considered to be "labor's God" despite the fact that in the entire Greek religious world-view there is little that can be seen as proletarian, socialistic, or revolutionary. Similarly, in his view of Judaism, Lunacharsky considered the Old Testament to be based upon a "religion of labor." In a chapter entitled "The Biblical Spirit and the Religion of Labor," he asserted:

> The biblical spirit appears in history more as
> a latent thirst for justice than as a desire
> for power. God is justice. He is the opponent
> of the scheming and grasping rich man and the
> supporter of the poor proprietor--a friend of
> equality. Therefore he gives victory to the
> moral, moderate, work-loving representatives
> of the lower levels of society over the dissi-
> pated, magnificent, proud people who have for-
> gotten the ascendency of God.[70]

Lunacharsky identified Satan with the acquisition of wealth: kings, lords, and millionaires are agents of the devil. God stands for justice; the poor and the down-trodden will achieve the Kingdom of Heaven. Just as God struck down Sodom and Gomorrah, so will the twentieth century proletariat destroy the contemporary worshippers of Mammon.[71]

Though he searched for similarities between the social-ist movement and many old religions, it was in Christianity that Lunacharsky found the most complete analogue with revo-lutionary socialism. Like Gorky, Lunacharsky considered Christ to be the ultimate symbol of proletarian revolution.

He explicitly identified Jesus Christ with the working class
and asserted that the desire for socialism was spiritually
identical with the desire for the Second Coming of the
Messiah![72]

Here Lunacharsky gave the purest expression of God-
building as an eschatological vision; he saw socialist revolution as the Millenium.

> And on the hill of Golgotha arises a new
> Messiah, his blood has been spilled and they
> have nailed him to the cross. And they mock-
> ingly say to him, "You, liberator of the world,
> liberate yourself from hard labor camps, prison,
> and the grave where we have put you for your
> deeds." But it is impossible to kill Labor,
> it is resurrected and continues its preaching,
> its heavy struggle; it carries once more its
> cross from Golgotha to Golgotha . . . for in
> truth the Savior of the World never dies.[73]

In his historical account of Christianity, Lunacharsky
found that it had always contained proletarian and socialistic elements. Indeed, he found that the earliest form of
Christianity was in fact a revolutionary movement of the
laboring classes.

> The basis of Christianity, in Jerusalem and
> everywhere else, was social-ness and brother-
> hood arising from the very lowest levels of the
> population. . . . Christianity in Rome and in
> Palestine was a movement of the proletariat.
> The happy and the powerful never make revolu-
> tions. Native Romans disappeared among Greeks,
> Syrians, Egyptians, and various Asians, whether
> freedmen or slaves. All these variegated ele-
> ments felt the need to create for themselves
> an artificial fatherland which could help them
> and augment their petty individuality. Such
> was the ground upon which quickly grew the family
> of Christianity. To all this mass of the poor,
> the enslaved, those who live in gloom and degra-
> dation, Christianity gave a bright light of hope,
> gladness, and a future. With Christianity arose
> the sense of a people and a feeling of brother-

hood among the unfortunate, the cast off, the despairing. Christian martyrs had more faith than common sense, but their heroism showed the height of enthusiasm that is awakened by the idea of communism.[74]

Furthermore, Lunacharsky dwelt at length upon the Christian millenarianism of the Middle Ages. He distinguished eschatalogical from "liberal" or "orthodox" Christianity as having a purely proletarian composition and motivation. The Christian millenarians of the Middle Ages, according to Lunacharsky's interpretation, believed in the brotherhood of the poor; they hated the rich; and they rejected secular culture. They longed for the utter destruction of the evil world and the subsequent reign of goodness and perfection of the Kingdom of Heaven.

The only significant difference between early Christians and contemporary proletarian revolutionaries, he said, was simply the political passivity of the Christians. They believed that a transcendent God would create the new, perfect world for them. Nevertheless, Lunacharsky insisted that their millenarianism was both communistic and revolutionary.[75]

> The communistic spirit of the first, popular socialism is beyond question. . . . At variance with the whole contemporary cultured world, it was a radical, uncompromising contradiction. In counterposing to [that world] a completely new form of life, it was revolutionary. Any ideology that truly reflects the downtrodden masses cannot but be revolutionary at heart.[76]

Though he included socialism under the general term of religion, Lunacharsky did not conceive of socialism as simply an equal member of that genus. Instead, he claimed that socialism was actually the pinnacle of human religious thought. Socialism represented all the hopes and desires that humanity had ever expressed in its religious yearnings. The difference, according to Lunacharsky, was that socialism was neither a myth nor a lie; socialism would in fact usher in the Kingdom of Heaven that past religions had always only promised.

Religions had always been attempts "to resolve the contradictions between life and nature."[27] Humanity had for all its previous existence been limited in its desires and aspirations by both the forces of nature and the oppression of ruling classes. In the past, the only solution to the contradiction between life and nature that religion had produced was a faith that in a life after death humanity would finally experience perfect joy, brotherhood, and abundance. Such a solution, said Lunacharsky, was of course only a delusion.

Scientific socialism, however, according to Lunacharsky, fulfilled the same needs that religion had arisen to satisfy, but socialism would resolve the contradiction between life and nature not in fantasy but in fact. Following the proletarian revolution--the "Day of Judgement"--the working class will create its own paradise. Lunacharsky here echoed the sentiments of both Bogdanov and Gorky: the proletariat will become God-like in its knowledge and its power over nature. Socialism will be that perfect existence that humankind had previously always called "heaven."

> The reconciliation of the laws of life and the laws of nature arises from the victory of life with the help of knowledge and technology. Labor, wide sociality, development of the sense or relatedness, hope for unlimited progress-- this is what gives religious confort to our epoch. If there is a God, then it is life and its highest representative, the human species. The religious task of the new man is to serve science and labor, the contemporary struggle for socialism--an all-encompassing struggle that destroys both the decrepit state of society and the decrepit state of the spirit and creates a new society and a new spirit.[78]

It was just this religious feeling--this eschatalogical expectation of an earthly paradise--that Lunacharsky believed to be the essence of the revolutionary movement. It was this religious desire that he thought motivated the revolutionaries in their struggle for socialism. Thus Lunacharsky concluded that socialism would not be the product of economic forces but of religious enthusiasm. In the conclusion to the first volume of Religion and Socialism, Lunacharsky explicitly emphasized that the future is not predetermined and that the religious enthusiasm of socialism was essential to those people who voluntarily undertook the creation of the new world of the future.

> But is the new religion only a dream? No, it is a hope; a hope with more foundation than supports any other religion. Hope, of course, can always deceive us. Religion has been rationalized and cleansed but it loses nothing in its depths, in its creative powers, in its exciting beauty. In it man sees the purest expression of his great species and understands by himself the great elemental Humanity and derives from it heroic resolution. It denies the self, over-comes "my self," to fight in the thousand year struggle for Humanity--regardless of the fact that the outcome of the struggle is hidden from our eyes by the thick mist of the future. Religion is enthusiasm and "without enthusiasm

people cannot create anything great."[79]

Bogdanov's Utopian Novels

Bogdanov was never an explicit proponent of God-building. Though the movement could not have stood without the philosophical foundation provided by Bogdanov's Empirio-monism, Bogdanov himself never compared the revolutionary socialist movement with religion nor did he ever use words with religious connotation (sacred, holy, martyr were three of Lunacharsky's favorites) to describe either the working class movement or their socialist goal. In later polemics with Lenin during the schism of the Bolshevik faction, Bogdanov actually publicly objected to the comparison of socialism with religion. In doing so, however, Bogdanov did not contradict anything that Lunacharsky or Gorky had said about religion or about socialism; he simply said that the religious analogy was not good for public relations between the Bolsheviks and their more orthodox Social-Democratic comrades.

Nevertheless, at the same time that his close friends and philosophical collaborators were yielding to the enthusiasm of the 1905 Revolution, Bogdanov, too, felt the spirit moving within him. While Gorky was writing The Confession and Lunacharsky was writing Religion and Socialism, Bogdanov tried his hand at fiction for the first time. He published Red Star in 1808 and Engineer Menni in 1909.[80] Both were science fiction, utopian novels describing life on Mars.

Red Star tells of a space journey of a Russian revo-

lutionary. In the process of preparing for an armed assault
on the autocracy (he is obviously a Bolshevik), this revolutionary meets a particularly dedicated and daring socialist.
Upon further acquaintance, the Russian discovers that his
new comrade is actually a Martian.

A group of Martians has been scouring the Earth for
the most advanced example of the human species, and in this
Russian Social-Democratic revolutionary they have found their
man. Since he is a scientific socialist, he has already
attained the knowledge of universal truth; consequently, life
on Mars will not be a shock to him.

The Martians take him up to their planet to show him
more or less what the Earth's future will be like and to
prepare him to announce this truth to the people on Earth
after he returns. Mars is a socialist utopia. The laws of
historical development that Marx discovered apply not only
to the Earth; they are universally true. Mars is just a few
centuries ahead of the Earth in its economic development.
The tribal, feudal, and capitalist stages of development are
already far in the Martian past; socialism is already about
three hundred years old.

Martian society is therefore perfect. It is a totally mechanized, automated society. There is an abundance of
material goods, and all Martians are equally well provided
for. There is a well-developed popular culture; museums,
art galleries, libraries, and laboratories (scientific study
is a form of recreation among the Martians) abound. There

are collective nurseries, collective schools, collective living quarters; there is no such thing as a family. Comradely cooperation gives a sense of family unity to the entire collectivity of Martians.

Peace and harmony exist among all the people. There is no such thing as crime. There are only a few, extremely rare cases of mental illness for which special hospitals have been established. There is no need for armies, police, or even any sort of government. Social administration is taken care of by scientific-statistical institutions which regulate all production and distribution of goods. But these institutions do not coerce; they only make recommendations. Martians are perfectly free to work whenever and wherever they want.

The Martians, however, are totally dedicated to (or even obsessed with) labor. The more heroic the task, the more anxious are the Martians to undertake it. The existence of laggards or shirkers on Mars is absolutely unthinkable. The statistical bureaus need only publish the number of workers needed to work at any given job at any given time and sufficient volunteers automatically appear for work.

The resolution of the class struggle has not made Martian society static and stagnant. There still remains the struggle with nature. There are occasional plagues and pestilences and some rare natural disasters, but the principal problem facing the Martians is that of dwindling natural resources. Martians must colonize other planets to obtain necessary raw materials. It is this task that inspires the labor of the most intelligent and dedicated Martians.

Struggle and conflict between individuals on Mars is limited because of the reign of reason among them. Martians are always logical and reasonable. Those who establish policy and make leadership decisions have no official rank and no physical means of coercion; they can exercise no sanctions against disobedience. There is, in fact, simply no question of disobedience. Superior intellect and knowledge is always followed; the most knowledgeable person in any particular field is deferred to by all others.

Engineer Menni, Bogdanov's second novel about socialism on Mars, was no more than an elaboration of a piece of Martian history already related in Red Star. The engineer Menni was the chief organizer in charge of the construction of the canals on Mars during its late capitalist era. It was Menni who first worked out the principles of the "organizational science" that shaped the world-view of the Martian working class and gave it the ideological tools for the creation of socialism. That "organizational science" that is expounded in Engineer Menni is, of course, Bogdanov's own philosophical system.

Thus, though Bogdanov was silent on the topic of religion and socialism, his utopian expectations for the future of human society after the proletarian revolution were high. He never compared his vision of the future with the "kingdom of heaven" described by religious chiliasts. Nevertheless, of all the Bolshevik God-builders, Bogdanov wrote the most explicit, systematic, and complete prediction of the coming socialist utopia. Just as Gorky wrote the first novel of Socialist Realism, Bogdanov was the originator of socialist science fiction--a genre that would flourish in the early years of the Soviet Union.[81]

S. Volsky and Socialist Ethics

Stanislav Volsky was yet another radical Bolshevik who contributed to God-building during the years immediately following the 1905 Revolution. He was a late arrival to the God-building movement; his single work, The Philosophy of Struggle, appeared in 1909. He was more influenced by Bogdanov, Lunacharsky, and Gorky than he was influential upon them. Nevertheless, his formulation of the ethical questions of the revolutionary socialist movement contributes to an understanding of the world-view of the radical Bolshevik idealists.

Volsky was approximately six years younger than Bogdanov, Lunacharsky, and Bazarov, but he shared their social origins and their revolutionary experience. He was born Andrei Vladimirovich Sokolov in March, 1880, in Volokolamsk. His father was a judge on the Moscow regional court. Volsky attended the Moscow Gymnasium and matriculated at the juridical faculty of the University of Moscow. However, in 1899, his first year at the university, Volsky was expelled for participating in student disturbances. After his expulsion, Volsky travelled to Germany; while in Berlin, he joined the

Social-Democratic party.

From the very beginning of the Bolshevik-Menshevik schism of 1903, Volsky adhered to Lenin's faction. During 1904 and 1905 he was a practical party organizer for the Bolshevik committee in Moscow. He was one of the initiators of the underground Bolshevik journal, Golos Truda, and he was invited to participate on the editorial board of Vpered. We have already noted his participation with Shantser and Liadov in leading the Moscow insurrection of December, 1905. Volsky's name will also be prominent in subsequent discussions of the Bolshevik schism of 1909. As the chairman of the Moscow Regional Bureau of the RSDRP, Volsky was a leading figure in the "otzovist" controversy and was a close ally of Bogdanov in the schism.[82]

Volsky was also a philosophical ally of Bogdanov-- or perhaps only a disciple. In the preface to The Philosophy of Struggle, he announced that he stood closest to the tendency in Marxism led by Bogdanov and Lunacharsky.[83] And in the first chapter of that book, Volsky showed that he adhered to Bogdanov's strict, empirical positivist epistemology. Volsky asserted that man has no access to knowledge of absolute reality; man does not know if the laws of nature are based upon material reality or on human perception alone. All that humankind can do, according to Volsky, is to formulate laws of nature based upon experience and then test the truth of those laws by applying them in practice.[84]

Later in the book, Volsky showed that he accepted

Bogdanov's understanding of how the human collective synthe-
sizes the experience of its many members into a single interpretation of the world--in other words, how the process of
human knowing actually creates the real world.

> We have seen how the experience of the separate
> individual is systematized and subsumed under
> the power of social experience, communally ac-
> knowledged and verified. Having strengthened
> the social bond to unprecedented degrees, the
> species becomes the master of individual con-
> sciousness, it changes from a simply collec-
> tive comprehension into an active creative
> force.[85]

The principal task that Volsky set himself in The
Philosophy of Struggle was to investigate ethics in the same
way that Bogdanov had treated knowledge or that Marx had
treated economic relationships. He wanted to investigate
the natural evolution of ethical systems, relate that development to the class struggle, and to predict the future of
ethics after the socialist revolution.[86] Just as Bogdanov
had done at the beginning of his philosophical speculations,
Volsky wanted to relate everything to cosmic evolution and
to purely objective criteria. He announced that "The evolution of the cosmos is the basis from which one can and must
extrapolate general human morality."[87]

Furthermore, in taking ethics as his theme, Volsky
followed the main subject of Lunacharsky's works. The latter's Religion and Socialism had been based on the premise
that scientific socialism was based as much on ethical judgements as on science. Lunacharsky believed that socialism
was actually dedicated to the very same religious-ethical

ideals that had been espoused by the religions and metaphysical philosophies of the past. For Lunacharsky, socialism was not a fact but a freely willed moral choice.

Yet Lunacharsky had never attempted to develop scientific socialism into a consistent ethical system. He had outlined a natural basis for ethics in "The Foundations of a Positive Esthetics," and he had written a history of working class idealism in Religion and Socialism. But he did not elaborate upon the role that ethics had played and would play in the history of the class struggle. Stanislav Volsky attempted to do just that.

Volsky began his Philosophy of Struggle with the same quotation from Marx that Lunacharsky and all the voluntarist Social-Democratic revolutionaries emphasized:

> In the author's view, the key to the moral philosophy of Marxism appears in Marx's words: "philosophy only explains the world in one way or another, the point, however, is to change it." Thus, "to change the world" does not mean to posit some sort of "immutable" law, nor to bow down to some absolute norm, but to learn the changing tendencies of social life in order to use them for the realization of mankind's practical goals--it is to this task that Marxist doctrine calls man.[88]

The significance that Marx's statement had for Volsky was that it introduced an important ambiguity into the science of historical materialism. The idea that mankind can change the world implies an act of human will. Will implies choice. And choice implies placing values on alternative actions. Finally, value implies a normative system--such as ethics.

However, a strictly determinist system cannot permit
the concept of ethics. If scientific investigation proves
that something will inevitably happen, then there can be no
alternatives, no choice, no free will, no objective ethical
norms. Thus the Marxist who attempts to place free will in
the process of historical development finds himself in the
same predicament as the Christian theologian who tries to
reconcile "free will" with "God's law." The only result can
be some variation on the theme of "perfect obedience is perfect freedom." As Volsky put it, "My necessity--precisely
because I realize it and make sense out of it--becomes my
freedom."[88]

But state the problem as he might, Volsky was as
unable as Berdiaev and Lunacharsky before him to solve the
paradox of human free will in a materialist and determinist
system. Indeed, Volsky echoed Berdiaev's sentiments:

> This synthetic expression--socialism--is
> simultaneously a doctrine of necessary war
> and a doctrine of ultimate ideal. In the first
> case, it is objective fact; in the second,
> it is a prediction which cannot pretend to
> accuracy and objectivity.[89]

Throughout The Philosophy of Struggle, Volsky's emphasis was
upon socialism as a doctrine of ultimate ideal.

What Volsky attempted to do in this work was to re-
interpret Marx's scheme of historical development by focusing
on the function of human ethical systems in social development. He did not suggest that ethics had any transcendent
value. Following the spirit of positivism, Volsky always saw
ethical systems as tied to practical human goals. But just

as Bogdanov had emphasized epistemology over material reality,
so Volsky emphasized human ethical development to the extent
that it seemed as if ethics must be superior to economic
conditions. Thus, capitalist ethics was directed at promoting capital accumulation and keeping the working class passive. Proletarian ethics was aimed at furthering the socialist revolution. Furthermore, the ideal society that Volsky
saw lying at the end of this historical process signified
the end of the need for ethical restraints. He understood
socialism as representing the complete liberation of human
will; mankind would ultimately be free of all necessity--
even free of the notions of good and evil.

Volsky began by looking at ancient cultures before
the sense of ethical norms had arisen.

> No contradiction arose between "world" and
> "society," nor between "subject" and "object,"
> nor between "I" and "not I." There was no
> place for problems of perception, since no
> contradictions of perception arose; moral norms,
> as conscious formulas for behavior, were ab-
> sent because there were no elements on the
> ground of which they could have been created.[90]

Volsky found that it was the process of labor that
began to separate the perceptions of individuals. Labor
required knowledge of nature and rational action based upon
that knowledge. The rational process of knowledge that began with the need to wrest a living from nature was ultimately extended to questions of human values.

> The mind . . . had ceased to believe. It turn-
> ed to itself, and by means of the construction
> of its own mind, it wanted to explain that which
> had been created by the collective reason.
> Myth had lost its old irrestibleness.[91]

However, this rational process of questioning did not begin a slow, direct development of critical thought down to contemporary times, as Volsky explained it. The labor process not only introduced knowledge and reason, it produced a society based upon economic class divisions. The ruling classes created ethical systems that they imposed upon the subordinate classes. Such systems formed boundaries which the members of the society could not question, and they served to preserve order among the oppressed classes. Thus the history of the class struggle is the history of ethical systems; ethical norms play a central role in that class struggle.

At the outset of his discussion, Volsky had said that "The goal of each class is to increase its own power, and its moral norms have value solely to the extent that they are conducive to the achievement of that task."92 Thus there can be no such thing as abstract morality. Good and bad are concepts that a ruling class creates (makes "true") to serve its own ends. Ethical development is inseparable from economic development. The victory of one class over another class in economic and social terms involves the re-placement of one ethical system with another. The new ethi-cal system is created to justify the economic objectives of the newly victorious class.

However, Volsky did not see ethics as a mere by-product of economic events; the ethical system that each class developed was also an important weapon in its struggle

against its oppressor. Therefore, in the process of the
emergence of the proletariat as a revolutionary force, it
must create for itself a goal and an ethical system that
obligates all the members of the working class to struggle
for that goal. The ideal that gives unity and direction to
the proletariat, according to Volsky, is the ideal of socialism.

> Thus an organizing center is found: class
> self-consciousness . . . Socialism becomes
> the subject of faith, faith that is all the
> more incontestable since it proceeds from the
> spontaneous economic conditions of its exis-
> tence.[93]

Here Volsky apparently wanted to have his cake and
eat it, too. He argued that socialism was a faith, but he
also said that socialism proceeded from the facts of existence.

> Theoretically [the proletariat] understands
> the whole historical conditionality of its
> faith; practically it believes in socialism
> as in something that is unconditional, as in
> a _duty_ expected of every thinking human.[94]

Since socialism is the ultimate ideal of the working
class, their ethical system must be oriented toward furthering the socialist revolutionary movement. What is "good"
is what brings the proletariat closer to socialism. "The
sole leading norm, admitted by all members of socialist
society, says: socialism is the freedom of struggle; all is
good that increases struggle, and all is bad that decreases
it."[95]

When Volsky discussed the morality of socialism, he
was really only talking about the morality of the socialist

revolution. Until that victory is achieved, all ethical values must be directed only toward revolution. "The morality of an armed camp . . . is an instrument of only one social class considered in a definite historical epoch, and outside of that epoch is devoid of any meaning."[96]

Consequently, once the socialist revolution had been accomplished, the ethics that had advanced that goal will no longer be valid. In the new classless society there can be no ethical system because there is no longer any need for one class to oppress another. "Therefore [the proletariat] cannot have a coercive ideology which it wants to carry into the future, no norms which pretend to eternal value, no boundaries which the individual cannot transgress."[97]

Socialism will introduce an ethical utopia in which there is absolute individual freedom. Whereas Bogdanov had imagined socialism to be a material, economic, and social utopia, Volsky saw it as the beginning of true freedom. He thought of socialism as a new era in which "all will be reborn."[98]

> The new man is not solely the product of contemporary historical reality: he also carries in himself the seed of the future, he begins the first act of free and conscious human history. This is not the last cry of a dying man: this is the first cry of a newly born baby to whom the future belongs.[99]

Volsky even thought of humankind as a God-like ruler of the universe in much the same terms as the God-builders had done.

> Precisely there, in the hazy distances of the
> future, lies that which is most precious and
> sacred for the individual . . . Only there
> is man proud, strong, bold, and beautiful;
> only there, in harmony of feeling and all-en-
> compassing knowledge, will grow the ruler of
> the universe for whom any contemporary reality
> serves as a mere pedestal.[100]

Volsky's ultimate conception of ethics in the ideal
socialist future was markedly Nietzschean. He found the concept of _agon_, or conflict, to be a central element in the
new society. It would be through the struggle and competi-
tion between men that nature would be subdued to human will.

> The freedom of struggle is our common task
> . . . and we work together in order to clear
> out of the way all extraneous obstacles, in
> order to master those elemental forces of nature
> which threaten our existence and interfere
> with our struggle: we are conscious co-workers
> precisely because we are conscious enemies.
> After all, it is he, in contradicting my
> ideas with his, who helps me to produce the
> greatest clarity in my thought. After all, it
> is he who forces me to experience the greatest
> exertion of will, the greatest ecstacy, when
> the soul, inspired with passion for victory,
> flies above the world like a whilrwind, thirst-
> ing for obstacles to destroy. After all, it
> is he who strikes a spark from me and makes
> from it a fire with which I will enflame man-
> kind.[101]

God-building Polemics Against

Orthodox Marxism and Fashionable Religion

For three years (1906-1909) God-building flourished
among the radical Bolsheviks. Besides the major works which
presented the main tenets of their thought, the God-builders
also published several collections of minor essays and polemical articles. These essays dealt with points of philosophical contention between the God-builders and their two

principal groups of opponents--the orthodox Marxists and the intellectuals of Russia's "New Religious Consciousness." Defending their position from the attacks of orthodox Marxists, such as Plekhanov, the God-builders published Outlines of the Philosophy of Marxism. The two volumes of Literary Decadence, on the other hand, were not as much a defense as an attack upon the futility of the Russian intelligentsia's search for a transcendent religion. As an alternative to this futile search, the God-builders offered their own religion of proletarian revolution.

The Outlines of the Philosophy of Marxism was devoted to the themes that had always engaged the interest of the left Bolshevik philosophers: the epistemological and ethical foundations of Marxism. Bazarov opened the collection with "Mysticism and Realism of our Times," an empirical epistemological attack upon the absolute materialist ontology of Plekhanov. Plekhanov's belief in an absolute material reality, argued the positivist Bazarov, was really a form of unconscious mysticism.[102] The concept of an absolute "thing-in-itself" is completely beyond the realm of human experience, and to believe that such a thing exists involves a faith that can only be considered to be religious.

Just as Berdiaev had suggested in Subjectivism and Individualism in Social Philosophy, Bazarov pointed out that the acceptance of the concept of absolute material reality implies belief in the possibility of a priori knowledge. Furthermore, if the possibility of a priori truth is allowed,

the philosophical ground was laid for idealism and ethical
absolutes. Bazarov then argued that Plekhanov's concept of
the "thing-in-itself" was no less abstract and idealist than
Kant's supposition of a noumenal world.

> Plekhanov himself admits that at the basis of
> his world-view lies not facts of experience,
> not a conclusion from experience, but a relig-
> ious presupposition independent of any exper-
> ience--a metaphysical "leap of faith."[103]

Bazarov went on to offer once again empirical epistemology as an alternative to Kant's idealism and Plekhanov's
mystical materialism. The only reality about which one can
speak is the reality of human perceptions; humankind organizes its experience into certain working hypotheses which
interpret reality and allow mankind to successfully deal with
the external world. But, cautioned Bazarov, the positivist
does not imagine that his perceptions constitute "elemental
matter" or that his hypotheses are "absolute laws of nature."

Bazarov concluded by arguing that Marx and Engels
were positivists of Bogdanov's empiriomonist type; they were
not crude materialists like Plekhanov. He quoted from Engel's
"From Utopian to Scientific Socialism."

> "Our knowledge is based on action. First,
> there is sensory perception of reality. Then
> we act on that preliminary knowledge. To the
> extent that our knowledge corresponds to real-
> ity, we will be successful in action.[104]

The concept of knowledge that Engels revealed was
identical with the epistemology the God-builders had espoused
from the beginning, as Bazarov pointed out.

> The materialism of Marx and Engels is strict-
> ly realistic; the materialism of Plekhanov is

hieroglyphic. Marx and Engels rise from empirically given facts and causes to general ideas;
Plekhanov descends from the transcendent idea
of "the thing-in-itself" to facts. The materialism of Marx and Engels is the living method
of scientific investigation, the materialism
of Plekhanov is a dead scholasticism which sets
aside any scientific investigation.[105]

It was this question of relativist epistemology ver-

sus absolutist ontology that was central to the entire de-

bate between the God-builders and the orthodox Marxists.

The distinction between the two points of view had practical

significance of immense importance for the revolutionary

movement. Accepting matter as an absolute "thing-in-itself"

committed one to a strictly monist universe of rigid deter-

minism. Such historical fatalism led to revolutionary pro-

grams that tended to be passive--to allow the laws of mater-

ial cause and effect to produce their historically inevitable

results without human interference. From the other point of

view, we have already seen how the choice of positivist

epistemology ultimately led both to frankly millenial expec-

tations and to extreme revolutionary voluntarism. The conser-

vatism of the Mensheviks and the radicalism of the Bolsheviks

were but reflections of their differing philosophies of

reality.

During this period, Bogdanov devoted an entire book,

The Adventures of a Certain Philosophical School, to discred-

iting Plekhanov's philosophy of absolute material reality.[106]

He used the same criticisms of materialism in "The Land of

Idols and the Philosophy of Marxism," Bogdanov's contribution to the Outlines of the Philosophy of Marxism.

Bogdanov's principal objection to Plekhanov's notion
of the "thing-in-itself" was that it was not really materialism and it really did not provide the foundation for a monist
world-view. By supposing the existence of absolute matter
quite independent of human consciousness, Bogdanov reasoned
that Plekhanov was actually suggesting that there were two
quite different sorts of reality--physical existence and
spiritual existence.[107] Plekhanov had tried to maintain
that although human mental consciousness had no direct knowledge of reality, its psychic impressions actually paralleled
the facts of absolute material reality.

Bogdanov responded by arguing that Plekhanov could
not prove that there was any kind of cause and effect between
the two quite different realms of material existence and
human consciousness. Such a universe would be a dualist one
which contained both spirit and matter--each acting according
to its own laws. There could be no question of causality or
objective inevitability.

Paradoxically, Bogdanov was actually accusing the
arch materialist, Plekhanov, of idealism. As Bazarov had
done, Bogdanov also pointed out the similarity between Plekhanov's notion of matter and Kant's supposition of a noumenal
reality. Bogdanov once again offered his own empiriomonism
as the only truly monist view of reality that could underly
the theories of scientific socialism. All that a human could
consider to exist is his perception and his own method of

organizing that perception into knowledge.

> The principle of <u>universal empirical substi-</u>
> <u>tution</u> is the extension into all of nature,
> into all the experience of people, of that
> method which makes up the essence of the social
> relations of people in the process of their
> common labor--<u>the method of their mutual under-</u>
> <u>standing</u> [of reality].[108]

In his essay, "Atheism," in <u>Outlines of the Philo-</u>
<u>sophy of Marxism</u>, Lunacharsky also joined in the attack
against ontological materialism. Typically, however, Lunacharsky looked at the question from a radically different
point of view. Bogdanov and Bazarov had dealt with materialism on strictly logical, philosophical grounds. They had
attempted to portray Plekhanov as a mystic and idealist,
while assuming for themselves the guise of objective monists.
(They stressed human perception as the sole foundation of
reality, and they insisted that human knowledge was objective
in respect to individual members of the human collective.)
Lunacharsky, however, did just the opposite. He faulted
Plekhanov for being too rigid a determinist and for robbing
the socialist movement of all the human idealism that gave
it life.

Lunacharsky began his critique by investigating the
moral implications of both idealism and materialism. Both
those schools of thought, asserted Lunacharsky, were pro-
foundly pessimistic doctrines. Although Kant had conceived
of the existence of moral ideals, he posited their existence
in some noumenal realm. Such ideals could never be perfectly
realized in the realm of human experience.[109] Lunacharsky

admitted that Kant's thought was certainly appropriate to capitalism--in bourgeois culture human ideals could never be realized. But, he insisted, such pessimism would not be valid for revolutionary socialism because socialism would in fact realize the ideals of the working class.[110]

The bulk of Lunacharsky's essay, however, was directed against the tenets of absolute materialism. He found materialism objectionable because it is inseparable from the concept of determinism and because of its ethical implications. Determinism, he asserted, produced only pessimism and passivity. Lunacharsky actually claimed that revolutionary activism and optimism could not proceed from a faith in materialism. The ultimate result of a purely materialist, mechanistic, and deterministic world-view must be senseless passivity. Lunacharsky quoted the words of a French materialist:

> "In nature there is neither beauty nor sense, only blind process. In us, ourselves, there is only this same process, plus unnecessary and tormenting consciousness. This consciousness soon is extinguished. . . . That is all. Existence is a great stupidity; life and thought are still greater stupidities."[111]

Lunacharsky suggested that there "is a synthesis, a saving synthesis of freedom and mechanism, ideal and necessity, creativity and automatism."[112] He suggested that the proletariat, as a class, is capable of making such a synthesis, of making sense out of life. The proletariat, in Lunacharsky's view, would not surrender to the supposed inevitable, but would first create an ideal for itself and then strive to realize that ideal in the real world. Lunacharsky summoned the founders of scientific socialism to his side.

> Marx and Engels chased idealism from history; they traced the intellectual development of humankind down to its economic development, but, by the same token, they lifted the idea and significance of economic progress to a high ideal value; I would say to a religious value.[113]

Once again Lunacharsky was translating Marxism into the terms of God-building. He asserted that "historical progress is a real movement toward freedom, by the means of economics, i.e., power over nature by understanding it."[114] The way in which Lunacharsky used the term "economics" reveals that he was deliberately misusing Marxism. For Marx, economics meant material causation; for Lunacharsky, it meant the exertion of human will over the material world.

Despite the fact that Lunacharsky appeared to be arguing from the opposite point of view of Bogdanov and Bazarov, he was really only revealing the consequences of the epistemology adopted by his fellow positivists. The substitution of human perception for materialist ontology could only result in the supremacy of human will in the process of history. Lunacharsky concluded his essay with new expressions of God-building.

> But the hope for attaining beauty and goodness, bliss and power, for joyful devotion to the highest ideals, breaking the bounds of alienated life, and raising the transience of life to an eternal meaning--this is the spirit of religion. God himself was only a representation of this spirit. It seems to me that we name the essence of socialism quite accurately when we say that it is religious atheism.[115]

> God, as all-knowing, all-blessed, all-power-
> ful, all-encompassing, eternal life, is really
> all that is human in its very highest poten-
> tial.
>   Thus we say that God is humanity in its
> highest potential.[116]

Outlines of the Philosophy of Marxism was fundamentally a philosophical work, directed mainly at intellectuals
within the Social-Democratic movement. Literary Decadence
was something else entirely. The essays in this collection
did not try to justify the religious enthusiasms of God-
building to other Russian Marxists; instead it suggested
some implications that the ideals of God-building had for
Russian intellectual culture as a whole. The articles in
Literary Decadence show that the God-builders were not interested only in economic transformation or in technological
control over the natural world by humanity. As the title
of the two volume collection indicated, the contributors
were concerned not just with Russia's political reaction and
economic oppression but with its cultural decay as well.
The socialist revolution that they envisaged would not only
liberate Russia materially, it would rejuvenate Russia's
spiritual culture.

   The subjects of Literary Decadence as well as the
audience toward which it was directed makes it clear that
God-building was offered as a solution to the spiritual un-
certainties of the Russian intelligentsia. The God-builders
were concerned with the mysticism and pessimism of the God-
seekers; they lamented the rise of personal, mystical, tran-

scendent religions for whose sake the intelligentsia had
abandoned its traditional commitment to the welfare of the
Russian people.

The God-builders tried to reawaken the intelligentsia's social consciousness--to show them that their
ideals could be realized only through the revolutionary socialist movement. The intelligentsia--as indicated by Problems of Idealism and Signposts (published one year after
Literary Decadence)--no longer believed that their ideals
could be realized through social action. Thus the God-
builders were the last representatives of the century-old
tradition of socially conscious Russian intellectuals who
identified their own ideals with the ideals of the Russian
people.

Gorky--who had never felt himself to be alienated
from the Russian people--believed that an individual, inward
looking religious experience was invalid. For Gorky, religion could be true only as an expression of collective spirit.
In "On Cynicism" in volume one of Literary Decadence, Gorky
said that,

> A whole personality is possible only when there
> are no heroes and no masses, when there are
> people who are tied together by feelings of
> mutual veneration.
> This feeling must arise from recollection
> of the great collective work which the people
> have wrought in the past, for the sake of its
> own resurrection; this feeling must become
> stronger in the consciousness of unity of ex-
> perience of each and all and the solidarity
> of the tasks of all together.
> And in time this feeling of respect of
> man for man will turn into a religion. The
> religion of humanity must be the wonderful

and tragic history of its successes and its
sufferings in the infinite, grandiose struggle
for spiritual freedom and for power over the
forces of nature.[117]

In "Gloom" in the same volume, Lunacharsky directed

his attention to the literary world. He pointed out that

the tendency in Russian culture in recent years was to ig-

nore social questions and to create an independent "free"

art. For this reason he felt it ignored the socially con-

scious writers of the previous century and paid particular

attention to non-socialists such as Pushkin or anti-social-

ists such as Dostoevsky.

Lunacharsky's main point in this essay was that the

contributors to the "free" Russian literature (such as

Briusov, Belyi, Merezhkovsky, and especially Andreyev) seem-

ed to be obsessed with the fear of death. Lunacharsky focus-

ed particularly upon the works of Andreyev, characterizing

him as a "grave digger." He claimed that Andreyev's fiction

was concerned with death and destruction and that his entire

world-view was colored with "black pessimism and hopeless-

ness."

Lunacharsky's purpose was not, himself, to offer an

alternative to this pessimism and despair. For that he

directed his readers to Religion and Socialism. In "Gloom,"

he simply wanted to demonstrate the hopeless depths to which

the intelligentsia had fallen in their religious search after

they had turned their backs on the people. Lunacharsky in-

sisted that even when they looked to Christianity for salva-

tion, they were only trying to fool themselves with fairy

tales of life after death. Indeed, Lunacharsky felt that
Christianity was particularly inappropriate for the decadent
Russian intelligentsia since Christianity was founded upon
socialist consciousness. He said of Christ:

> If we try to reconstruct him historically
> as an individual, we see in him an original
> leader of the proletarian masses of Galilee.
> If we think of him as a hero of legend, then
> he is the ideal of the proletarian masses of
> the Roman Empire during its decline . . .
> Even if he is too passive a hero for our con-
> temporary spirit, he is nevertheless a prole-
> tarian hero . . .[118]

According to Lunacharsky, no progressive or optimistic values or ideals could be found outside the revolutionary
movement.

In the second volume of Literary Decadence, Bazarov
chose Merezhkovsky as the particular object of his attention.
He argued that Merezhkovsky's vision of the imminent apocalypse was elitist, mystical, and logically untenable, and,
moreover, that Merezhkovsky's vision of the future ideal
world would be realized even more perfectly in the new world
of the socialist revolution.[119]

The most significant article of the whole collection
also appeared in volume two. Lunacharsky's "Twenty-third
Collection of 'Znanie'" was a review of Gorky's The Confession. Lunacharsky began his review by reiterating his
distress at the anarchy of Russia's literary decadence; he
lamented the fact that Russian literature lacked any guiding
principles. Why, asked Lunacharsky, can there be no artistic
geniuses as great in literature as Marx and Engels had been

in economics and politics?[120]

"There can be, must be, will be . . . !" said Lunacharsky, "It has already begun. Marxism above all gives the
artist the basis for an original and tragic understanding of
existence."[121] He listed the topics that would be available
to the new novelists. The list would be endless: the growth
of capitalism, the struggle among capitalists, the struggle
of the proletariat to become masters of their destiny, and
the construction of the new socialist world. "As a science,
Marxism turns the attention of the artist to the most important phenomena of life . . ."[122]

However, Lunacharsky did not have in mind a simple
empirical description of the reality of the capitalist world
or the reality of the working class movement. He wanted the
new socialist art to breathe with the ethical spirit of God-
building.

> Thus, the basic socio-psychological fact
> of our time is, in our view, the birth of a new
> type of soul. Just this process of noticing,
> expressing and illuminating with bright colors
> such a huge, exciting, poetical, and joyful
> task which can inspire the talent of the writer,
> which at last sifts through the dry sand of
> individualism to the fresh spring that quenches
> the thirst of the soul.[123]

The body of Lunacharsky's essay was an enthusiastic
appraisal of Gorky's most explicit God-building novel. He
asserted that Gorky's work should be the model for the new
proletarian art. In The Confession, Gorky had given concrete
expression to the religion inherent in socialism and had
promoted the worship of collective humanity as a God. "The

power of the collective, the beauty of the ecstasy of collective life, the miracle-working power of the collective--
that is what the author believes in, that is what he summons
us toward."[124]

Thus in "The Twenty-third Collection of 'Znanie',"
Lunacharsky contributed further to the theoretical foundation
of Socialist Realism. He had, as we have seen, already in
1903 in Foundations of a Positive Esthetics stressed the
importance of art in furthering the socialist revolution and
in constructing the new culture of socialism. In Gorky's
novels of the revolutionary movement, Mother and The Confession, Lunacharsky had found his literary prescriptions
marvelously filled.

Their concern with the works of writers influential
in contemporary Russian culture shows that the God-builders
felt themselves to be a part of the general Russian intellectual milieu. They had always felt it to be natural to en-
gage in polemics with the idealists, such as Berdiaev and
Bulgakov, as it was to argue with other Social-Democrats.
Their philosophical interests had always been the same as
those of non-party Russian intellectuals.

It was surely no coincidence that at the same time
that God-building flourished, Russia's religious renaissance
was also at its peak. Rozanov, Berdiaev, and Merezhkovsky
were presenting their own apocalyptic visions of the end of
history, numerous Religious-Philosophical Societies were
founded, and the Russian Orthodox Church was flourishing.

The God-builders were asking the same ethical, religious questions as the God-seekers were asking; the difference was that they were answering those questions with the tenets of scientific socialism.

But their involvement in culture and their preoccupation with cultural problems had another significance as well. Bogdanov's epistemology had originally been based upon a belief in some sort of external reality, but as time went on both Bogdanov and his philosophical followers so emphasized the power of human thought in shaping reality that they ignored the existence of objective, material reality. In just the same way, the God-builders had begun with the orthodox Marxist notion of a materially determined proletarian revolution. But in so stressing the importance of human will and human ethical judgement in the historical process, they ultimately conceived of the proletarian revolution as a product of the mind and not of matter.

Although they had held the most extreme revolutionary positions and programs and cherished the most optimistic hopes for immediate socialist revolution, the God-builders had never been concerned with the political aspects of revolutionary change. They had never dwelled upon the mechanisms of the direct siezure of political and economic power, nor had they pondered the future of the dictatorship of the proletariat. Instead, the goal toward which they labored was humankind's future life of freedom, comradeship, and unlimited creativity. As time progressed, the God-builders became concerned exclusively with questions of culture and ideology.

As we shall see, the principles of "Socialist Realism" would soon replace, for the God-builders, the principles
of What is to be Done?. The Bolshevik millenarians ultimately saw the preparation for the socialist revolution as an
educational and not an organizational matter. They translated
Lenin's organizational theories into educational principles.
They began to believe that socialist consciousness was the
only necessary prerequisite to revolution.

Thus the God-builders soon sought to instill in the
workers those religious values of collectivity, control of
nature through science and technology, and faith in the
future of mankind that they believed to be essential to the
workers' movement. Such education (or cultural transformation) would be sufficient to promote the socialist revolution.
They sought to create a new "proletarian culture" that would
lay the foundation necessary for the construction of socialism. Socialist Realism would be only one aspect of such an
education; they would also attempt to create a workers' university. These new tendencies, however, did not appear until
after the schism in the Bolshevik faction--the subject of
the next chapter.

NOTES TO CHAPTER IV

[1]A. Bogdanov, "Normy i tsely zhizni," in Novyi Mir (Moscow: Izdanie S. Dorovatovskago i A. Charushnikova, 1905), pp. 55-59.

[2]Ibid., p. 135.

[3]A. Bogdanov, "Prokliatye voprosy filosofii," in Novyi Mir, p. 169.

[4]Akademiia Nauk SSSR, Institut Mirovoi Literatury, Letopis' zhizni i tvorchestva A. M. Gor'kogo, 7 vols. (Moscow: Akademiia Nauk SSSR, 1958), vol 1, p. 209.

[5]Ibid., p. 238.

[6]Ibid., p. 372.

[7]Ibid., p. 404.

[8]Ibid., p. 372.

[9]Ibid., p. 642.

[10]Ibid., p. 458.

[11]Ibid., p. 466.

[12]Maxim Gorky, Seven Plays of Maxim Gorky (New Haven: Yale University Press, 1945), p. 38.

[13]Ibid.

[14]Ibid., p. 57.

[15]Ibid., p. 66.

[16]Letopis', vol. 1, pp. 553-62.

[17]Ibid., p. 617.

[18]Ibid., p. 536.

[19]Liadov, p. 115.

[20]Letopis', vol 1, p. 562.

[21]Ibid., p. 593.

[22]Ibid., p. 584.

[23]Maksim Gorky, Mother (New York: D. Appleton-Century, 1936), p. 106.

[24]Ibid., p. 155.

[25]Ibid., p. 306.

[26]Ibid., pp. 305-6.

[27]Ibid., p. 41.

[28]Ibid., p. 46.

[29]Ibid., p. 174.

[30]Ibid., p. 20.

[31]Ibid., p. 220.

[32]Ibid., p. 77.

[33]Ibid., pp. 274-75.

[34]As quoted by Bertram D. Wolfe in The Bridge and the Abyss (New York: Praeger, 1967), p. 45.

[35]Ibid., p. 51.

[36]A. V. Lunacharsky, Religiia i sotsializm, 2nd ed., 2 vols. (St. Petersburg: Izdanie Shipovnik, 1908), vol. 1, p. 7.

[37]Letopis', vol. 1, p. 564.

[38]Ibid., p. 564.

[39]N. A. Trifonov, "Soratniki (Lunacharskii i Gor'kii posle oktiabria)," Russkaia Literatura, no. 1 (1968), p. 26.

[40]Velikii perevorot, p. 32.

[41]Maxim Gorky, The Confession (New York: Frederick A. Stokes, 1916), p. 23.

[42]Ibid.

[43]Ibid., p. 33.

[44]Ibid., p. 46.

[45]Ibid., p. 47.

[46]Ibid., p. 59.

[47]Ibid., p. 173.

[48]Ibid., p. 154.

[49]Ibid., p. 209.

[50]Ibid., p. 210.

[51]Ibid., p. 247.

[52]Ibid., p. 59.

[53]Ibid., p. 195.

[54]Ibid., p. 292.

[55]Ibid., p. 292.

[56]Ibid., p. 291.

[57]A. V. Lunacharsky, "Budushchee religii," Obrazovanie, no. 1 (1907), pp. 1-25.

[58]Ibid., p. 6.

[59]Ibid.

[60]Ibid.

[61]Ibid., p. 7.

[62]Ibid., p. 22.

[63]Religiia i sotsializm, vol. 1, p. 10.

[64]Ibid., p. 14.

[65]Ibid.

[66]Ibid.

[67]Ibid., p. 16.

[68]Ibid., p. 10.

[69]Ibid., p. 8.

[70]Ibid., p. 184.

[71]Ibid., pp. 186-87.

[72]Ibid., p. 101.

[73]Ibid., pp. 101-2.

[74]Ibid., vol. 2, pp. 61-62.

[75]Ibid., p. 61.

[76]Ibid., p. 139.

[77]Ibid., vol. 1, pp. 41-42.

[78]Ibid., p. 95.

[79]Ibid., pp. 227-28.

[80]A. Bogdanov, Krasnaia zvezda (St. Petersburg: Tov-arishchestvo Khudozhestvennoi Pechati, 1908), and Inzhener Menni, 3rd ed. (Petrograd: Izdanie Petrogradskogo Soveta Rabochikh i Krasnoarmeiskikh Deputatov, 1918).

[81]A. F. Britikov, Russkii sovetskii fantasticheskii roman (Leningrad: Izdanie "Nauka," 1970), p. 55.

[82]For biographical information see Deiateli revoliu-tsionnogo dvizheniia v Rossii, bio-bibliograficheskii slovar', 5 vols. (Moscow: Izdatel'stvo Vsesoiuznogo Obshest-vo Politicheskikh Katorzhan i Ssyl'no-poselentsev, 1931), vol. 5, pt. 2, pp. 971-974.

[83]Stanislav A. Vol'skii, Filosofiia bor'by (Moscow: Knigoizdatel'stvo "Slovo," 1909), p. vi.

[84]Ibid., p. 4.

[85]Ibid., pp. 92-93.

[86]Ibid., p. 5.

[87]Ibid.

[88]Ibid., pp. 306-7.

[89]Ibid., p. 11.

[90]Ibid., p. 113.

[91]Ibid., p. 128.

[92]Ibid., p. 9.

[93]Ibid., p. 265.

[94]Ibid., p. 266.

[95]Ibid., p. 302.

[96]Ibid., p. 281.

[97]Ibid., p. 271.

[98]Ibid., p. 302.

[99]Ibid., p. 300.

[100]Ibid., p. 12.

[101]Ibid., p. 309.

[102]Ocherki po filosofii marksizma (St. Petersburg: n.p., 1908), p. 1.

[103]Ibid., p. 14.

[104]Ibid., pp. 64-65.

[105]Ibid., p. 71.

[106]A. Bogdanov, Prikliucheniia odnoi filosofskoi shkoly (St. Petersburg: Izdatel'skoe Tovarishchestvo "Znanie," 1908).

[107]Ocherki po filosofii marksizma, p. 235.

[108]Ibid., p. 242.

[109]Ibid., p. 108.

[110]Ibid., p. 109.

[111]Ibid., p. 116.

[112]Ibid., p. 140.

[113]Ibid.

[114]Ibid., p. 141.

[115]Ibid., p. 157.

[116]Ibid., p. 159.

[117]Literaturnyi raspad, 2nd ed., 2 vols. (St. Petersburg: Izdatel'stvo "Tovarishchestva Izdatel'skoe Biuro," 1908), vol. 1, p. 299.

[118]Ibid., p. 155.

[119]Ibid., vol. 2, pp. 5-38.

[120]Ibid., p. 85.

[121]Ibid., pp. 85-86.

[122]Ibid., p. 86.

[123]Ibid., p. 88.

[124]Ibid., p. 96.

CHAPTER V

THE SCHISM IN THE BOLSHEVIK FACTION

In the period between Stolypin's effective coup d'etat of 1907 and the general political amnesty granted in 1913, the Russian Social-Democratic Labor Party was in a shambles. Government reaction methodically decimated local party organizations within Russia. The passivity of the working class added further discouragement to revolutionary activity. The number of active Russian Social-Democrats fell from 100,000 in early 1907 to less than 10,000 in 1910. In the summer of 1909, only five or six Bolshevik committees were in regular operation.[1]

The greatest disability of the RSDRP was to be found in the separation of the central party leadership in exile in Europe from the local organizations in Russia. Difficulties in communication both between the central organs and the localities and among the various local groups prevented any semblance of party unity. During the years of reaction, even convocations of Russian delegates abroad were impossible. The Fifth Party Congress was held in London in 1907; the sixth was not convened until the summer of 1917.

Thus the party was split. In Russia was the body of the party; in Europe was its head. The local organizations had to depend upon irregularly smuggled issues of

214

various emigre journals to learn what programs its leadership was recommending. Otherwise, those few Social-Democrats who did not abandon the revolutionary movement improvised and generally followed their own inclinations. The leadership was isolated from practical activity.

Indeed, the Central Committee had fewer than twenty agents within Russia with which they were in communication.[2] The various factions of the party had to depend upon occasional correspondence with those acquaintances in Russia who were not in prison. Communication was irregular and haphazard to say the least. In 1912 a bureau was formed to travel to Russia and circulate among all the local organizations to attempt to reinstate some degree of Party unity. But its delegates found nothing but harrassment and arrest. (Some individuals were arrested five or six times in two years.) The results of the plan were nil.

The absence of any practical organizational work to occupy the attention of the party leaders led to excessive preoccupation with theory. Those revolutionaries who escaped abroad after 1907 to keep the revolutionary fires burning were its leaders. Since political leaders tend to be strong of will and independent of thought (else they would be followers and not leaders), there was no lack of viewpoints among the emigres to be bitterly contested. The bitterness engendered in such disputes caused numerous divisions in the emigre RSDRP.

And because all the emigre revolutionaries were

leaders, they could dissociate themselves from other "Bolsheviks" or "Mensheviks" without believing that they were
abandoning "Bolshevism" or "Menshevism." There was no real
organization for them to leave since the organizations were
in Russia and no emigre group had close enough ties with the
local organizations to function as their head. Both sides
of any division could claim to speak for their nominal organizations within Russia--it was never themselves, but their
opponents, who were renegades from the "true" movement.

Thus the major form of emigre organization was the
"literary group." Whenever a group of like-minded Social-
Democrats found themselves opposed to the principles of a
larger group, they split off and established their own literary group and their own journal in which to voice their
opinions to the rank and file of the party. Such groups were
so essential a part of the RSDRP that the Central Committee
gave them official recognition, financial support, and the
right to send their own delegates to official party conferences.

During the 1905 Revolution the party as a whole relegated theoretical matters to the background and presented a
relatively united front. The Social-Democrats of whatever
persuasion found that they had more in common with one another
than with any other political groups. This unity was reflected in the relatively cooperative Fourth (Unification) Party
Congress which was held in 1906 while revolutionary enthusiasm were still high.

However, by May, 1907, the time of the Fifth Congress, the revolution was past all hope of revival and the splintering of the RSDRP had begun in earnest. The first split to occur was the recurrence of a sharp division between the Bolsheviks and Mensheviks. Subsequently even those two major sub-groups began to argue among themselves, and the process of splintering continued.

It was at this time that the emigre Bolshevik faction suffered a devastating schism that it did not resolve until several months after the February Revolution of 1917. The controversy within the faction first began to appear in early 1907 and ultimately resulted in an open break in the early summer of 1909. In the dispute, Lenin found himself at odds with a group of radical Bolsheviks led by the God-builders Bogdanov, Lunacharsky, and Gorky.

In essence the controversy was over tactics. What was the proper course for the Social-Democratic party to follow during the years of reaction? The division between the two camps of Bolsheviks was a division according to optimism for the future of the working class revolution. One side viewed the reaction in Russia as an insuperable obstacle that had to be endured indefinitely; they cautioned restraint, urged careful rebuilding of the local party organizations, and insisted on the full use of legal opportunities to further the principles of Social-Democracy. The other side of the dispute refused to believe that the revolutionary wave had receded or even yet crested; they firmly demanded

that the Bolsheviks immediately summon the working class to
armed insurrection against the autocracy.

Nevertheless, the tactical dispute soon acquired
political and philosophical overtones. Because of the personalities of those involved, the dispute became a struggle
for the leadership of the Bolshevik faction. Also, the controversy assumed a philosophical dimension. Each side of
the schism believed that the deficiencies in their opponents'
tactical program was the direct result of their philosophical
wrong-headedness.

In its origin, the controversy among the Bolsheviks
concerned Social-Democratic participation in the elections
to the newly formed Duma in 1906. The Bolshevik faction had
opposed participating in the First Duma and had voted to
boycott the electoral campaign. However, other revolutionary parties had won a significant number of seats in that
election, and when the Duma was convened, the revolutionaries
were able to use their freedom of speech on the floor of the
Duma as a means for propaganda. This success led the Bolsheviks to reverse their position, and they decided to participate in the elections to the Second Duma.

However, in June, 1907, the Second Duma was dissolved,
the constitution and the electoral laws were revised, and the
Social-Democratic representatives in the Duma were arrested.
Consequently, the Bolsheviks once again came out strongly
against participating in the next Duma. The Mensheviks did
not agree. They remained in favor of Duma participation, and

they constituted a majority of the party. At the Second
All-Russian Conference of the RSDRP in August, 1907, it was
resolved that the party should campaign in the coming autumn
elections for the Third Duma. Of eleven Bolshevik delegates
to the Conference, ten advocated boycotting the election.
Those ten Bolsheviks chose Bogdanov to be their spokesman.[3]

However, the single Bolshevik who voted with the Mensheviks in favor of Duma participation was a very important
Bolshevik: V. I. Lenin. As we have already seen in What is
to be Done? and Two Tactics, Lenin had been at the very forefront of Social-Democratic radicalism both before and during
the 1905 Revolution. Indeed, it was because of Lenin's
radicalism that Bogdanov and the other God-builders had
originally adhered to Bolshevism.

But Lenin was a political realist; even his revolutionary idealism and voluntarism did not dull his political
acumen. He was the first Bolshevik to understand accurately
Russia's new political and social situation. As early as
the fall of 1906 (even while the First Conference of Military-Fighting Organizations was in session), Lenin perceived
that the revolutionary fires were dying out and that the
RSDRP faced a long period of retrenchment as it awaited the
next social conflagration. He was already retreating from
the extreme position he had held in the first half of the
decade and was moving toward the moderation of the Mensheviks
in general and Plekhanov in particular.

In June, 1906, for example, in the article "On the

Eve," Lenin wrote that "We are on the eve of great historical events, we are on the eve of the second great stage of
the Russian revolution."[4] One year later--to the month--
Lenin was writing "Against Boycott"--and was expressing an
opinion current among the Mensheviks.

"Against Boycott" was a masterpiece of polemics.
Lenin had to defend the principle of boycott (since the Bolsheviks had boycotted the First Duma), but he wanted also to
argue that the times were no longer appropriate for a boycott. Simultaneously, Lenin wanted to distinguish himself
from the Mensheviks. They, too, were against a boycott, but
Lenin thought they were against it for the wrong reasons.
Lenin argued that a boycott is not wrong in principle (as
the Mensheviks believed), but he also asserted that summoning
the workers to rise up in armed insurrection was not always
right (as the Socialist-Revolutionaries and a large part of
the Bolshevik faction were urging).

A Marxist, Lenin stressed, must "examine the historical conditions of the boycott's applicability," and not continue to mouth old revolutionary slogans simply to appear
radical.[5]

> If anyone wants to persuade the Social-Demo-
> cratic proletariat that the slogan of boycott
> is a correct one, he must not allow himself
> to be carried away by the mere sound of words
> that in their time played a great and glorious
> revolutionary role. He must weigh the objec-
> tive conditions making for a sweeping, univer-
> sal, powerful, and rapid revolutionary upswing.
> But in periods such as we are now living in,
> in periods of a temporary lull in the revolu-
> tion, such a condition can in no circumstances
> be indirectly assumed.[6]

But such a capitulation to the exigencies of the
real world was precisely what the less practical, more impatiently radical Bolsheviks refused to do. They were so
impatient for the revolution to arrive that they saw any retreat from the demand for immediate insurrection not as a
simple, temporary change in tactics but as an outright betrayal of the working class.

Indeed, the God-builders were just as upset with
Lenin's new (apparent) conservatism as he was bothered by
their continued radicalism. They emphatically did not share
Lenin's appraisal of the revolutionary situation in Russia.
On the contrary, they were convinced that the resurgence of
the revolution was imminent, and they felt that involvement
in legal parliamentary affairs would only divert energy and
resources away from direct revolutionary activity.

However, in their writings, the God-builders did not
discuss the reality of social conditions in Russia as Lenin
had done. Instead, they stressed the importance of maintaining the spirit of the revolution regardless of material conditions. Lunacharsky recalled:

> It seemed to me necessary to support the exalt-
> ed mood of the proletariat, not to allow the
> atmosphere of world revolution to be extinguish-
> ed, which, as it seemed to me, dwarfed that
> false practical work [of Duma activity]. That
> is why I immediately joined the group "Forward"
> of which Bogdanov was the organizer.[7]

Gorky, too, was much too impatient an optimist to
passively endure the torpor that overcame the Social-Democratic movement during the period of reaction. It seemed to him

that the left Bolsheviks "confessed philosophical activism" at the same time that Lenin and Plekhanov "preached historical fatalism."[8] By so stressing the importance of spirit over matter, the God-builders once again revealed the idealism and voluntarism that lay at the foundation of their world-view.

Bogdanov was equally dismayed by Lenin's moderate and cautious proposals for Bolshevism. As Lunacharsky reported, Bogdanov interpreted Lenin's new conservatism not as a temporary concession to material necessity but as an actual betrayal of the revolution. "At that time Bogdanov was so annoyed that he predicted that Lenin would inevitably leave the revolutionary movement, and he even tried to prove to E. K. Malinovskaia and myself that Lenin was bound to end up as an Octobrist."[9]

Bogdanov was particularly upset by the rapprochement between Lenin and Plekhanov. Not only did Plekhanov represent conservative political policies, he was also the principal proponent of orthodox Marxism. As a result of his rigidly dogmatic materialism and determinism, Plekhanov had become Bogdanov's chief philosophical opponent.

The year of 1908 was a tumultuous one for the Bolshevik faction. It was a year of vigorous protest from the local Bolshevik organizations in Russia against Social-Democratic participation in the Duma. The same people who had demanded a boycott of the elections to the Third Duma now demanded that the Social-Democratic deputies to that Duma

be immediately recalled (hence the term otzov-ism). The
otzovists were unable to gain a majority of any one local
organization, but they were particularly numerous and vocal
in St. Petersburg and Moscow. The most vociferous of the
otzovists were the same people who had attempted to lead
the Moscow insurrection of December, 1905: Shantser, Liadov,
and Volsky.

Bogdanov, who had been the spokesman for the boy-
cotters at the Second Party Conference in 1907, had changed
his attitude somewhat by the middle of 1908. In June of
that year, he wrote an article for Proletarii (the official
organ of the Bolshevik Center) that was critical of otzovism.
His criticism was probably more a concession to his fellow
editor, Lenin, than a real change in policy, for Bogdanov
was still unenthusiastic about party activity in the Duma.

Bogdanov, however, announced a new policy which
another left Bolshevik, G. Aleksinsky, elaborated upon. They
called for an "ultimatum" to be issued to the Social-Democratic deputies to the Duma requiring them to unquestioningly
submit to the leadership of the Central Committee. Bogdanov
believed that the Duma faction should be considered to be
an organ of the party, and its activity should be strictly
subordinated to overall party strategy.

Despite this more moderate "ultimatism," Bogdanov was
still chosen by the otzovists to speak on their behalf at the
Party Conference held in Paris in late 1908.[10] What both
the otzovists and the ultimatists feared was that the entire

activity of the party would become channeled into legal, parliamentary activity, and the party would lose sight of its traditional revolutionary objectives.

The year of 1908 was also a crucial year in the development of Bolshevik philosophy. The previous year had seen the initial publication of Religion and Socialism, and it was during 1908 that God-building burst into full bloom with the appearance of The Confession, Red Star, Outlines of the Philosophy of Marxism, and Literary Decadence. Since the God-builders had allied themselves with the politically radical otzovists, it was perhaps natural that the two schools of thought were considered to be related. Indeed, it was this association of the idealists with the radicals that led Lenin to assume that political radicalism was due to idealist philosophy. It was for this reason that Lenin began to involve philosophy in the factional dispute over tactics.

During the course of 1908, Lenin's attitude toward the God-builders underwent an abrupt about-face. Very early in the year, Proletarii reaffirmed the principle of philosophical neutrality among Bolsheviks. Yet by the spring of 1909, Lenin had published Materialism and Empiriocriticism (a vehement and scornful attack upon the philosophy of the God-builders), was waging war against otzovism in the pages of Proletarii, and was making preparations to cast both the otzovists and the God-builders out of the Bolshevik faction.

Throughout 1908 the tensions between Lenin, on one hand, and Bogdanov and Gorky, on the other hand, mounted

steadily but were largely concealed from the public eye.
The three leaders of Bolshevism did not want their faction
to be weakened in relation to Menshevism by internal dissension. Try as they might, however, neutrality was impossible
to maintain. The final showdown was precipitated by Gorky's
and Bogdanov's insistence on using Lenin's Bolshevik central
organ, Proletarii, as a vehicle for their religious and philosophical views.

In the spring of 1908, Gorky had written an article
with pronounced God-building overtones and had submitted it
to Proletarii for publication. There were at that time three
editors of the journal: Lenin, Dubrovinsky, and Bogdanov.
Over Bogdanov's protest, Lenin and Dubrovinsky voted not to
publish Gorky's article. Bogdanov was furious. No doubt
both Lenin and Bogdanov were only more convinced of the impossibility of their future collaboration.

Lenin wrote to Gorky:

> When, after reading and rereading your article,
> I told A. A. that I was against its publica-
> tion, he grew as black as a thundercloud.
> The threat of a split was in the air. Yester-
> day our editorial trio held a special meeting
> to discuss the matter.[11]

What prevented--or rather postponed--the split was a
common desire to maintain Bolshevik solidarity against the
Mensheviks. They strove to deny the rumors of an impending
split between Lenin and Gorky that were already being voiced
in the German Social-Democratic press.[12] Lenin still believed
that neutrality on philosophical matters could be maintained.
He again wrote to Gorky:

> To hinder the application of the tactics of
> revolutionary Social-Democracy in the workers'
> party for the sake of disputes on the question
> of materialism or Machism, would be, in my
> opinion, unpardonable folly. We ought to fight
> over philosophy in such a way that <u>Proletarii</u>
> and the Bolsheviks, as a faction of the <u>party</u>,
> <u>would not be affected by it</u>. And that is
> quite possible.[13]

Lenin then asked Gorky to write only on neutral subjects for <u>Proletarii</u> and to publish his "Machist" opinions
elsewhere.

In March, 1909, the three men met at Gorky's villa
on the Isle of Capri to try to resolve their differences.
It was a futile attempt. Lenin and Bogdanov were too far
apart to continue as co-leaders of the Bolshevik faction.
As would soon be revealed to the public at the meeting of
the Bolshevik Center in June, each man regarded the other as
a danger to the faction. The Bolshevik faction would not
continue to contain both of them for very much longer.

The reason why Lenin was forced to drive Bogdanov,
Lunacharsky, and the radical God-builders out of the Bolshevik faction in 1909 was the same reason why he had welcomed
them into his faction in 1904. The God-builders were prolific writers. Lenin had needed good polemicists when he
left <u>Iskra</u> five years earlier, and Bogdanov and his comrades
had served that function with distinction.

Nevertheless, their prolixity was precisely the reason
why Lenin could no longer observe philosophical neutrality
and grant the God-builders the freedom to publish their philosophical writings in <u>Proletarii</u>. Even if he were to have

accepted the principle of "freedom of criticism," Lenin's own point of view would have been drowned out. Lenin could not have hoped to produce singlehandedly a sufficient volume of verbiage to outweigh the barrage of words that Gorky, Bazarov, Bogdanov, and Lunacharsky were capable of producing. Lenin explicitly admitted to Gorky that this was one of the factors that made the split in Bolshevism inevitable.[14]

It was Lenin who finally brought the crisis to a head. In June, 1909, he called a meeting of the "Enlarged Editorial Board of _Proletarii_," the organization that served as the effective central committee of the Bolshevik faction. Of the fourteen members of that committee only three were representatives of the left Bolshevik position. Those three --Bogdanov, Krasin, and Shantser--watched and protested help-lessly as the Board passed a series of resolutions that effectively expelled the entire left Bolshevik tendency from the faction.

The Board went down the list of leftist heresies and denounced in turn God-building, anarchism, otzovism, and the call for armed uprising. Lenin and his supporters also voted against the idea of a party school that Bogdanov and his associates had recently proposed. The Board concluded by specifically expelling Bogdanov from the Bolshevik faction.

> . . . Once Comrade Maksimov [Bogdanov] flatly rejected all the resolutions on key issues adopted by such a large majority of the con-ference, he had to realize that there was not that unanimity of opinion between himself and the conference which is an elementary condi-tion for the existence of a section within the party.[15]

The conference disclaimed "all responsibility for the political activities of Comrade Maksimov," and declared "that the question here is not of a split in the section but of Comrade Maksimov's break away from the Enlarged Editorial Board of _Proletarii_."[16]   Lenin made it clear that he was not trying to expel all otzovists or other leftists from the local Bolshevik-oriented party organizations in Russia. He tried to depict the expulsion of Bogdanov and the God-builders as the independent leave-taking of a few individuals from the emigre Bolshevik Center.

It became clear in the debates of the Expanded Edit-orial Board that it was Lenin who was expelling Bogdanov and his associates and not the left Bolsheviks who were trying to cause a division in the faction. Bogdanov, Krasin, and Shantser did not try to defend any of the leftist tendencies that Lenin so roundly condemned. They admitted that the God-builders chose poor terminology and should not have talked about religion in regard to the socialist movement.[17] They further pointed out that otzovism was not at issue at all. None of the emigre left Bolsheviks advocated otzovism.

Shantser insisted that the entire question was one of theory. None of the issues involved had overriding politi-cal importance, he said, and they should have been dealt with through intra-factional debate. There was no need, Shantser asserted, to make the debate an organizational issue and so split the faction.[18] Bogdanov claimed that the left Bolshe-viks included only one God-builder, Lunacharsky, and only one

otzovist, Gorky. He and his comrades had no desire to sub-
vert or to disrupt the faction. He concluded: "We have
been loyal, and we are now loyal. Here we are at our
posts."[19]

But it was too late for apologies. The three leftists at the conference were both outnumbered and outmanouver-
ed throughout the confrontation and found themselves help-
lessly and unceremoniously cast out of the Bolshevik faction.
Bogdanov's only remaining hope of maintaining his position
and influence in the party was through democratic representation of the local Bolshevik committees. He repeatedly insisted that the Bolshevik Center had no right to expel him
since he had been elected to the Center by the Bolshevik
factional caucus at the Fifth Congress. He also insisted
that the resolutions that were approved by the Enlarged Editorial Board of Proletarii were contrary to the desires of
the local committees within Russia.

To resolve the matter fairly, Bogdanov demanded that
a new party congress be convened in which the views of the
Bolshevik members of the local organizations could be heard.
Lenin and the Bolshevik Center simply refused to consider
such a proposal. In the first place, gathering another Congress would have had tremendous obstacles to overcome.
Police suppression of the socialist movement was effective;
there were few active organizations left, and the convocation
of a party congress in 1909 was physically inconceivable.

Furthermore--and more to the point--Lenin had firm

control over the Bolshevik Center and _Proletarii_, and there was no reason for him to risk his position by presenting his case to the rank and file for their approval. Lenin had shown at the second and third party congresses that he understood very well the ways in which such a gathering could be manipulated, and he no doubt did not want to give Bogdanov the opportunity of doing so.

In fact, there was evidence that there was considerable support for Bogdanov's radical position among the local Bolshevik committees. In his polemics against otzovism, Lenin had been careful to distinguish between the emigre leaders and the rank and file revolutionaries in Russia. He emphatically did not want to alienate the Bolsheviks at the local level. Lenin explicitly announced that his quarrel was only with those intellectuals who were otzovists on principle; worker otzovists should be persuaded to change their minds and not evicted from the faction. Thus Lenin recognized that the number of otzovists was significant; had he allowed a congress to be called he might well have found himself in the minority. Bogdanov could then have taken over as the leader of the Bolshevik faction.

Thus, along with the other aspects to the factional schism (tactical, theoretical, and political) there was the question of personal authority. Who should lead the Bolsheviks? From the very beginning, Bolshevism had been the personal organization of Lenin. He had always established its policies. But after the 1905 Revolution the people whom

Lenin had recruited to fill literary positions in the faction began to think of the faction as their own. They resented the notion that the faction belonged only to Lenin.

At the meeting of the enlarged board, Bogdanov specifically denounced the tendency of the Bolsheviks to think of their faction as a vehicle for Lenin's thought alone. He asserted:

> Kamenev says that we cannot follow anti-bolshevik tendencies under the bolshevik flag. But he is confusing the bolshevik faction with Lenin. They must not be lumped together, for the bolshevik flag and Lenin are not one and the same thing.[20]

During the discussions of the enlarged editorial board of _Proletarii_, Bogdanov remained on the defensive; his desire was to avoid a schism. He believed that there was room in the faction to accomodate a number of different points of view. All he seemed to ask for was the freedom of criticism and discussion among Bolsheviks.

However, once his expulsion became imminent and he walked out of the conference, Bogdanov went on the attack. He issued a series of ringing revolutionary appeals to the Bolshevik rank and file. In them, he did not attempt to argue any of the issues that had been raised by the enlarged board; he did not defend God-building, otzovism, or ultimatism. Instead Bogdanov doggedly appealed to the radical left wing of the RSDRP to reaffirm the principles they had stood for during the 1905 Revolution.

In his "Report to the Bolshevik Comrades by the Expelled Members of the Enlarged Editorial Board of _Proletarii_,"

Bogdanov stressed that instead of waiting passively the proletariat should be encouraged to seize the initiative. He
demanded preparations for immediate revolution, and he looked
beyond the mere democratic revolution toward the ultimate
socialist revolution.

> Democratic revolution in Russia cannot com-
> plete and give the country the greatest pos-
> sible development of its productive forces as
> would the hegemony of the industrial proletar-
> iat over other revolutionary forces . . . In
> unity with the rural proletariat and supported
> by the land-poor peasantry, the factory work-
> ing class, as the avant garde and leader of the
> democratic revolution, is summoned by history
> to carry to the end the rejuvenation of Russia
> and the creation of the best conditions for
> the furthest struggle for socialism.[21]

Bogdanov maintained that the chief failure of Bolshevism at the present time was that it had lost sight of its
principal goal--socialism.

> Fundamentally [the Bolshevik Center] has simply
> ignored [socialist propaganda]. In the sixteen
> months of emigre work, the current editorial
> board of _Proletarii_ has _not_ published _even one_
> propaganda book or brochure--regardless of the
> fact that it has under its purview many lit-
> erary forces and more significant material
> means than at any time previously.[22]

Bogdanov concluded from this that the leaders of
Bolshevism were becoming politically moderate. He felt that
they were abandoning their old maximalistic revolutionary
goals and were moving toward a unification with the Mensheviks and the liberal Duma parties.

> The distinction between the two political lines
> is clear. And on this ground is now being pre-
> pared a new grouping of party forces.
>   Its essence is contained in the formation
> of a new _faction of the center_. Between the
> "duma" Bolshevism of the new _Proletarii_ and

> the left party Menshevism, the border is becom-
> ing ever increasingly obliterated.
> The announcement of the editorial board of
> the schism with all "left Bolsheviks" removes
> the last obstacle to the unification of the
> "right Bolsheviks" with the part of the Menshe-
> vik tendency that is close to them.[23]

Bogdanov further asserted that there could be no middle ground between left Bolshevism and Menshevism--in fact, between himself and Lenin. Until the revolution pro-duced peaceful, organic development, said Bogdanov, there could be only two possible paths: revolutionism or oppor-tunism. Arguing that Lenin and the right Bolsheviks had al-ready chosen the path of opportunism, Bogdanov summoned his readers to join him and reaffirm their commitment to the proletarian revolution.[24]

Bogdanov called for a return to the underground party organization of the pre-1905 period. He insisted upon the necessity of a conspiratorial organization and illegal activ-ity, the dissemination of socialist propaganda, and the prepa-ration for an armed insurrection. He spoke of,

> . . . the extremely important but extremely
> difficult task during the present time of re-
> action: to preserve, regardless of the weight
> of oppression, and to strengthen, regardless
> of all obstacles, the illegal party organiza-
> tions; to carry on through all this inexpressib-
> ly heavy and gloomy period of the people's
> life so that when the epoch of new, decisive
> struggle comes, it will be ready for the task
> of leading the mass movement. Until that time,
> it must be consistently and unwaveringly pre-
> paring the conditions that are necessary for
> the success of the struggle.[25]

Bogdanov did admit that actual armed uprising was impossible at the present time, but he stressed the impor-

tance of preparing for it by working out the theoretical questions of armed insurrection, by teaching practical, military-
technical matters to the party rank and file, and by actively
spreading propaganda among the troops of Russia's armed
forces. Bogdanov further stressed that the leadership of
the armed insurrection should not be abandoned by the Social-
Democrats lest it pass into the hands of the anarchists.[26]

Bogdanov's first tactic in his struggle to keep his
vision of Bolshevism alive was--just as Lenin had feared--
to convoke a sixth congress of the RSDRP. He was convinced
that the representatives from the local Bolshevik committees
would affirm his position. But summoning a congress proved
to be impossible.

When he realized that such a congress was out of the
question, Bogdanov sought to create an independent faction
within the party that would rival both the Mensheviks and the
Bolsheviks. It would provide a new organization for all
radical, disaffected Bolsheviks to join. Thus Bogdanov borrowed the strategy that Lenin had followed after he had been
forced off the editorial board of Iskra in 1903. Bogdanov,
with the help of the God-builders and a number of otzovists,
founded a factional organ, Vpered. He intended that its
editorial board should function as the organizing center for
the new faction. The activities of the "Vpered Group" is
the subject of the next chapter.

Before following the further development of the God-
builders, however, it is important to consider Lenin's phil-

sophical relationship with them. Although the Bolshevik
schism took on philosophical overtones, and although Lenin
wrote a long philosophical attack upon empiriomonism, the
schism did not in fact indicate any real philosophical incompatibility between Lenin and the God-builders.

In looking at Lenin's polemical objections to God-
building, otzovism, and empiriomonism, it is clear that he
was arguing against them in a tactical sense and not in a
philosophical sense. Lenin did not say that the God-builders
were logically or factually wrong but that their ideas were
expressed in poor terms politically. Lenin's essential objection was that the left Bolsheviks were bad politicians.

From the very beginning of his association with Bogdanov and the millenarian Bolsheviks, of course, Lenin had
known that their philosophical speculations went far beyond
the bounds of orthodox Marxism. Nevertheless, before and
during the 1905 Revolution, Lenin was preoccupied with organizational issues and concrete revolutionary programs. He
cared nothing for philosophy as long as the philosophers were
active supporters of his political activities.

As late as February, 1908, Lenin admitted in a letter
to Gorky that philosophy was subordinate to political tactics.

> In the summer and autumn of 1904, Bogdanov
> and I reached a complete agreement, as Bolshe-
> viks, and formed the tacit bloc, which tacitly
> ruled out philosophy as a neutral field, that
> existed all through the revolution and enabled
> us in that revolution to carry out together
> the tactics of revolutionary Social-Democracy
> (=Bolshevism), which, I am profoundly convinced,
> were the only correct tactics.[27]

Lenin later added:

> I consider it necessary to give you my opinion
> quite frankly. Some sort of fight among the
> Bolsheviks on the question of philosophy I
> regard now as quite unavoidable. It would be
> stupid, however, to split on this. We formed
> a bloc in order to secure the adoption of def-
> inite tactics in the workers' party. We have
> been pursuing these tactics up to now <u>without</u>
> disagreement . . .[28]

Thus Lenin did not feel it necessary to combat empiriomonism as long as its adherents supported the revolutionary
strategy and program that Lenin believed to be correct. When
he finally did decide to evict the millenarians from the faction, it was not because their philosophical views had become
any more unpalatable to him, but because they were threaten-
ing to draw the Bolshevik faction into totally inappropriate
political activity. Or rather it was because they began to
endorse an opposing political program that Lenin began to
use their unorthodox philosophy as a means to discredit their
position in the Social-Democratic press.

Lenin began to attack in print the philosophy of the
empiriomonists and God-builders only after he had begun a
campaign against their political program. His philosophical
polemics were only one aspect of his political struggle to
remove the radical Bolsheviks from influential positions in
his faction. Moreover, the terms in which he refuted their
philosophy show that Lenin did not regard it as technically
faulty. He found it invalid simply because it provided the
foundation for a counter-revolutionary political program.

Indeed, in his major work of rebuttal against the

heresies of the millenarians, <u>Materialism and Empiriocriti-</u>
<u>cism</u>, Lenin completely dodged the real philosophical issues
that were at stake in the controversy between the materialists and the positivists. As in all his other polemics,
Lenin's principal rhetorical technique was not to logically
or factually refute the views of his opponents but rather to
demonstrate that those views did not contribute to the revolutionary movement and were therefore invalid.

In this manner Lenin relied principally upon "guilt
by association" to vilify the millenarians. He began <u>Mater-</u>
<u>ialism and Empiriomonism</u> by pointing out the similarities
between the empiriocritical critique of materialism and the
critique offered by "Bishop George Berkely." Lenin thus
associated the "Machists" (as he often referred to them) not
only with early eighteenth century idealism but with a leading
figure of the Anglican Church.

A typical example of Lenin's technique in discrediting the standpoint of the millenarians can be seen in this
passage in which he tried to associate Mach, a founder of empiriocriticism, with idealism and religion:

> "I openly declare that the inner sense, the
> soul of my philosophy consists in this, that
> a human being possesses nothing save experience;
> a human being comes to everything to which he
> comes only through experience . . ." A zealous
> philosopher of pure experience, is he not? The
> author of these words is the subjective ideal-
> ist Fichte . . . We know from the history of
> philosophy that the interpretation of the con-
> cept "experience" divided the classical mater-
> ialists from the idealists. Today professorial
> philosophy of all shades disguises its reaction-
> ary nature by declaiming on the subject of

"experience." All the immanentists fall back
on experience. In the preface to the second
edition of his Knowledge and Error, Mach praises
a book by Professor Wilhelm Jerusalem in which
we read: "The acceptance of a divine original
being is not contradictory to experience.[29]

Here, as he does innumerable times throughout Materialism and Empiriocriticism, Lenin refused to come to grips
with the real problems of materialism and idealism and their
implications for the philosophy of Marxism and the practice
of proletarian revolution. It is sufficient for Lenin to
show that the ideas he disagrees with are similar to the
philosophical positions taken by famous idealists, clerics,
or reactionaries. "The Catholic priests," said Lenin at one
point, "go into raptures over this philosophy."[30]

The conclusion that Lenin drew from this was that
the philosophy of the God-builders could not serve the working class in making its revolution. He feared that such a
philosophy could not serve as that revolutionary theory without which a revolutionary party could not exist. God-building could only lead (as in fact it already appeared to Lenin
to do) to "petty bourgeois" adventurism or terrorism.[31]

Materialism and Empiriocriticism should therefore not
be interpreted as anything but a political polemic; one should
not judge Lenin as a philosopher or logician from the arguments presented in that book. Lenin really presented no technical arguments for materialism or against idealism. He was
simply trying to discredit the empiriomonists in the eyes of
other revolutionary Social-Democrats and not trying to dis-
prove the theories of empiriomonism to the satisfaction of

professional philosophers.

At certain times--for instance when he demonstrated
that Bogdanov's philosophy was not an elaboration of Marxism
but essentially a contradiction of it--Lenin showed that he
had a knowledgeable understanding of the principal issues of
epistemology, causality, and ontology that were involved in
the dispute between the idealists and the materialists.[32]

On the other hand, whenever Lenin felt it necessary
to defend any particular aspect of the basic philosophy of
historical materialism, he was purposely obtuse. That a
material world exists independently of human thought and
that it is governed by natural laws was a belief that Lenin
understood to be self-evident and unnecessary of defense or
explanation. Lenin avoided the issue despite the fact that
he fully understood the issues at stake and despite the fact
that this particular point was the crux of the difference
between the empiriomonists and the materialists. Lenin refused to deal with the question except to hold idealism up
to ridicule.

No doubt the reason Lenin did not refute the God-
builders in philosophical terms was because he actually
shared their philosophical point of view. In What is to be
Done? Lenin's use of Karl Kautsky's idea of a scientific
socialist intelligentsia showed that he really agreed with
Bogdanov's assertion that ideology arises independently from
material existence. From this position it is a logical and
inevitable step to the conclusion that ideas have an inde-

pendent existence from material reality and that human will can therefore influence the course of events in the material world. Throughout his life Lenin proved through his practical political activities that he believed that he and his fellow Social-Democratic revolutionaries could bring socialism to Russia quite in defiance of the material social and economic conditions.

Lenin simply avoided discussing his own basic philosophical beliefs. For him orthodox Marxism was more a statement of revolutionary intentions than a personal system of beliefs. When Lenin defended Marxism in Materialism and Empiriocriticism, he did so in the terms in which he always argued: Marxism must be maintained because it is a revolutionary theory. Lenin believed in Marxism not as a philosopher but as a practical political manager and organizer. Marxism was based upon a consistent, apparently scientific world-view and it promised the inevitability of socialist revolution. It was thus a perfect world-view to inspire party workers and the working classes with revolutionary confidence and fervor. To diminish Marxism was to diminish the working class movement as Lenin understood it.

In fact Lenin was a politician and not a philosopher. He had the desire neither to think out patiently all the logical ramifications of Marxist philosophy nor to be overly concerned with whether or not any particular strategy or program that he advocated might violate some principle of Marxism. Lenin based his policies and made alliances accord-

ding to his strategy for furthering the revolutionary movement and not according to a dispassionate reading of Marx.

NOTES TO CHAPTER V

[1] *Protokoly sovershchaniia rasshirennoi redaktsii "Proletarii"* (n.p.: Partizdat, 1934), p. 139.

[2] Ibid., p. 48.

[3] Elwood, pp. 115-16.

[4] V. I. Lenin, "On the Eve," CW, vol. 11, p. 16.

[5] V. I. Lenin, "Against Boycott," CW, vol. 13, p. 18.

[6] Ibid., p. 36.

[7] *Velikii perevorot*, p. 41.

[8] N. A. Trifonov, "A. V. Lunacharskii i M. Gor'kii," in M. *Gor'kii i ego sovremenniki*, ed. K. D. Muratova (Leningrad: "Nauka," 1968), p. 144.

[9] *Velikii perevorot*, p. 71.

[10] K. Ostroukhogo, "Otzovisty i ul'timatisty," *Proletarskaia Revoliutsiia*, no. 6 (1924), p. 21.

[11] V. I. Lenin, "A Letter to A. M. Gorky," CW, vol. 13, p. 453.

[12] V. I. Lenin, "Statement of the Editors of Proletarii," CW, vol. 13, p. 447.

[13] "A Letter to A. M. Gorky," p. 454.

[14] *V. I. Lenin i A. M. Gor'kii: Pis'ma, Vospominaniia, Dokumenty* (Moscow: "Nauka," 1969), p. 32.

[15] *Protokoly*, p. 81.

[16] Ibid.

[17] Ibid., p. 42.

[18] Ibid., pp. 22-24.

[19] Ibid., p. 58.

[20] Ibid., p. 72.

[21] Ibid., p. 251.

[22] Ibid., p. 248.

[23]Ibid., p. 249.

[24]Ibid., p. 250.

[25]Ibid., p. 243.

[26]Ibid., pp. 244-45.

[27]"A Letter to A. M. Gorky," p. 449.

[28]Ibid., pp. 454-55.

[29]V. I. Lenin, Materialism and Empiriocriticism, CW, vol. 14, p. 149.

[30]Ibid., p. 211.

[31]Ibid., p. 358.

[32]Ibid., pp. 226-32.

CHAPTER VI

THE TRANSITION FROM POLITICAL TO CULTURAL REVOLUTION:
THE PARTY SCHOOLS AND THE "VPERED" GROUP

After their expulsion from the Bolshevik faction, the
first independent activity of the left Bolsheviks was to
establish a "Propagandistic-Agitational School for Workers."
In itself this school was not a direct result of the schism
in the Bolshevik faction; the idea for such a party school
had originated some time before the disputes within the Bolshevik faction appeared to be divisive. Indeed, one of the
originators of the party school and several of the students
were firm Bolshevik centrists and supporters of Lenin.
Nevertheless, the idea of the school fit in perfectly with
the attitudes of the millenarian Bolsheviks, and after it
was created the school became a natural center for the radicals' campaign against Lenin and the Bolshevik Center.

The idea to form a special school to train Social-
Democratic propagandists and agitators first arose as a solution to the disintegration of the party that had followed
the collapse of the 1905 Revolution. The ranks of the party
had been decimated. Particularly harmful to the revolutionary movement was the loss of the intelligentsia from party
leadership. The official report of the first party school
admitted the crucial role the intellectuals had played in the

past:

> . . . In view of the weak theoretical prepara-
> tion and slight political experience of the
> working class, professional party leaders
> from the intelligentsia could not but play
> very important and outstanding roles in the
> [local] organizations. They were the secre-
> taries of committees, "responsible" regional
> organizers, "responsible" propagandists, agi-
> tators, literateurs, and technologists. In
> their hands also were concentrated the finan-
> cial connections that nourish the organiza-
> tion, that give it the necessary means for
> work. It is self-evident that the desertion
> of the party intelligentsia cannot but have
> its effect on the disarray of party activity.[1]

As it was originally conceived, the purpose of the

party school was to create a new contingent of Social-Demo-

cratic party organizers. Since the intelligentsia had

proven undependable, members of the working class would be

educated to organize and manage their own revolutionary move-

ment. The party schools would train its worker-students to

write propaganda articles, to edit, publish, and distribute

underground newspapers, manage their financial affairs, and

in general manage the machinery of an illegal revolutionary

organization.

The plans to create such a party considerably ante-

dated the schism in the Bolshevik faction. It was in Septem-

ber, 1908--while Proletarii still professed philosophical

neutrality and before otzovism had become a really divisive

issue--that G. Aleksinsky and a group of Social-Democrats in

Geneva presented a plan for a party school to the Bolshevik

Center.[2] The idea was presented again in a report to the

Fifth All-Russian Conference of the RSDRP in December of the

same year. And in early 1909, Gorky and the Geneva Social-
Democratic circle once again wrote to Proletarii insisting
upon the need for such a school.[3] But the leaders of Russian
Social-Democracy did no more than discuss the idea.

None of the Social-Democratic emigre groups would
take the initiative, and the practical organization of a
party school waited until a Russian worker by the name of
Vilonov arrived in Europe. Vilonov was of working class ori-
gen although he had spent the years since 1902 as an active
party organizer in the Social-Democratic movement. Vilonov
had suffered several arrests and periods of exile for his
revolutionary activities. He had contracted tuberculosis
during his years of exile, and by 1908 Vilonov was so ill
that his most recent exile was cut short. The Tsarist
authorities allowed him to travel to Italy--presumably to
die in a warm climate. (The authorities probably believed
that so ill a man could be of no more harm to the government, and Vilonov did die before two years had passed.)

Arriving in Italy in the fall of 1908, Vilonov soon
was attracted to the Isle of Capri and the villa of Maksim
Gorky.[4] It was Vilonov who excited Aleksinsky's and Gorky's
interest in the idea of a party school. He convinced them
to join him in forming an organizing committee to create a
school to train party organizers.

Bogdanov and Lunacharsky were soon converted to the
idea, and they were quick to enlist in Vilonov's organizing
committee. Indeed, they were soon to make the idea of the

school their own and to dominate its ideological course.
The concept of a party school was particularly attractive
to the left Bolsheviks because it gave them a positive alternative to Lenin's program of legal parliamentary activity.
After all, the Bolshevik radicals could not long continue
to plead for immediate armed insurrection; that was becoming
clearly impossible even in the minds of the most radical
Bolsheviks.

The idea of a party school was appealing to the left
because it was dedicated to illegal revolutionary activity.
The organizers of the school emphasized direct involvement
with the working class, and they promised to rebuild the
party into a revolutionary force once again. The spirit of
the party schools recalled the atmosphere of the local RSDRP
circles as they had existed before 1905.

Nevertheless, despite the enthusiasm for the idea
among the leaders of left Bolshevism, the school would still
probably never have occurred without Vilonov. While the intellectuals on the organizing committee were still haggling
over how the students for the school should be selected,
Vilonov personally travelled to Russia, selected twenty workers to be students, and arranged for their travel to Capri.[5]

By this time, however, it was already the spring of
1909 and the schism in the Bolshevik faction was fast taking
shape. The issue of a party school began to take on divisive overtones--if for no other reason than the fact that the
organizing committee for the school was composed almost

entirely of left Bolsheviks. Lenin was already denouncing
the school.

Still, the idea of the school was not inherently
anti-Leninist. Vilonov himself was a Bolshevik centrist
and a staunch supporter of Lenin's policies. He must not
have been aware that his comrades on the organizing committee
were the nucleus of Lenin's opposition. Little did Vilonov
realize that they would soon use his school as a weapon in
the factional controversy.

Indeed, from the very beginning Vilonov insisted
that the school be officially sanctioned by the RSDRP. The
organizing committee drew up four principles designed to
give the school the authority of a party institution and to
maintain its independence from any faction of the party.
The course of studies and the teaching personnel were to be
approved by local organizations within Russia (and hence not
subject to the control of either the Central Committee or
the Bolshevik Center), and "in its activity and internal organization the school must enjoy the usual autonomy within
the bounds of the party charter."[6]

Since Gorky, Bogdanov, Lunacharsky, and Aleksinsky
were all on the organizing committee, it must have seemed
obvious to Lenin that the party school would never represent
Social-Democracy as he conceived it. Those four were among
the most extreme proponents of the three Bolshevik heresies
of 1909: God-building, empiriomonism, and otzovism. Lenin
did his best to thwart the creation of the school by opposing

its approval by the Central Committee, by having it officially condemned by the Bolshevik Center, and by asking the
regional RSDRP organizations in Russia to neither sanction
the school nor allow any of their members to participate in
it.

Lenin was successful with the Central Committee and
with the St. Petersburg and Moscow regional committees. But
the Moscow Regional Bureau of the Northern and Central Industrial Districts was a hotbed of otzovism. Stanislav Volsky,
a leading left Bolshevik, was the secretary of that Bureau.
The Bureau both approved the idea of the school and set up
procedures for choosing students to attend it.[7]

Meanwhile, the real organizer of the school, Vilonov,
probably knew very little of this political manouvering.
He had left Capri for Russia long before the open break between Bogdanov and Lenin. In fact, by the time of the convention of the Enlarged Editorial Board of Proletarii, in
which the Bolshevik schism became public and official, Vilonov had already made preparations for the students to travel to Capri and was himself already back in Italy.

The "First Highest Social-Democratic Propagandistic-
Agitational School for Workers" opened on the Isle of Capri
on August 5, 1909 and lasted for four months. The course of
studies included both practical and theoretical training.
In regard to the practice of revolutionary organization,
the students studied the structure of the RSDRP, the techniques of propaganda and agitation, how to organize study

circles and party cells, how to write editorials that would interpret current events in terms of Marxism, how to edit and publish an underground newspaper, and how to manage the accounting of party finances.

The school also devoted considerable attention to the theoretical basis of the proletarian revolutionary movement. Bogdanov taught economic science and the history of social thought, Lunacharsky handled the history of the international socialist movement, Liadov lectured on the history of the RSDRP, Pokrovsky taught the history of Russia, and Gorky read lectures on the history of Russian literature.[8]

This first party school completed its four mounth course of studies as scheduled. Before the term was over, however, the school had suffered an internal schism in which it lost almost half of its students and very nearly fell apart. The internal dissension among the students and teachers was a direct result of the struggle between the two factions in Bolshevism.

Lenin had been strongly opposed to the existence of the school from the very beginning. In his campaign against it he found a very unlikely associate--Vilonov, the principal founder of the school. Vilonov had never given up his attempts to gain recognition and approval for his school from the Bolshevik Center. He spent most of his time while the school was in session trying to get the students and faculty to announce their support for Lenin's program. Lenin had meanwhile stepped up his campaign against the school; half

way through the term <u>Proletarii</u> printed its strongest attack
castigating its lecturers and students as "otzovists, ultimatists, and God-builders."

It was this editorial that caused the final break
between the original organizer of the school and the left
Bolsheviks who had taken over his idea. The governing committee of the school drafted a strong reply to <u>Proletarii</u>
and submitted it to the students for their approval. After
a stormy meeting, eight of the thirteen students supported
the committee's position while the remaining five stood
with Vilonov on the side of Lenin and <u>Proletarii</u>. Those
five students were immediately expelled from the school.
Accompanied by Vilonov the five travelled to Paris to hear
lectures from Lenin, Kamenev, and Zinoviev.[9]

However, even though the remaining eight students
sided with their left Bolshevik teachers at the time, they
did not feel any particular animosity toward Lenin and the
Bolshevik Center. Indeed, after the course of studies at
the Capri school was completed, those eight students also
went to Paris to attend lectures given by Lenin and his collaborators.

Lenin's lectures could hardly be called a school,
however. His talks were not devoted to lessons on theory,
program, or tactics or to methods and techniques of revolutionary organization but solely to a detailed and thorough
attack upon otzovism and empiriomonism. Other Bolshevik centrists lectured on the current state of Social-Democracy in

Russia, and the history of the Social-Democratic movement.[10]

The practical results of the first party school were small. One of the students was arrested immediately after he and his comrades returned to Russia. He revealed the names of the other students, and a majority of them were soon arrested and imprisoned. Only one of the students, F. I. Kalinin, later became prominent in the Bolshevik faction. The principal effect of the first party school was simply to add fuel to the Bolshevik intra-factional strife.

The original idea of a party school that would raise party leaders up from the ranks of the working class may not have originated as a weapon in the Bolshevik factional struggle, but it was inevitable that it should have played such a role. The content of the theoretical aspects of the course of studies could not but be colored by the lecturers' attitudes toward otzovism, empiriomonism, and God-building.

Bogdanov's influence upon the theoretical standpoint of the school was particularly evident. All the official pronouncements of the Capri school committee strongly echoed the positions that Bogdanov had taken in his published writings since his expulsion from the Bolshevik Center. He was the author of the sharply worded response to _Proletarii_'s critical editorial that prompted the schism in the school.[11] Also, the official _Report_ of the school if not actually written by Bogdanov was at least written by someone who shared Bogdanov's philosophical and political views and who copied his style of expression.

Bogdanov also excercised complete control over the school's course of studies on the subject of scientific socialism. Indeed, the name of Marx was not even mentioned in any of the course outlines given in the Report. The only purely theoretical courses offered were Bogdanov's "economic science," and "history of social thought." The students were clearly being taught empiriomonism and not Marxism.

Even the practical aspects of the course could not but become vehicles through which the left Bolsheviks expressed their political program. Part of the students' practical training was a review of the organizational structure of the RSDRP. Lecturers covered such topics as "The Question of Centralism and Democratism in the RSDRP," "The Party and the Duma Faction," "Kautsky's View on the Parliamentary Faction in Relation to the Party," and "The Ultimate Goal and the Course of Tasks of the Workers' Organization."[12] Such topics would inevitably be colored by the lecturers' attitudes toward the schism.

Furthermore, no matter how non-partisan the idea of a party school in general might have been, the demand for such a school at that particular time was clearly rooted in the otzovist attitude of uncompromising dedication to immediate armed insurrection by the Russian working class. In the appeal that Bogdanov had addressed to Russian Bolsheviks after he had been expelled from the faction, he had explicitly declared that a party school for workers would assume a leading role in advancing the proletarian revolution.

> . . . The second extremely important task of
> our faction during the current interrevolution-
> ary period [is] the task of broadening and
> deepening socialist propaganda . . . This
> necessitates, first, the creation of propa-
> gandistic literature, both legal and illegal,
> much more definitive and encyclopedic in con-
> tent than that which has existed until now
> . . . It is necessary to work out a new type
> of party school which, in completing the party
> education of the worker, filling the gaps in
> his knowledge . . . , and harmoniously syste-
> matizing [that knowledge], would create a
> reliable and conscious leader who would be
> prepared for all forms of proletarian struggle.[13]

By the time of the Capri school, even the most radical of the Bolsheviks had ceased to seriously campaign for
immediate working class insurrection. They were constrained
by the disintegration of the RSDRP organization in Russia
to devote their primary attention to questions of party rebuilding. This, of course, was the position that Lenin had
long held. Since 1907 Lenin had argued that the reaction in
Russia was so severe and the party organization was in such
disarray that the party had to slowly and patiently rebuild
itself. He added that the party should not disdain to rely
upon such legal and parliamentary means of propaganda as
were available.

The left Bolsheviks simply expressed Lenin's program
in more radical terms. They insisted upon the recreation of
an underground revolutionary party such as the RSDRP had been
before 1905. Further reflecting the revolutionary extremism
which had previously been manifest in otzovism, the millenarians ceased to talk about the rekindling of the bourgeois-
democratic revolution that had begun in 1905. Instead they

began to anticipate the actual socialist revolution. The
Report of the first party school held the preparation for
socialism to be the primary task of the school.

> [Bogdanov] characterized propaganda and agi-
> tation of the 90s of the last century as ele-
> mentary socialist and that of the first half-
> decade of the present century as primarily
> democratic-revolutionary. Purely socialist
> propaganda must now be implemented in this
> third period. Class deepening of Social-Dem-
> ocratic propaganda is now the first task of
> the school. The party school must prepare
> not only political revolutionaries but con-
> scious socialists . . .[14]

The party school on Capri was thus an ideological
weapon wielded by the left Bolsheviks in their struggle
against Lenin and the centrists. Such a school could also
have organizational significance. It could serve as a center around which Bogdanov could build a factional organization which could compete with the editorial board of Proletarii (the effective central committee of the Bolshevik faction) for the allegience of the rank and file Bolsheviks in
Russia.

Early in the preparations for the Capri school, Lenin
perceived the danger that such a school might present to his
leadership of the Bolshevik faction. Already at the meeting
of the expanded editorial board of Proletarii in June, 1909,
Lenin warned that the school could easily become a political
organization.

> . . . All the initiators [of the school] side
> with the opposition in our faction. To or-
> ganize a school--this means to enter into re-
> lations with local organizations, to have
> continuous contacts. This is nothing other

than a center, and even stronger than the
Central Committee, for the Central Committee
doesn't have twenty agents and the school
wants to have that many.[15]

Lenin certainly appears to have been right. Taking

over the leadership of the Bolshevik faction seems to have

been Bogdanov's intention. After all, Bogdanov and the

school committee--and indeed all the Bolsheviks who had

been excluded by the Bolshevik Center in the June schism--

did not act as if they had been expelled from anything.

They continued to refer to themselves as Bolsheviks. They

claimed to uphold the principles for which Bolshevism had

stood during the 1905 Revolution. They portrayed themselves

as the true Bolsheviks and Lenin as the renegade.

Furthermore, no sooner had the first school ended

than the lecturers and students formed themselves into a

political organization. In December, 1909, the group petition-

ed the Central Committee to recognize them as a "literary

group" publishing the journal Vpered. Their petition was

granted. Thus Bogdanov had established that institution

that Lenin had always argued was so essential to a central-

ized, effective revolutionary organization: "a theoretical

journal with a network of agents in Russia."[16]

Vpered, the title of their journal, was ironic.

Vpered had been the first Bolshevik journal to appear after

Lenin lost control over Iskra to the Mensheviks in 1903.

Thus Vpered had been the journal of radical Bolshevism of

1905, and its use by the left Bolsheviks in 1909 recalled

the optimism and extremism of early Bolshevism. It was also

significant that Lenin had founded Vpered after he had been
expelled from both Iskra and the Central Committee, and he
created it in order to form the center for a faction that
had resulted from a recent party schism--in other words,
Lenin's position in 1903 and Bogdanov's position in 1909
were the same.

At its founding the Vpered Group included sixteen
people. Only two of them, Shantser and Izrailovich, had
been neither students nor lecturers at the Capri school.
The former lecturers were Bogdanov, Lunacharsky, Gorky,
Volsky, Liadov, Pokrovsky, and Menzhinsky. The remaining
members of the group were former students.[17]

The Vpered Group turned out to be a quite disparate
association of individuals. A Soviet scholar of the group
has claimed that "among them we literally can find no two
comrades whose views on questions of theory and tactics were
in complete agreement."[18] He asserted that the sole thing the
members of the Vpered Group had in common was their insistence upon the freedom to think whatever they pleased, and
he was certainly correct. All the left Bolsheviks were intellectuals with firm convictions. They refused to defer to
anyone else's interpretation of scientific socialism.

However, though the Vperedists did not share a positive program, they were at least united in what they opposed.
All the members of the Vpered Group considered themselves to
be the faithful heirs of revolutionary Bolshevism, and they
were unanimously opposed to the conservative direction in

which Lenin seemed to be moving. Bogdanov was the principal spokesman for the group, and the others rallied around him as long as he spoke in general terms of radical Bolshevism. But when Bogdanov (and other Vperedists) began to propose specific new programs, the unity of the group came to an abrupt end.

In early 1910 Bogdanov drew up a preliminary summary of the positions and program of the Vpered Group, "The Contemporary Situation and the Tasks of the Party." Bogdanov began by repeating the evaluation of party affairs that had been expressed in the report of the first party school. He voiced a concern about the drastic shrinkage of the Social-Democratic party during the period of reaction. He, too, felt that the defection of the intelligentsia from the revolutionary movement was particularly debilitating for the RSDRP since the intelligentsia had traditionally supplied the party's organizational, editorial, and leadership forces.

Nevertheless, Bogdanov's proposed solution to this loss of leadership was emphatically not to summon the intelligentsia back into the movement. Indeed, Bogdanov considered the loss of the intellectuals from the RSDRP to be a positive development. Whereas the intelligentsia was manifest-its essential cowardice in the face of government reaction, Bogdanov thought that the workers were still staunch revolutionaries. Local party circles were becoming more purely proletarian and among them ". . . clearly appears the greatest spiritual courage, the deepest faith in the power of the

proletariat, and the staunchest fighting mood."[19] He thought
that the only thing that prevented the local circles from
recreating a vital revolutionary movement was a lack of
trained leaders and organizers. Socialist education--such
as that supplied by the party schools--was all that was necessary to produce proletarian leaders for the revolutionary
socialist movement.

Bogdanov further asserted that the working class was
already beginning to take over the movement. While the
local intellectuals had simply deserted the movement, the
emigre intellectuals were subverting it by ". . . devoting
most of their attention and energy to inter-factional struggle."[20] Contrary to the splintering of the emigre RSDRP
leadership, Bogdanov insisted that the local party organizations were overcoming their differences and becoming unified.
He claimed that the right wing Mensheviks were simply abandoning the revolution while the left Mensheviks were uniting
with the Bolsheviks.

Thus, in Bogdanov's analysis, the Social-Democratic
movement was becoming predominantly Bolshevik. But it was
the Bolshevism of the 1905 Revolution, he said, and not the
parliamentarism of Lenin, that was inspiring the local party
circles. Bogdanov represented his own _Vpered_ Group as the
true upholders of the Bolshevik tradition and hence as the
proper leaders of the RSDRP.

He then reiterated the main differences between the
left Bolsheviks and the centrists: the _Vpered_ Group insisted

upon the necessity of freedom of criticism within the party,
the need to spread purely socialist propaganda, and the need
to actively prepare for an armed uprising. On this last
revolutionary note, Bogdanov was adament.

> We suggest that the strategy and tactics of
> popular insurrection must become one of the
> subjects of study for conscious workers. . . .
> We must never lose sight of these tasks, must
> never abandon what needs to be done for the
> preparation and facilitation of the coming
> decisive struggle.[21]

Despite the fact that he dissociated himself from
Lenin on programmatic questions, Bogdanov reaffirmed his belief in the organizational principles upon which Lenin had
founded Bolshevism. Bogdanov emphasized the importance of
democratic centralism and leadership by a politically conscious elite.

> The Bolsheviks recognized that Social-Democ-
> racy is before all else a party of conscious
> revolutionary proletarians based upon the en-
> tire experience of international socialism;
> it must raise the working masses up from an
> elemental movement to the level of the high-
> est socialist consciousness, and not lower
> its organization and tasks to compromise with
> the elemental movement.[22]

Part of the problem facing Social-Democracy was the
fact that this democratic centralism had broken down and
that members of the higher level RSDRP institutions were
being coopted and not elected. Bogdanov demanded that local
organizations be rebuilt as quickly as possible, that all
local, regional, and national bureaus be elected, and that
a new congress be convened upon the basis of such a reorganization. He further demanded that the RSDRP cease its fac-

tional in-fighting.

> Different ideological tendencies must inevi-
> tably exist in any strong and vital party;
> they are a mark of its growth and development.
> They find their expressions in literary groups,
> in free groupings of like-minded people at
> congresses, conferences, etc. But among us
> they have attained a completely abnormal form
> --a party within the party that destroys the
> general unity of the party and under present
> conditions interferes with the free develop-
> ment of those very ideological currents.[23]

The current leaders of the RSDRP, Bogdanov said,
were from the old bourgeois intelligentsia and retained the
harmful habits typical of that class: too much pride and
self-will, unwillingness to accept comradely criticism, and
excessive deference to authorities. Bogdanov scorned not
only loyal Leninists but dogmatic Marxists as well when he
criticized ". . . the widespread habit among party workers
to blindly believe in famous authorities . . ."[24] This, too,
was a characteristic of the intelligentsia. The RSDRP would
be strengthened as it lost the intelligentsia from its ranks.

Bogdanov concluded "The Contemporary Situation and
the Tasks of the Party" by repeating the leftists' maximalist
demands for immediate revolution. He insisted that "Life
itself definitely and insistently sets this task for the en-
suing inter-revolutionary period: to supply the military-
revolutionary preparation for the time of a new upsurge."[25]

But his conception of the contemporary situation
was paradoxical. Bogdanov enthusiastically noted the transformation of local Social-Democratic groups into purely proletarian circles, but he also expressed a distrust of the

elemental workers' movement and insisted that the movement must be directed by conscious socialists.

Bogdanov tried to resolve this apparent contradiction by arguing that the new party leaders who would lead the elemental working class revolution would themselves be of proletarian origin. They would, however, be educated in scientific socialism and would have achieved socialist class consciousness. It must have been obvious that Bogdanov conceived of the Capri school as the model of a means of educating the future proletarian leaders of the RSDRP. It must also have been obvious that the people who would educate the workers was a small, elite group of socialist intellectuals--Bogdanov's own faction of left Bolsheviks.

Thus Bogdanov raised the elitism of What is to be Done? yet one step higher. The real leaders of the revolutionary movement that Bogdanov was imagining would not be party organizers but the teachers of the party organizers. The first party school thus provided the model for a new system of party organization based not on a central journal but on an educational institution. Lenin's "theoretical organ with a network of agents" would be replaced with a party school with an organization of its students.

In this way Bogdanov began to transform the proletarian revolution into a question of socialist education. The main thrust of his program was no longer arming the workers but rather educating them. He believed that if the working class was properly educated, it could handle the details

of the organization and implementation of the revolution
without direct leadership by the intelligentsia.

Bogdanov emphasized the necessity of spreading socialist propaganda among the workers. Instead of agitating by
means of specific slogans and demands, the workers should
be given a complete socialist education. Teachers should
address not only economic or political questions ". . . but
as much as possible questions of everyday life and general-
cultural life."[26] For this purpose local groups must set
up propaganda circles, develop new popular literature, publish popular newspapers, and set up schools to train party
workers in socialist propaganda and agitation.[27]

The program expressed in "The Contemporary Situation
and the Tasks of the Party" was the embryo of a new approach
to revolution. Bogdanov expressed the essence of his future
Proletarian Culture movement:

> There is only one solution: to use the former
> bourgeois culture and counter-pose it; to
> create and spread among the masses a new pro-
> letarian [culture]; to develop proletarian
> science, to strengthen pure-comradely relations
> in proletarian circles, to develop proletarian
> philosophy and to direct art in the direction
> of proletarian striving and experience.[28]

The idea of cultural revolution preceding economic
revolution may have raised some orthodox Marxist eyebrows at
the time--even among the members of Bogdanov's own Vpered
Group. After all, if existence determines consciousness,
then true socialist, proletarian culture could not arise
until the ownership of the means of production and distribution of material goods had passed into the hands of the

working class. Nevertheless, Bogdanov's suggestion that proletarian culture was a necessary preparation for socialist revolution was simply a logical development of his epistemological insistence upon the primacy of thought over matter and of consciousness over existence. The important revolution would be made in the way workers thought; the material revolution would be a mere consequence.

This conclusion was only implicit in Bogdanov's statement of program in 1910, however. It was not until he elaborated on his idea of proletarian culture and made explicit its social implications and theoretical suppositions that it led to an open break in the Vpered Group between the positivist and the orthodox Marxists.

During the single year of its effective existence, the Vpered Group managed only two successful projects. It established its own factional journal, Vpered, and it arranged another "Highest Propaganda-Agitational School for Workers" similar to the first party school on Capri. The journal was intended to be a popular organ for distribution in Russia explaining the Vpered Group's program to the local Social-Democratic organizations. There is no record indicating its success in penetrating Russia or its welcome by Social-Democrats there. Vpered was published only three times; the last issue appeared in May, 1911, after the people most responsible for writing it had already left the group.

The second party school was moved from Capri to Bologna. It was not officially an undertaking of the Vpered

Group since the organizers of the school wanted to create
the impression that the school was non-factional. Nevertheless, all of the organizers and most of the lecturers
were members of the Vpered Group. The organization of this
second school was begun immediately following the conclusion
of the Capri school.

An organizing committee had been formed which included Bogdanov, Lunacharsky, Volsky, Aleksinksy, and Liadov.
In January, 1910, they appealed to the Central Committee of
the RSDRP for funds to support another school, but the Central Committee refused. As an alternative the Central Committee suggested that it set up its own organizing commission
to create a really non-partisan, party-wide school. The
Vpered Group was invited to send two of its members as delegates to the commission. The two delegates, Aleksinsky and
Pokrovsky, soon saw that they would have too small a role to
play in the school. Insisting that the lecturers and the
curriculum should be chosen by the students and not by any
central party institution, Aleksinsky and Pokrovsky walked
out of the commission.[29]

Realizing that it was impossible for them to control
the ideological point of view of an official RSDRP school,
the Vperedists again decided to go their own way. The major
problem they faced was lack of money--it had been for financial support that they had applied to the Central Committee
in the first place. However, once again they were provided
for by the generosity of Gorky; the latter both provided his

own money and solicited donations from a few of his rich friends.[30] A second source of income for the Bologna school came from a band of Bolshevik bandits in the Urals. In exchange for the three thousand dollar proceeds from a recent robbery, the organizing commission promised that four of the expropriators could attend the school.

F. I. Kalinin, a graduate of the first party school who was on his way to becoming an important member of the left Bolsheviks, was put in charge of selecting students and helping them to travel to Italy. The number of students was greater at the second school than at the first, and their origins were more diverse. Twenty one students were selected by Bolshevik organizations from St. Petersburg, Moscow, the Urals, and Odessa.[31]

When the second party school was convened in Bologna on November 21, 1910, it had much the same appearance as its predecessor. Once again Bogdanov took full charge of the theoretical and philosophical curriculum. The other lecturers were also veterans of the Capri school; Aleksinsky, Pokrovsky, Lunacharsky, Liadov, and Volsky all repeated their previous courses. The main difference in the curriculum was a greater emphasis upon practical organizational work. Another difference in the school's format was the presence of a number of prominent non-Bolshevik Social-Democrats as guest lecturers. Maslov, Kollontai, Volonter, and Trotsky all agreed to lecture at the Bologna school.[32]

The course of studies was completed by March, 1911,

and this time no internal dissensions rocked the school.
At the conclusion of the course, the faculty and students
did not disperse before they had planned to establish yet
a third party school as soon as possible. That third school
was not destined to be, however. The Vpered Group was
being racked with both personal and ideological conflicts
and its disintegration was imminent. After the Group finally
collapsed later in the spring of 1911, there was no longer
a large enough a contingent of left Bolshevik intellectuals
to manage a new school.

Neither was there any more money available. The
principal financier of the left Bolsheviks had been Maksim
Gorky, and Gorky had begun to distance himself from his God-
builder comrades even before the Bologna school had begun.
Even though he agreed to fund the school, Gorky refused to
be involved personally. Perhaps Gorky was heeding the many
letters that Lenin was writing to him at this time trying to
win him from God-building back to Bolshevism. Gorky began
to perceive Bogdanov as a political manipulator seeking only
to advance his personal position within the party. Furthermore, Gorky's wife had quarrelled with the wives of Bogdanov
and Lunacharsky.[33] The latter families had already moved to
Bologna before the school convened. It was, indeed, Bogdanov's and Lunacharsky's philosophical and personal estrange-
ment from Gorky that caused the location of the school to be
moved. Gorky refused to lecture at the new school on the
grounds of ill health. He was headed in a new direction and

had no future role to play in the intellectual development
of Bolshevik millenialism.

The _Vpered_ Group turned out to be a totally ineffec-
tual organization. Though the group had been formally recognized as a literary group by the Central Committee, it was
totally unable to cooperate with the central party institutions, and its role in party affairs was negligible. The
Vpered Group received little sympathy from the emigre Social-
Democratic groups, and it found no organizational following
among local Social-Democratic circles in Russia. There had
been two _Vpered_-oriented circles in St. Petersburg and Tiflis
for a short time, but they had ceased to exist by early
1913 and had never been influential. [34] The radical rank and
file Bolsheviks in Russia simply did not rally around the
banner of the _Vpered_ Group as Bogdanov had expected them to.

The group did not even have a consistent, unifying
point of view among its own members. It existed in name until 1917, but the original membership did not hold together
for much longer than a single year. Formed in December,
1909, the _Vpered_ Group had disintegrated due to internal conflicts by May, 1911.

In a letter to Gorky written in early 1910 (about a
year before his analysis was proven accurate), Lenin said
that he suspected that the _Vpered_ Group was really composed
of two contradictory elements: a Marxist, party-oriented
group motivated primarily by otzovism and a Machist (empiriomonist), anti-party group who had nothing in common with the

Social-Democratic party.[35]

To an extent Lenin was correct. Men such as Menzhinsky, Pokrovsky, and Liadov were orthodox Marxists who
withdrew from Lenin's faction only because they perceived
him to be moving away from radical Bolshevism toward the
right wing of the party. During the First World War they
were all firm internationalists and joined Trotsky's left-
wing Mezhduraionnyi Komitet. After Lenin's April theses
in 1917 in which Lenin announced his return to a radical
program, these left Bolsheviks again enthusiastically rejoined him.

The other members of the Vpered Group--Bogdanov,
Lunacharsky, Lebedev-Poliansky, and Kalinin--were far from
Marxist orthodoxy even though close to the spirit of revolutionary Bolshevism. Indeed, it was their closeness to
Bolshevism and their desire for philosophical consistency
that led them to revise Marxism. Although all of them but
Bogdanov rejoined the Bolshevik faction after Lenin's left-
ward turn in 1917, this group of radicals did not become as
loyal party men as did their former Vperedist comrades. They
preserved their own unique interpretation of the socialist
revolution independent of the official Bolshevik program.
They all (this time including Bogdanov) formed the core of
the Proletkult that strove to socialize Russian culture independently of the new Communist Party.

It was the objection of the orthodox Marxist members
of the Vpered Group to Bogdanov's notions of Proletarian

Culture that led to the dissolution of the Vpered Group.
Lunacharsky claimed that Bogdanov was actually the first to
leave the group because of an argument with Aleksinsky. Indeed, Lunacharsky blamed Aleksinsky's abrasive personality
for the collapse of the group. He claimed that Pokrovsky
and Menzhinsky also clashed with Aleksinsky and departed
from the group soon after Bogdanov did.[36]

Soviet scholars assert that Pokrovsky was the first
to leave. Pokrovsky strenuously objected to Bogdanov's
ideas on the subject of Proletarian Culture and to Bogdanov's
insistence on using Vpered as a means of propagating his
philosophy of revolution.[37] Whatever the real reason for
its dissolution, after the spring of 1911 the Vpered Group
had lost all but one of its original left Bolshevik members
and was no longer a significant literary group within the
RSDRP.

Aleksinsky maintained a branch of the Vpered Group
in Paris until it dissolved in 1913. He vigorously objected
both to Bogdanov's unorthodox philosophy and to Lenin's moderate political policies. At the same time Lunacharsky was
associated with a splinter organization of the Vpered Group.
in Geneva. Lunacharsky's group devoted its attention solely
to developing the theory of Proletarian Culture; it was not
active in Social-Democratic factional politics.[38] In fact,
soon after the break-up of the original group, Lunacharsky
began to seek a personal rapprochement with Lenin.

The collapse of the _Vpered_ Group signified the final, ignominious conclusion to revolutionary Bolshevism as it had been originally conceived by Lenin, Bogdanov, Liadov, and others in 1904. The Bolsheviks had considered the Russian Revolution of 1905 to be not merely a bourgeois attack upon feudalism, but rather a revolutionary-democratic movement in which the working class could play an essential and even leading role. They did not actually believe it would be a socialist revolution, but their anticipation of a fundamental change was high, and they hoped that the revolution would at least establish the basic preconditions for the ultimate socialist revolution. They were intransigent in their demand for armed insurrection by the working class. The Bolsheviks believed in the positive good of violent revolution; it was, indeed, the foundation of their program.

Lenin had been the first of the Bolsheviks to recognize the collapse of the elemental revolutionary movement and the rise of counter-revolution and official reaction. Lenin quickly realized the futility of promoting armed insurrection during a period of reaction and appreciated the values to be gained by participating in the Duma and pursuing legal party activities.

The reality of counter-revolution and all that it implied was precisely what the left Bolsheviks had stubbornly refused to see. They continued to believe in the imminence of armed insurrection; they perceived any retreat from this maximalist stance to be cowardly surrender and not concession

to the inevitable. It was simply in their opposition to
moderation and their clinging to obsolete policies that the
leftists were united as a group. The disintegration of the
Vpered Group began when they finally began to comprehend
the reality of reaction and working class passivity within
Russia. As their demands for armed struggle, underground
organization, and boycott of the Duma became more and more
obviously foolish, the Vperedists lost the burning issues
that kept them united. Each of the revolutionaries began to
move in a different direction.

Pokrovsky remained in Paris and began to devote his
time to the study of literature, science, and history.
Liadov returned to Russia not to be heard of again until he
became prominent in the Baku uprising in 1917. Aleksinsky
continued a Vperedist organization in Paris until the World
War began. He supported Plekhanov's defensist position
during the war. After 1917 Aleksinsky became a rabid anti-
Bolshevik and emigrated to the United States. Bazarov involved himself in a number of Menshevik circles and joined
Gorky in editing Letopis' and Novaia Zhizn' during the war.
Stanislav Volsky became a left Menshevik.

Gorky had been the first of the left Bolsheviks to
abandon not only the Vpered Group but the RSDRP. Though he
had sided with Bogdanov during the Bolshevik schism, Gorky
soon became disaffected with both the philosophy of God-
building and the continued political in-fighting of the
Vpered Group.

Turning away from politics and the revolutionary movement entirely, Gorky ceased trying to create a revolutionary art. He devoted the decade from 1910 to 1920 to writing his apolitical autobiography. He opposed both the World War and the Bolshevik seizure of power in 1917. Gorky wrote articles critical of the Bolsheviks in the pages of his newspaper, Novaia Zhizn', until Lenin had it shut down in the summer of 1918. It was not until 1921 that Gorky again donated his name and his art to the services of politics.

For Bogdanov and Lunacharsky the years immediately following their expulsion from the Bolshevik Center was a period of fundamental intellectual reorientation. The most significant consequence of their experience was a disillusionment with the political aspect of the proletarian revolution. Their own political powerlessness within the Bolshevik faction and their inability to organize a rival factional center combined with the patent impossibility of political revolution in Russia in those years caused Bogdanov and Lunacharsky to seek an alternative to political revolution.

The two party schools, in which both men played instrumental roles, were both a culmination of their revolutionary thought of the past decade as well as the genesis of an entirely new approach to revolution which would engross them for the next decade. On one hand, of course, the schools were no more than the means to recreate the spirit of Bolshevism as it had existed before and during the 1905

Revolution. The object of the schools was to create a new
group of dedicated party organizers and journal editors
who would create a new, vital underground revolutionary
organization committed to promoting the socialist revolution. But at the same time, their emphasis upon educating
the working class as the principal means of preparing for
socialism shed a new light on the millenarian Bolsheviks'
concept of revolution. More and more Bogdanov focused not
upon the simple education of revolutionary organizers but
upon the instillation of the working class with an entire
socialist world-view--a complete Proletarian Culture.

In the next chapter we will see how Bogdanov began
to reap the harvest of his earlier philosophical reformula-
tion of scientific socialism. By contradicting the notion
that existence determines consciousness, Bogdanov made the
proletarian revolution not an inevitable physical act but
an act of creative human collective will. The change in the
ownership of the means of production would not give rise to
socialist consciousness in Bogdanov's understanding of it;
instead, socialist consciousness would impel the workers to
seize the means of production. Thus spiritual education
would be more important than political organization. The
spiritual revolution would precede the physical revolution.
It was to the spiritual revolution that Bogdanov and Lunacharsky devoted themselves after 1911.

NOTES TO CHAPTER VI

[1]Otchet pervoi sotsialdemokraticheskoi propagan-
distsko-agitatorskoi shkoly dlia rabochikh (Paris: "Soiuz,"
1910), p. 1.

[2]S. Livshits, Partiinye universitety podpol'ia
(Moscow: Izdatel'stvo Vsesoiuznogo Obshchestva Politkat-
orzhan i Ss.-Poselentsev, 1919), p. 11.

[3]Ibid., p. 12.

[4]Ibid.

[5]Ibid., p. 23.

[6]Otchet, p. 2.

[7]Livshits, p. 18.

[8]Otchet, p. 9.

[9]Livshits, p. 58.

[10]Ibid., pp. 61-63.

[11]Ibid., p. 2.

[12]Otchet, p. 10.

[13]A. Bogdanov, "K vsem tovarishchem," in Protokoly,
p. 248.

[14]Otchet, p. 3.

[15]Protokoly, p. 48.

[16]CW, vol. 5, p. 23.

[17]K. Ostroukhova, "Gruppa 'Vpered'," Proletarskaia
Revoliutsiia, no. 1 (1925), p. 198.

[18]N. Voitynskii, "O gruppe 'Vpered' (1909-1917),"
Proletarskaia Revoliutsiia, no. 12 (1929), p. 76.

[19]A. Bogdanov, Sovremennoe polozhenie i zadachi partii (Paris: Izdanie Gruppy "Vpered," 1910), p. 2.

[20]Ibid.

[21]Ibid., p. 30.

[22]Ibid., p. 15.

[23]Ibid., p. 18.

[24]Ibid., p. 16.

[25]Ibid., p. 29.

[26]Ibid., p. 23.

[27]Ibid., pp. 20-21.

[28]Ibid., p. 17.

[29]Livshits, pp. 65-66.

[30]Ibid., p. 67.

[31]Ibid., pp. 69-70.

[32]Ibid., pp. 78-79.

[33]M. Gor'kii i ego sovremenniki, pp. 146-47.

[34]Voitynskii, p. 110.

[35]Letopis', vol. 2, p. 124.

[36]Velikii perevorot, p. 52.

[37]Ostroukhova, p. 213 and Voitynskii, p. 109.

[38]Voitynskii, pp. 109-10.

CHAPTER VII

BOGDANOV AND THE IDEA OF "PROLETARIAN CULTURE"

The dissolution of the Vpered Group signified the end
of Bogdanov's political involvement in the Social-Democratic party. Bogdanov had been one of the most prominent Social-Democrats of the preceding decade, and within the Bolshevik faction, his prestige had been second only to Lenin's.
He had been a member of the Central Committee of the party
during the 1905 Revolution, a member of the Bolshevik Center
from 1904 to 1909, an editor of all the significant Bolshevik journals from 1903 to 1909, and the spokesman for the
most radical members of the most radical faction within the
Russian Social-Democratic movement. But only two years
after he was expelled from the Bolshevik Center, Bogdanov
had fallen from the highest levels of party leadership to
near oblivion. In 1911 Bogdanov found himself with no organization, little rank and file support, and only a few emigre
allies.

Bogdanov's position in 1911 was much the same as it
had been ten years before when he was defending his positivist Marxism from the idealists. Only the subject of debate and the personnel had changed. Bogdanov's opponent
was now Lenin. Bogdanov and Lunacharsky were still inseparable comrades. Though they had lost Bazarov as an ally, they

were joined by F. I. Kalinin (a graduate of the Capri school)
and V. Lebedev-Poliansky (another left Bolshevik and former
associate of the Vpered Group). Once again Bogdanov and his
comrades elaborated a positivist revision of Marxism to
serve as the foundation of an impatient and radical revolutionary world-view.

One of the things that Bogdanov must have learned in
his fall from influence in the RSDRP between 1909 and 1911
was that politics was not his metier. He was conspicuously
lacking in the organizational and managerial skill and political acumen that was so prominent in Lenin's personality.
Henceforth, Bogdanov would play no political role in the
revolutionary movement. Instead, he turned to cultural activity, the realm in which he was temperamentally suited to
excel. It was not politically but intellectually that Bogdanov excercised his influence upon Russia's working class
revolution.

Indeed, culture was to Bogdanov as politics was to
Lenin. Both men were voluntarist revolutionaries impatient
for the arrival of socialism. But while Lenin elaborated
the principles according to which a revolutionary party must
use to seize and maintain political power, Bogdanov elaborated the cultural and philosophical principles upon which the
new socialist society should be based. Bogdanov's imprint
on Soviet culture would be no less profound that Lenin's influence upon Soviet political development. The genealogy of
socialist realism, the idealism of the first five year plan,

and the utopian fervor of Soviet society in the 1920's is
not to be found in the science of Marxism but in the philosophy of empiriomonism. Soviet socialist idealism was the
child of Bogdanov's Proletarian Culture movement.

The party schools at Capri and Bologna were significant landmarks in Bogdanov's transition from political to
cultural concerns. The schools were not important for their
positive results; both schools were really dismal failures.
They were important instead for the direction in which they
encouraged Bogdanov's thought to progress.

Indeed, failure seems too mild a word to describe the
party schools. All the expense of money and energy, the
detailed planning, and the elaborate curriculum was devoted
to the education of merely 34 workers. Few of them would
ever play an important role in the RSDRP. It was unreal-
istic to have hoped that the graduates could--on the basis
of a few months' study--set up their own schools in Russia,
share their learning with other workers, and thereby create
a new, vital revolutionary organization.

The notion that the party schools might revitalize
the RSDRP and further the socialist revolution in Russia
was no more than a fantasy created by men who were more ped-
agogues than politicians. In a sense, the party schools
were no more than wish fulfillment by the lecturers. In any
healthy society, men of the intellectual capacities and attainments and philosophical temperament of Bogdanov and his
friends would have been prominent scholars and academicians.

For a short time in 1910 and 1911, these revolutionary the-
orists created an artificial world in which they could freely excercise their pedagogical ambitions.

The two schools at Bologna and Capri were a high bur-
lesque of academia. The students were Russian workers who
had less than high school education, and the principal purpose of the schools was to produce political technicians to
organize local propaganda and agitational circles in Russia.
Yet the schools themselves could have been models for a progressive European university. The structure of the schools
was elaborate and founded upon the full equality of students
and teachers. Both the students and their teachers cooperatively worked out the curriculum, the students elected the
teachers, and a school committee, composed of students and
teachers, administered the affairs of the school.

These Russian workers were also treated to courses
that would have been an asset to any university in Europe.
Pokrovsky taught Russian History, Gorky taught Russian Literature, Bogdanov taught the history of philosophy, and Lunacharsky taught world literature. Having established a school
to teach propaganda, agitation, and organizational skills,
the lecturers could not resist the temptation to lecture on
the subjects of their expertise.

No matter that the schools failed miserably in attain-
ing their stated goals--Bogdanov and Lunacharsky were nevertheless fired with the enthusiasm for socialist education.
Realizing in this way a basic temperamental inclination--the

desire to teach--the Bolshevik millenarians began to change
their ideas about how the socialist revolution could be
achieved. They now began to carry to its logical conclusion
Bogdanov's suggestion that consciousness determines existence.

Asserting the primacy of culture over politics as
early as 1908, Lunacharsky had announced in Religion and
Socialism that "the ideological hegemony of the proletariat
serves as the real preparation for the dictatorship of the
proletariat."[1] Bogdanov and Lunacharsky, following their
experience at the party schools, began to substitute education for organization, change of spirit for armed uprising,
and cultural transformation for political revolution.

Bogdanov was the first to elaborate an agenda for the
Proletarian Culture movement. We have already seen how, in
the summer of 1910 in his platform for the Vpered Group,
Bogdanov had first tentatively expressed the idea that a new
proletarian culture was an essential prerequisite to the socialist revolution. In 1911, Bogdanov began in earnest to
develop the foundation of what would ultimately become the
Proletkult. In the February, 1911 number of Vpered, he published an article "Socialism in the Present." It was the
first complete statement of Bogdanov's concept of cultural
revolution. Also, according to a Soviet scholar, the article
was the immediate cause of the split between the God-builders
and the orthodox otzovists in the Vpered Group.[2]

Bogdanov began "Socialism in the Present" as he began

all the essays he wrote in this period: he expressed his great concern with the depression, disillusionment, and passivity of the Russian Social-Democrats. The tide of opportunism, long vigorously denounced by Bogdanov, now seemed to him to have risen only higher. Those opportunists, he asserted, believed that class conflicts were lessening, that socialism could be achieved by peaceful evolution, and that violent revolution would be unnecessary.

The question that Bogdanov posed at the outset of "Socialism in the Present" was this: How does one answer the backsliding socialist who argues that socialism is a mere utopia for his generation? How can one maintain the old sense of self-sacrificing idealism? Bogdanov believed that the contemporary Social-Democrats were renouncing lives of hardship and deprivation and seeking an easier path to socialism through cooperation, compromise, and gradual improvement.[3]

Once again Bogdanov's impatient revolutionary idealism was evident. Perhaps one of the reasons he had continued to call for the preparation for armed uprising from 1907 to 1909 was not because he believed that there was any hope of success but because he did not want the Social-Democratic movement to lose its enthusiasm. It was clear in the opening of "Socialism in the Present" that Bogdanov did not believe that revolutionary idealism could be kept alive as long as the prospects for revolution were put off into the indefinite future.

Bogdanov noted that at that time the collectivists, trade unionists, and cooperativists believed that they could start with an inherently socialistic economic unit at the local level (such as a consumers' coop) and gradually extend it to city, regional, and ultimately national level. The gradual expansion of such organizations, according to the thinking of the time, would eventually produce socialism.

Bogdanov vigorously opposed such a conception because:

> They understand the class struggle not as socialists, but as people who join forces to persue personal interests. The more successful a cooperative or a union is the more conservative it will become--restricting entry, making profits, and creating a new "aristocracy."[4]

But Bogdanov's rejection of such gradualism was not due only to his insistence upon the unselfish idealism of the socialist revolutionary movement. He also did not believe that a totally new society could be achieved except through abrupt, radical change. Bogdanov maintained an apocalyptic conception of the genesis of socialism. He argued that something that is essentially different cannot simply evolve into being. It must arise fully developed, and everything that contradicts it must be destroyed. The evil of the present world must be done away with at a single stroke; it cannot be done piecemeal.

Once again Bogdanov's rejection of the principles of materialism was evident. One of the reasons why he opposed trade unionism and the cooperative movement was because

of the essentially bourgeois spirit that inspired them.
Bogdanov argued that the simple possession of the means of
production is <u>not</u> the ultimate determinant of the nature of
society. Even if the gradualist social reformers were to
ultimately gain possession of all the means of production,
socialism would still not necessarily exist. What is important, Bogdanov said, is not the material situation but the
spiritual culture of the people. Socialism depends not
upon material possessions but ". . . <u>the comradely organization of all production</u>, that is, the rule of comradely labor
relations among the people."[5]

In claiming that socialism can exist only when it is
based upon comradely organization of production in its entirety, Bogdanov was once again arguing from the assumption
that consciousness determines existence. In the past he
had been content only to elaborate upon the basic principles
of positivist epistemology; he had allowed Lunacharsky and
Gorky to spell out the implications that his empiriomonism
had for revolutionary practice. Now, for the first time,
Bogdanov applied his principles to such questions.

Since consciousness determines existence, Bogdanov
now argued that the proletarian culture upon which socialism
would be based must precede the revolution and not follow it.

> The struggle for socialism is not at all
> embodied in a single war against capitalism
> and in the simple collection of [material]
> forces for that task. This struggle is a
> positive and creative work--the creation of
> the new elements of socialism in the prole-
> tariat: in its internal relations, in its
> unifying, living conditions. It is the work-

ing out of a socialist, proletarian culture.[6]

Furthermore, Bogdanov did not have in mind the rise
of "comradely relations" in economic and political life
alone. He considered that the true prerequisite for socialism was the transfiguration of the entire world-view and
entire culture of the working class.

> Socialism demands also new science and
> philosophy. We know that science and philo-
> sophy consist in the consistently organized
> experience of the people as a whole. But pro-
> letarian experience is different from old
> classes, and former knowledge is not sufficient
> for the proletariat. Marx had to lay down
> the basis of a new social science and a new
> historical philosophy. It may be thought that
> all science and all philosophy will obtain
> a new look in the hands of the working class
> because other conditions of life give birth
> to other concepts of perceiving and under-
> standing nature . . .[7]

"The proletariat," Bogdanov also asserted, "needs
its own socialist art, imbued with its own feelings, own desires, own ideals . . ."[8]

> [The proletariat] will make its own new forms
> in all aspects of life: in work, in social
> activity, in the family, in philosophical un-
> derstanding, and in art. In uncompromising
> struggle with the old society, the proletariat
> will increasingly live according to itself
> and will thereby remake all humanity in the
> spirit of socialism.[9]

He further argued that the new culture of the proletariat could be forged only in the uncompromising class
struggle. It was this struggle with a common enemy, according to Bogdanov, that would unite the workers in spirit and
provide the environment for the elaboration of the new working class culture. Thus the continuation and intensification

of the revolutionary struggle against existing society (and
not the amelioration of that struggle) could be the only
passage to socialism. He insisted that revolution is good
not simply because of the goal the revolutionaries want to
attain but because the very process of violent revolution
is an essential part of the final goals.

In this way Bogdanov channeled all his intransigent,
impatient desire for socialist revolution from the realm of
political action to the realm of cultural life. Physical
revolution--in a political, economic, or social sense--was
inconceivable (surely even to an optimist like Bogdanov) in
Russia in 1911. By stressing cultural revolution, Bogdanov
had found an area in which the revolutionaries could still
be active and feel confident that they were in the vanguard
of the revolutionary movement. It seemed to Bogdanov in
those years that the political leadership of the RSDRP had
abandoned the revolution. If socialism were to be achieved,
the intellectuals and artists would have to take up the task
of creating it.

In the same issue of _Vpered_, immediately following
"Socialism in the Present," was an article by Stanislav Volsky on much the same subject. In "On Proletarian Culture"
Volsky presented Bogdanov's thesis in a slightly different
way. Volsky was fully as radical a Bolshevik as Bogdanov,
but he had a more strictly orthodox Marxian point of view.
The crucial point, of course, was the question of material
determinism, and Volsky took the view that existence deter-

mines consciousness.

Thus Volsky was obliged to argue that as long as
capitalism prevails the proletariat cannot fully develop
their unique class culture. Only after they are free to
excercise their labor creatively will the working class be
able to realize true socialist culture. As an orthodox
Marxist, Volsky insisted that proletarian culture could not
arise while the means of production were still in the hands
of the capitalists.[10] Until such a time as the revolution
was completed, Volsky asserted, there could be no thought of
socialist science or socialist philosophy but only proletarian-revolutionary science and philosophy.[11]

It was by using terminology such as this that Volsky
was able to retain the aura of Marxian orthodoxy. He refused to speak of socialism in the present, but Volsky used
the term "proletarian-revolutionary" to signify the same
sort of socialist culture that Bogdanov meant when he said
"proletarian culture." Furthermore, also like Bogdanov,
Volsky was strenuously opposed to any suggestion that socialism could be achieved by any means other than violent struggle and radical change.

In The Philosophy of Struggle, as has been seen,
Volsky asserted that struggle was a creative act in and of
itself. In "On Proletarian Culture," he revealed syndicalist
tendencies; he pointed to the general strike as a particularly effective means of raising revolutionary-proletarian consciousness.[12] And, contradicting Marxian economic determism,

Volsky did not really portray proletarian culture as arising from the working conditions of capitalist production.
He believed that the culture of the proletariat could only
arise from the struggle against capitalism. For Volsky it
is not class consciousness that produces class struggle; it
is the struggle against capitalism that produces class consciousness. He asserted that "Proletarian art, proletarian
science, and proletarian philosophy arise inevitably from
the process of the socialist revolution."[13]

For Volsky, as for Bogdanov, the act of violent
revolution was a kind of magical act without which the new
world could not come into being.

> Struggle with the old order everywhere
> high and low! Struggle with its torture-cham-
> bers, struggle with its misery, struggle with
> its hypocrisies, with its ways of thought,
> with its scientific fetishes, with its philo-
> sophical scarecrows, with its slavish belief
> in God, with its slave-like unbelief in man!
> From this struggle will be born a new man
> tempered and powerful.[14]

The theories of cultural revolution were simply new
guises for the idealistic enthusiasms of revolutionary Bolshevism. Ardently immoderate and uncompromising, both Volsky and Bogdanov believed that socialism could arise only
through the purging fire of the apocalypse.

Soon after the appearance of "Socialism in the Present," Bogdanov published The Cultural Tasks of Our Time, a
much more thorough presentation of his cultural conception
of proletarian revolution. The Cultural Tasks of Our Time
was to the Proletarian Culture movement what What is to be

Done? had been to the Bolsheviks. Bogdanov's work resembled Lenin's in that it was a passionate castigation of the contemporary revolutionary movement and a presentation of the means by which the working class revolution could be hastened. Though its revolutionary spirit equalled that of *What is to be Done?*, its conclusions seemed to contradict Lenin's.

Like Lenin, Bogdanov began by railing against trade unionism and opportunism that he saw subverting the revolutionary movement. But instead of finding the fault to be in the mentality of the working class, Bogdanov blamed opportunism upon the leadership of the Social-Democratic party. Flatly contradicting Lenin's argument, Bogdanov asserted that the revolutionary intelligentsia were fundamentally incapable of escaping their bourgeois ideology. He found not the workers but the revolutionaries to be suffering from a trade union mentality. The solution that Bogdanov offered was a program to help the workers to organize their own proletarian culture and thus establish the foundations of socialism free from the taint of the bourgeois intelligentsia.

The Cultural Tasks of Our Time was a synthesis and a culmination of Bogdanov's thought up to that time. It revealed how his positivist epistemology, Marxian sociology, and revolutionary voluntarism came together in a basically religious view of revolutionary change. He opened the work with a presentation of the basic epistemology of empiriomonism: that language and knowledge have their source in human perception and originate in the process of labor. The

culture that is created by the class of people who possess
the technology of production organizes the labor process and
the society as a whole. This knowledge "directs, regulates,
and controls" all "activity, productivity, and culture."[15]
Thus change in knowledge (or culture, which is the same
thing) must precede change in material economic relationships.

In the past Bogdanov had differed from the God-builders only in his choice of terminology. It is also clear in
The Cultural Tasks of Our Time that his idea of a revolutionary proletarian culture was only a continuation and
further elaboration of the religion of socialism that Gorky
and Lunacharsky had presented four years previously. Bogdanov began his pamphlet by frankly asserting that the role
that religion had played in past societies and the function
that the culture of the proletariat would play in future
socialist society.

Culture, he said, is simply the means by which a
class makes sense out of its world. Culture is the total
organization of the perceptions of all members of a class.
Religion was historically the first form of culture: it
served as an organizing principle for ancient peoples. "Religion organizes the people for the protection of their life-
interests."[16] Cultures based upon belief in the supernatural
were later replaced by cultures that explained reality according to concepts of philosophy and science--but which
were, according to Bogdanov--no less mythical and symbolic

than religion.

The culture that would provide the organizational foundation of socialist society would be the ideology of the working class. And here Bogdanov explicitly asserted that proletarian consciousness must precede not only socialism but the socialist revolution as well. He marvelled at what he called a "curious psychological enigma," namely, that he ". . . could not find in the literature of Marxism a clear expression of the idea that ideology, or spiritual culture, excercises an organizational function in the life of societies, groups, and classes."[17]

Bogdanov asserted that it was illogical of Social-Democratic revolutionaries to attempt to develop class self-consciousness of the Russian working class without first understanding and developing the ideology of the collective. Organizing a workers' revolutionary party would only be a mechanistic, superficial undertaking if the workers' spiritual culture were ignored. ". . . Our conception [of ideology as an organizing force] immediately removes this misunderstanding: to develop class self-consciousness means to organize class force."[18]

Here Bogdanov recognized that an active revolutionary party acts according to the implicit assumption that consciousness can determine existence. Clearly, those Social-Democratic revolutionaries (like Lenin in What is to be Done?) who accepted Karl Kautsky's thesis that socialist consciousness arises out of the bourgeois intelligentsia must believe

that human thought is a cause and not just an effect. Bogdanov took the idealist assumption of revolutionary practice
and developed it to its logical conclusion. He argued that
it is through change of spirit that the working class will
rise up to make its revolution, and it is only after the
development of a purely proletarian culture that socialist
society will arise.

The program that Bogdanov proposed for Social-Democracy was accordingly not political but educational. Since
"culture is the highest means of organization," the energies
of the revolutionaries must be immediately directed toward
the development of proletarian culture.[19] Russian Social-
Democrats should ". . . consistently and systematically
unite the results and methods of contemporary knowledge with
the collective-labor experience of the working class."[20]

The key to the creation of the new culture, Bogdanov
insisted, was the "democratization of science," and the
chief tool for this purpose would be the creation of a "new
encyclopedia." This encyclopedia would not only express
science in popular terms, it would also unite all sciences
into a consistent whole--as they were used by the working
class.

Such a new encyclopedia would function for the working class movement just as the great French Encyclopedia
had served the bourgeoisie in their revolution. Of the
French Encyclopedia, Bogdanov said:

> Henceforth the liberation movement had a firm
> ideological ground: a person, having read

> and understood the "encyclopedia" could confi-
> dently say that he knew his place in nature
> and society, that he knew whence mankind came
> and where it was going, and what each ration-
> al, active human being should do. The answers
> that they gave are not for us, of course--
> after all, each epoch has its own nature--but
> the "encyclopedia" was the crystallization
> of the truth of its times.[21]

But, paradoxically, after making a beginning so obviously based upon voluntarism and idealism, Bogdanov went
on to base the rest of his program upon material determinism. Whereas Lenin had spoken often in orthodox Marxist
terminology and yet founded his practical policies upon
idealist presuppositions, in <u>The Cultural Tasks of Our Time</u>
Bogdanov talked like an idealist and yet advocated policies
that assumed materialism.

Bogdanov gave the revolutionaries only a small role
to play in the creation of the new encyclopedia. Proletarian culture could only arise from the proletariat. The
"alien" intelligentsia, Bogdanov asserted, could aid the
proletariat in matters of political organization (even though
they tended toward opportunism), but they could not lead
the working class culturally. The proletariat alone could
give the new encyclopedia "consistency, wholeness, and a
true class psychology."[22]

Indeed, in an earlier article in <u>Vpered</u>, Bogdanov
had said:

> Thus the working class cannot trust any-
> one in its difficult, great struggle, but
> must evaluate everyone and everything with
> its own mind, with its own general class con-
> sciousness. It can depend on no one save its
> own mass force. This means that the libera-

tion of the workers is the affair of the workers themselves.[23]

The sole task of the revolutionary intelligentsia would be to establish proletarian universities. These would be organized on lines similar to the structure of the party schools that Bogdanov himself had so recently administered. The working class students would be in full control of the universities. The lecturers would be bourgeois intellectuals and specialists in their separate fields, but because the lecturers would teach only those topics demanded by the students, the entire tone and content of the curriculum would be determined by working class interests. By requiring the teachers to answer their questions, the proletariat would give its own point of view to the factual content of the courses. Though the factual data would come from bourgeois scientific knowledge, it would be organized and focused by working class experience. It would be this proletarian reorganization of bourgeois knowledge that would provide the content for the new encyclopedia. The new encyclopedia would be written by the students of the proletarian universities.

This democratization of science was only the first element of Bogdanov's program for proletarian culture. Art would also play an important role. Bogdanov understood art to be a powerful force in organizing and developing proletarian consciousness.

> . . . The universal meaning of art—its cultural task—constitutes the same social spirit as knowledge and speech. It organizes and

> unifies collectives of various levels and types
> by means of uniting human experience and by
> giving form to the experience and feelings of
> people.[24]

It was unclear exactly where Bogdanov thought the
source of proletarian art would be. He suggested no program for training workers to be artists, though he did assert that the new encyclopedia and the proletarian universities would aid in the artistic development of the working
class. Bogdanov's emphasis, however, was upon the spontaneity of proletarian art.

> Without a doubt the new university and
> the new encyclopedia will aid in the devel-
> opment of proletarian art. But only the im-
> mediate life of the collective can give birth
> to it--a collective in which is concentrated
> richly gifted artistic natures. Its ties
> will become more close and harmonious, its
> magnetic energy will grow. In the realm of
> art [the proletariat] will also achieve mag-
> nificent victories over the old society, the
> creative powers of which have withered.[25]

Here in Bogdanov's revolutionary program can be seen
the same idealist attitudes toward art that Lunacharsky expressed in his esthetics and that Gorky tried to manifest
in his own artistic work. Once again one of the millenarian
Bolsheviks helped to establish the fundamental principles of
Socialist Realism.

> All social norms of proletariat culture lead,
> in the final analysis, to the principle of
> comradely solidarity. The new art makes its
> hero not an individual but a collective or
> a person in a collective. The subject of
> knowledge, the carrier of truth is here not
> individuality but the collective, and the
> criterion of truth is in its [collective]
> practical life.[26]

Bogdanov concluded his proposed program by leaving

no doubt but that the transformation of spiritual culture was the primary prerequisite of socialism. He had earlier argued that revolutions cannot be moments of direct creation of new techniques and new ideology; he believed that both had to be already developed by the "productively advanced class." "Culture," said Bogdanov, "is the highest means of organization."[27]

In The Cultural Tasks of Our Time, Bogdanov had revealed a basic contradiction that had plagued his writing from the very beginning. It was the same paradox that is evident in Lenin's thought as well as in the attitudes of all Marxists who wish to actively influence the course of history. At the turn of the twentieth century, Berdiaev had pointed out that the desire for socialism was an ethical choice and not simply confidence deriving from scientific proof that socialism would inevitably arise. Berdiaev admitted that if he had to choose between his own ideals and the desires expressed by the working class, he would follow his own conscience. Lenin implicitly supported Berdiaev's conclusions in What is to be Done? when he affirmed his own socialist consciousness over the trade union mentality of Russian workers.

Bogdanov's development since his first arguments with Berdiaev had been complex. He was a firm supporter of Lenin's organizational program for Social-Democracy, and so he must have shared Lenin's idealism emotionally if not intellectually. Nevertheless, alone of all the left Bolsheviks,

Bogdanov had always stressed the spontaneously revolutionary nature of the working class. He had not accepted Lenin's
assertion that the proletariat could not rise above trade
unionism without the aid of socialist intellectuals. During
the controversy over otzovism, Bogdanov had consistently
demanded that the question be voted on by the rank and file
of the faction. During the years of severest reaction following the 1905 Revolution, he optimistically continued to
call for armed proletarian insurrection. In his theory of
the party schools, he insisted that the working class students should have the right to elect their teachers and
choose the subjects for study. As the leader of the <u>Vpered</u>
Group, Bogdanov also repeatedly asserted that the working
class was far more radical than was the leadership of the
RSDRP. And, of course, in <u>The Cultural Tasks of Our Time</u>,
Bogdanov expressed a faith in the working class worthy of
a true believer in Marxian economic determinism.

Yet from the very beginning, Bogdanov had consistently argued against the principles of economic determinism.
We have seen how his initial espousal of positivist epistemology logically led him to revise the basic materialist
propositions of Marxism and to assert that human thought is
the basis of reality and that the development of human thought
is the basis of history. Bogdanov's life work had been to
create a system of idealist determinism in which human consciousness was the motive force but whose development operated according to certain objective laws and whose process

was inevitably directed toward socialism. By 1913 Bogdanov
had largely completed his system.

In The Cultural Tasks of Our Time, Bogdanov had
focused upon the role that the intelligentsia revolutionaries should play in developing proletarian culture and in
justifying his conception of proletarian culture as the
organizing force of the socialist revolutionary movement.
But he did not deal with the "objective" foundations of
human society that made his Proletarian Culture movement--
and, of course, the socialist revolution that it would usher
in--inevitable. This explanation Bogdanov presented in two
works written soon after, The Science of Social Consciousness and The Philosophy of Living Experience.

The Science of Social Consciousness was subtitled
"A Short Course of Ideological Science in Questions and Answers." Bogdanov proposed to answer the questions: "What
exactly is the social consciousness of a people, where does
it originate, what forms does it take, how has it developed
in the history of mankind, where is this development now
heading."[28]

He began with Marx. The theory of ideology had
begun when,

> Fifty four years ago Marx formulated the basic
> law of the development of ideas, laws, moral-
> ity, politics--in general all social conscious-
> ness and ideologies. They are dependent upon
> the means of production and distribution.
> From this law issues the general path of [my]
> investigation.[29]

But Bogdanov did not introduce Marx in order to agree

with him. He hastened to point out that ideology can not
be considered to be merely a superstructure; he argued that
ideology is an integral part of the process of economic
production. The entire ideology of a class, argued Bogdanov,
and including such seemingly abstract aspects of culture as
art and morality, is an essential element in social labor
and economy "without which they could not exist."[30]

Reiterating his earlier arguments that proletarian
culture must be an essential element in social change, Bogdanov insisted that ideology is the "means of organizing
society, production, classes, and in general all social
forces or elements--the means without which this organization is impossible."[31] The objective of his book, Bogdanov
claimed (thereby implicitly contradicting the very "objectivity" of the process he was attempting to describe) was
to impart to the Russian working class the understanding of
the science and history of ideology that they needed in
order to create a new socialist ideology for their class.

The main part of The Science of Social Consciousness
was a history of ideology. Bogdanov took Marx's three major
divisions of economic history (tribal, feudal, and capitalist) and showed how their particular cultures (as manifested
in philosophy, religion, science, art, myth, etc.) served
as a system of organizing principles according to which each
social system's economic and political relations were formed.
Thus human history had progressed according to the development of human consciousness.

In conclusion, Bogdanov summarized his ideas of
what the culture of the future, the "Ideology of Collectiv-
ism," would be like. He argued that the collectivist ideology
would arise from the scientific technology of machine production. In the vein of left Bolshevik millenialism, he did
not restrict his discussion to only the coming proletarian
revolution or the building of socialist society. He promised that the working class would assert a God-like mastery
over the natural world. Bogdanov predicted ". . . the con-
scious-organizational unification of all human forces for
the struggle with nature and the unending development of the
power of labor over it."[32]

It was, however, Bogdanov's second major work of
1913, The Philosophy of Living Experience, in which he most
clearly expressed both the objective-determinist basis and
the God-building potential of Proletarian Culture. The book
was sub-titled "Popular Outlines," and it was largely a re-
capitulation in popular language of Bogdanov's philosophical
principles of Empiriomonism.

The basis of this philosophy was, of course, a strict
empirical theory of knowledge which rejected the possibility
of any sort of ontology (whether material or ideal) and which
refused to admit the possibility of any absolute, objective
natural laws.

> Upon this basis one rejects not only a mater-
> ialist foundation and, in general, the idea
> of "substance" in all its aspects but also
> the principle of causation. Any relationship
> in experience can be expressed as a function-
> al dependence of one piece of data on another.

. . . The idea of causality is no more than a false hypothesis.[33]

Bogdanov held that the source of knowledge--and hence the essence of reality, since there could be no reality other than knowledge--resided exclusively in the perceptions of human experience. The human mind organizes its experience in order to make sense out of it. This organization, in turn, enables men to act successfully in the real world. It is in this activity that the validity of hypotheses can be tested.

> Contemporary empiricism strives to be solely a philosophy of experience, critically verified, liberated from all additions, inventions, and distortions. It seeks its scientific foundation in the methods of the most up-to-date natural sciences. The social foundation of this philosophy is formed by the conditions of the labor life of intellectual-technological personnel of heavy industry and scientific enterprises.[34]

His last sentence here reveals the crucial role that labor played in Bogdanov's system. He insisted that labor was the primary source of experience (of activity in the natural world) and hence the true origin of knowledge. In the very beginning of the human species, both language and thought originated in the process of labor.

> In the first phase [of human history] were born the very elements of thought: from the cries of labor--involuntary sounds accompanying the various acts of collective labor--there developed words, concepts which served as the designations of those acts. Subsequently, having stood apart from the process of labor, they become complicated and perfected according to the practical necessities of life.[35]

Bogdanov argued that knowledge that results from

labor is a collective creation that serves all the members
of the society.

> Social existence and social consciousness
> are the same since the social struggle is direct-
> ed toward a fixed goal. In production, in
> communication . . . , in law, in morality,
> man acts to attain the same end. Such activity
> represents effort. Hence, the social process
> is a process of work. Every social phenomenon
> is a form of toil and nearly all labor is
> social. Work is social when it contributes
> to the survival of the social organism.
> Society, as a whole, is a system of cooper-
> ation in the widest meaning of the word.[36]

Bogdanov added, however, that historically the technology of labor has always been possessed by a single class,
and that class had always used its possession of knowledge
to rule and oppress the laboring classes. The course of
historical development has thus been the rise and fall of
technological-ideological systems and the classes that developed them. The victorious class has always been the
class that had possession of the technology of the next
stage of economic development.

It was crucial to Bogdanov's ultimate teleology that
the source of human knowledge be in the process of labor.
By associating thought and labor, Bogdanov could still follow Marx's stages of economic development. But instead of
relating each economic stage to a particular material foundation, Bogdanov related it to a particular world-view. Thus
the bourgeoisie overthrew feudalism because it possessed
the scientific knowledge and the labor technology that could
create an economic system more viable than that of feudalism.
Similarly, the working class would ultimately displace the

owners of capital because it would create a more viable
labor technology.

Thus, in Bogdanov's view, socialism would not arise
when the working class seized the means of production. Instead, it would seize the means of production only after it
had attained its own unique understanding of reality, mastered the technology of the future, and created a class culture that embodied its new knowledge in a consistent world-
view.

What makes the working class unique of all previous
social classes, in Bogdanov's understanding, was that it is
bringing human knowledge to its ultimate perfection. The
proletariat would undertake the last social revolution because it would attain universal knowledge. Bogdanov asserted that the principal obstacle in the path of such universal
knowledge was the fragmentation of knowledge among the many
disciplines of science. Because of bourgeois individualism,
each field was so specialized that scientists of different
fields were unable to communicate with one another. He said
that "It is just in our time that the final type of special-
ization has arisen, a man with narrow, one-sided experience,
routine methods, and a total lack of understanding of nature
or of life as a whole . . ."[37]

The difficulties tending to prevent the unification
of human knowledge include the mammoth quantity of factual
data and the fact that each discipline of knowledge had to
create its own method of organizing and understanding its

data. "Philosophy--not as the study of department specialists but as the real generalization of experience--would in
the end become absolutely impossible if new forces of life
were not to bring about a turn in the direction of development."[38] This is the obstacle which bourgeois individualist
culture cannot surmount and which sounds the death-knell of
capitalism.

The working class will accomplish this unification
of knowledge. Bogdanov asserted that "The starting point of
this transformation lies in labor practice and specifically
in machine production."[39] He argued that machine production would contribute to the organization and unification of
all the sciences because such production involves all the
sciences in its construction and process of operation.

Machine production involves chemistry, physics,
mathematics, and biology. As machines become more developed,
workers will cease to be purely menial laborers and become
machine operators. They must excercise "observation, judgement, and consideration." Simple administrative labor will
be replaced by "the organizing labor of educated specialist-
engineers." Ultimately all workers will be engineers, and
as they come to understand the totality of the equipment
and machinery which they operate in their work, they will
synthesize and organize the sciences upon which the technology is based.[40]

> We have seen that the progress of machine
> production makes workers' activity a continually
> more fully and clearly expressed organizational
> character. This is completely in harmony with

the historical task of the class as a whole:
the _organizational_ task of unprecedented breadth
and complication. The resolution [of this
task] cannot be accidental or anarchical but
must be systematic and scientific. And this
presupposes the unification of all organizational experience into a special _general science of organization_. Such a science must
be universal.[41]

More explicitly than ever before, Bogdanov empha-

sized the reality of human thought over the reality of the

external world. In mastering knowledge, the working class

will also master the forces of nature. Thus the proletariat

was not preparing only to create a new culture or social

system--it was on the threshold of mastering the natural

universe.

. . . [The universal science] must observe
and neatly systematize all those means and
devices of organization which are _factually_
applied in society, in life, and in nature.
The regularity which will be found and proven
will give universal leadership for the mastering of the totality of the forces of nature
and of the totality of the facts of experience.[42]

Thus the whole spirit of Bogdanov's philosophy was

identical with the optimism that the God-builders had ex-

pressed when they asserted that humankind had the ability to

create a new world.

The highest stage on the ladder is, for
us, the human _collective_; in our time it is
already a many-millioned system composed of
individuals. In labor and in knowledge humankind creates its own "reality"--its own objective reality with its own strict orderliness
and its systematic organization. The practical activity of the great social organism is
none other than _world-building_ . . .[43]

Bogdanov had never been an explicit proponent of God-

building, but he had written its fundamental philosophy.

When Gorky and Lunacharsky had expressed their belief that
socialism was a religion, they depended upon Bogdanov's empiriomonism for their concepts, terminology, and basic philosophy. When Gorky and Lunacharsky had written about the
religious essence of the coming socialist world, they stressed humanity's unlimited power of creativity--its ability to
create reality through its will. What made the proletariat
God-like in the eyes of the God-builders was its power to
transform the real world into a paradise.

It was just such an all-creative power that Bogdanov
attributed to the proletariat in The Philosophy of Living
Experience. Though Bogdanov did not use the word "God," his
vision of humanity possessed all the attributes of God: the
power to create and recreate the universe. Bogdanov's term
of "world-building" echoed Gorky's "God-building." Bogdanov
attempted to evoke the same spirit that had infused The Confession.

> Philosophy is living out its last days.
> Empiriomonism is already not wholly philosophy,
> but rather a transitional form because it knows
> where it is going and to what it will yield
> its place. The foundations of the new, univer-
> sal science will be established in the near
> future, it will blossom up from that gigantic,
> feverish organizational labor which will create
> a new society and which will conclude the agon-
> izing prologue to the history of mankind. That
> time is not far off . . .[44]

At this point the socialist revolution pales greatly
in significance; the revolution will only be a side effect
in the progress of the working class toward control over the
very universe.

Though Bogdanov's following in the RSDRP was virtually non-existent in 1913, his program for Proletarian
Culture was not ignored entirely. A branch of the _Vpered_
Group was temporarily revived in Geneva from 1915-1917.
Lunacharsky was associated with this circle, but it was led
another former left Bolshevik, Lebedev-Poliansky. Though
it is doubtful that he maintained contact with Bogdanov
during those years, he had supported Bogdanov in the break-
up of the _Vpered_ Group in 1911. Under Lebedev-Poliansky's
leadership, the Geneva group adopted Bogdanov's cultural
program.

In the first issue of its journal, _Vpered_, in 1915,
the group announced that "The idea of proletarian culture
has become the distinguishing characteristic of Vperedism."[45]
It asserted that the crisis that the world war had introduced into international socialism was due to "defects in
the scientific-socialist education of the working class."
And it claimed that opportunism was caused by "the reign of
bourgeois-elaborated forms of thought over proletarian experience."[46] The solution that _Vpered_ offered was to help the
proletariat to develop its own culture free from the corrup-
tions of bourgeois ideology.

Following the principles of _The Cultural Tasks of
Our Time_, the Geneva group focused upon the education of the
working class.

> In general and as a whole, the proletariat
> has done very little for the establishment of
> schools. It must fight for [schools] even

> more than it fights to arm itself. Coopera-
> tives and syndicates must give the lion's
> share of their income for the organization
> of socialist schools of all levels. Party
> higher schools and scientific organs will
> crown this system. Besides schools and clubs,
> a huge educational role must be played by a
> wide network of ideological clubs.. . .[47]

The groundwork was already being laid for the rise of the

organization of the Proletkult in 1917.

During these same years, Bogdanov's closest comrade

also began to be fired with the enthusiasms of Proletarian

Culture. Lunacharsky led a "Proletarian Culture Circle" in

Paris from 1911 to 1915. The circle was principally liter-

ary in orientation and was probably focused more toward

helping proletarians to become creative writers than toward

developing a consistent working class culture. Lunacharsky's

group included such prominent proletarian writers of the

future as Bessalko, Gerasimov, and Gastev. F. I. Kalinin

was also a member of the circle.[48]

In 1915 Lunacharsky moved to Geneva. It is not known

if he became an official member of the Geneva circle of the

Vpered Group mentioned above, but he was certainly close to

its members. Since that group did not arise until Lunachar-

sky moved to Geneva, it is possible that he had a hand in

its creation. It may also have been more than coincidence

that the Geneva group promoted the same Proletarian Culture

movement that Lunacharsky had been involved in.

Of the writings that Lunacharsky published during

these years that are now available few concern Proletarian

Culture. As far back as 1907 he had written an article,
"The Task of Social-Democratic Artistic Works," for <u>Vestnik
Zhizni</u>. In it Lunacharsky foreshadowed many of the themes
that would later become prominent in the Proletarian Culture
movement. Typically, he associated the culture of the working class with religion.

> I insist that Social-Democratic creative writing
> must exist and will exist and <u>already</u> has its
> role to play. It will not be <u>proper</u> to talk
> of party art , however, for Social-Democracy
> is not simply a party but a great cultural move-
> ment. It is actually the greatest of all [cul-
> tural movements] that have ever been. Only
> mighty religious movements can so much as be
> compared with it. After all, no one laughs
> when one speaks of Christian art.[49]

However, Lunacharsky's conception was of an agitational rather than an organizational art. He saw art not
so much contributing toward the creation of an entirely new
culture as much as simply inspiring the working class to
struggle for socialism. The goals of Social-Democratic art,
as Lunacharsky presented them, were to portray the evils of
the present world, glorify the struggle against that evil,
and to depict the paradise of socialism that lies in the
future.

Furthermore, Lunacharsky was not as pure a populist
as was Bogdanov. Bogdanov expected the proletariat to produce its own culture while Lunacharsky stressed the importance of the revolutionary intelligentsia. He said that,
". . . the creators of this art will [not] be exclusively
physical laborers. For the most part all classes recruit
their ideologues from the intellectual proletariat—that

curious product of the disintegration of the petty bourgeoisie."[50]

Lunacharsky's other extant writings on cultural matters and proletarian art from the period between the Bolshevik schism and the 1917 Revolution were principally studies
and reviews of socialist literature in Western Europe. It
was only after the February Revolution that Lunacharsky
began to contribute significantly to the literature of the
Proletarian Culture movement.

Thus, before the world war broke out, Bogdanov had
already established the theoretical foundations of the future
Proletkult, and a number of left Bolsheviks had adopted his
revolutionary program. Then, between 1913 and 1917, Bogdanov was silent. He had returned to Russia after his political
failures in the emigre RSDRP. Bogdanov was a physician
(he had earned his medical degree in 1899), and early in the
war he was drafted into the army to serve as a doctor at the
front. It was only after the February Revolution that Bogdanov made his way to Petrograd and became a part of the
revolutionary movement again.

NOTES TO CHAPTER VII

[1]Religiia i sotsializm, p. 14.

[2]Ostroukhova, p. 214.

[3]A. Bogdanov, "Sotsializm v nastoiashchem," Vpered, no. 2 (1911), p. 62.

[4]Ibid., p. 63.

[5]Ibid.

[6]Ibid., p. 68.

[7]Ibid., p. 70.

[8]Ibid.

[9]Ibid., p. 71.

[10]S. Vol'skii, "O proletarskoi kul'ture," Vpered, no. 2 (1911), p. 73.

[11]Ibid., p. 81.

[12]Ibid., p. 75.

[13]Ibid., p. 82.

[14]Ibid.

[15]A. Bogdanov, Kul'turnye zadachi nashego vremeni (Moscow: Izdanie S. Dorovatovskago i A. Charushnikova, 1911), p. 14.

[16]Ibid., p. 13.

[17]Ibid., p. 44.

[18]Ibid., p. 45.

[19]Ibid., p. 97.

[20]Ibid., p. 68.

[21]Ibid., p. 58.

[22]Ibid.,pp. 69.

[23]A. Bogdanov, "Proletariat v vor'be za sotsializm," Vpered, no. 1 (1910), p. 5.

[24]Kul'turnye zadachi nashego vremeni, pp. 17-18.

[25]Ibid., p. 80.

[26]Ibid., p. 91.

[27]Ibid., p. 92.

[28]A. Bogdanov, Nauka ob obshchestvennoi soznanii (Moscow: Knigoizdatel'stvo Pisatelei v Moskve, n.d.), p. 5.

[29]Ibid.

[30]Ibid., p. 6.

[31]Ibid., p. 7.

[32]Ibid., p. 199.

[33]A. Bogdanov, Filosofiia zhivogo opyta (St. Petersburg: Izdanie M. I. Semenova, n.d.), p. 177.

[34]Ibid., p. 176.

[35]Ibid., p. 32.

[36]Ibid., p. 291.

[37]Ibid., p. 260.

[38]Ibid., p. 265.

[39]Ibid.

[40]Ibid.

[41]Ibid., p. 267.

[42]Ibid., pp. 268-69.

[43]Ibid., p. 256.

[44]Ibid., pp. 271-72.

[45]N. Voitynskii, "O gruppe 'Vpered,'" Proletarskaia Revoliutsiia, no. 12 (1929), p. 78.

[46]Ibid., p. 78.

[47]Ibid.

[48]Velikii perevorot, p. 51.

[49]A. V. Lunacharskii, Sobranie sochinenii: kritika
estetika, literaturovedenie, 7 vols. (Moscow: "Khudozhest-
vennaia Literatura," 1967), vol. 7, pp. 154-55.

[50]Ibid., p. 155.

CHAPTER VIII

PROLETARIAN CULTURE AND EARLY SOVIET SOCIETY

Proletarian Culture on the Eve of the October Revolution.

After the February Revolution of 1917, as revolutionary optimism and enthusiasm were being rekindled among
Russia's professional revolutionaries, the left Bolsheviks
again joined together to advance their revolutionary program. No one valued the periodical press as a means of political influence more highly than did the Bolshevik millenarians. Their literary and polemical talents had already allowed them to excercise an influence within the Social-Democratic movement far out of proportion to their numbers.
It was natural, therefore, that when the revolutionary wave
once again began to rise the former Vperedists coalesced
around a journal. In 1917 they were too few in numbers and
too poor in resources to publish an organ of their own, so
they had to seek an alliance with another group. The journal that they found most hospitable belonged to their old
friend, Maksim Gorky.

Gorky established Novaia Zhizn' two months after the
February Revolution. It drew its editors and contributors
principally from Letopis'--yet another of Gorky's publications. Founded in 1915, Letopis' had been primarily a literary endeavor; it published the works of the most important

314

Russian writers of the period. To the extent that its contributors had a political orientation, they were united in
their opposition to imperialism, war, and chauvinism.

After February, 1917, Gorky felt it necessary to
supplement the monthly Letopis' with a daily commentary
upon social and political questions; such was to be the task
of Novaia Zhizn'. N. Sukhanov was named the editor-in-
chief, and the main contingent of editors and contributors
were left Mensheviks. It was this group of Social-Democrats
at Novaia Zhizn' which formed the nucleus of the "Organization of Left Social-Democratic Internationalists,"--a radical Menshevik organization that cooperated with the Bolshevik government after October.

A second (and very small) group within Novaia Zhizn'
was composed of the former God-builders and culture-oriented
members of the Vpered Group. Included were Bogdanov, Lunacharsky, Lebedev-Poliansky, and Kalinin. (There were also
two writers who fit partially into both camps. Volsky and
Bazarov had been God-builders but now were left Mensheviks.)
The two groups kept aloof from one another. The Mensheviks
were sufficiently tolerant to accept the former left Bolsheviks, but the latter were not very comfortable associating
with so timid a revolutionary party as Menshevism.

Lunacharsky had been a contributor to both of Gorky's
journals from abroad and continued to write for Novaia Zhizn'
after he returned to Russia in May. Novaia Zhizn' was not
radical enough for him, however, and he prefaced his first

article published after his arrival in Russia by announcing
that he did not agree with the editorial stance of the
journal and would be responsible only for articles signed by
himself. Despite this air of radical condescension, Gorky
made Lunacharsky the head of the "cultural-socialist" division of Novaia Zhizn'.[1]

In 1917 Gorky was calling for the amelioration of
the class struggle and a shift of emphasis from political to
cultural activity.[2] Lunacharsky and Bogdanov, of course,
were also concerned with cultural matters to the exclusion
of all else, but their point of view could not have been
more dissimilar from Gorky's. Their emphasis on culture was
intended to intensify and not diminish the class struggle.
In their conception of the coming revolution, a purely proletarian culture would sharply delineate itself from the old
bourgeois culture and would serve as the leading force in
destroying that culture and the economic and social system
for which it was the foundation. Gorky, on the other hand,
was more interested in creating an environment in which literature and the arts could thrive regardless of the political attitudes or social origins of the artists. Gorky's
notion of culture was completely non-partisan and apolitical;
he wanted to preserve the cultural heritage of the past and
build upon it.

Thus the principal reason why the advocates of Proletarian Culture were anxious to collaborate with the editors
of Novaia Zhizn' was simply because there was no other publi-

cation in which they could disseminate their ideas. Their
thinking had already been pronounced unacceptable by Lenin,
so there would be no room for them to elaborate upon Proletarian Culture in the pages of Bolshevik journals. However,
no other Russian journal would have been politically radical enough to wish to associate with Bogdanov and Lunacharsky. Thus they and their Proletarian Culture comrades had
to adapt themselves to the most politically amenable group
and await the time when they would have the means to publish
a journal of their own. It was probably their personal
friendship with Gorky rather than philosophical or political
compatibility that allowed them to publish their work in
Novaia Zhizn'.

It was thus on the pages of Novaia Zhizn' that Lunacharsky and Bogdanov began to popularize their ideas of Proletarian Culture in the spring of 1917. At this time Lunacharsky first began to reveal a full and complete acceptance of
Bogdanov's assertion that cultural revolution was the prerequisite for socialist revolution. In the preceding five
years, Lunacharsky had written little on working class culture or on religion and socialism; his work had been principally devoted to analyses of Western European culture. His
interest in proletarian art had been limited to its inspirational or agitational function: he saw it as manifesting
the holy ideals of socialism and helping to stimulate revolutionary activity. By the spring of 1917, however, Lunacharsky had come to accept Bogdanov's conclusion that prole-

tarian art--and its culture in general--would be an organizing force that would provide the foundation for socialist
society.

Furthermore, Lunacharsky saw in Proletarian Culture
those same religious elements that he had discovered in the
revolutionary socialist movement a decade previously. In
June, 1917, he published "The Cultural Tasks of the Working
Class" in Novaia Zhizn'. In it Lunacharsky drew an extended
analogy between the culture of the proletariat and the spirit
of the Christian church.

> The famous theologian, Foma Akvinsky, vividly
> and clearly drew a picture of the similarities
> and differences between the victorious church,
> a community of the holy and blessed, and the
> fighting church, an assembly of martyrs and
> evangelists.
> The first, Ecclesia triumphans, is entirely
> infused with the spirit of victory, peace,
> concord and blessedness. Ecclesia militans,
> on the other hand, is preoccupied with ordeals,
> political defeats, and the zeal for suffering.
> . . . [In the first case] all hopes have been
> realized; [in the second] all is seen as if
> in a crystal ball. On one hand success is
> manifest; on the other hand there is only
> faith and hope.
> Such a division is not relevant only to
> the church in the Christian understanding of
> it. [The division] is inherent in any move-
> ment that proceeds beneath the banner of an
> ideal . . . The socialist culture of the
> future will be an all-human, classless cul-
> ture--a classical culture--in which content,
> established and developed through a healthy
> organic process, achieves a fully appropriate
> form.
> The culture of the struggling proletariat
> is a sharply aloof class culture oriented to-
> ward struggle. It is a romantic culture in
> which content . . . outstrips its form, for
> there is no time to worry about a sufficient-
> ly accurate and true form for that stormy and
> tragic content.[3]

Recalling his enthusiasm of the period of the 1905
Revolution, Lunacharsky once again portrayed the working
class revolution as a "movement that goes forth under the
banner of an ideal." He emphasized struggle and glorified
the militancy of the socialist martyrs and evangelists.
This fighting spirit (reminiscent of the the left Bolsheviks
in 1905) had not been emphasized in Bogdanov's works on
Proletarian Culture, but it soon became a distinguishing
characteristic of the Proletarian Culture movement.

In this enthusiasm, Lunacharsky was a bellwether for
the revolutionary socialist movement in Russia in 1917. Both
the working class and the Bolshevik faction developed a sudden interest in culture. On the part of the workers, their
interest in culture was manifested principally in a spontaneous interest in education and knowledge of their world.
The February Revolution engendered an elemental surge of interest in education. As John Reed reported:

> All Russia was learning to read and read-
> ing--politics, economics, history--because
> the people wanted to know . . . In every city,
> in most towns, along the Front, each political
> faction had its newspaper--sometimes several.
> Hundreds of thousands of pamphlets were dis-
> tributed by thousands of organizations, and
> poured into the army, the villages, the fac-
> tories, the streets. The thirst for education,
> so long thwarted, burst with the Revolution
> in a frenzy of expression. . . . Russia ab-
> sorbed reading matter like hot sand drinking
> water, insatiable. And it was not fables,
> falsified history, diluted religion, and the
> cheap fiction that corrupts--but social and
> economic theories, philosophy, the works of
> Tolstoy, Gogol, and Gorky . . .[4]

Russians wanted to learn, and it was this desire that

provided a hospitable environment for Bogdanov's Proletarian Culture movement to grow and flourish. No matter that the Russian people were motivated only by a straightforward desire to learn to read and to study science, history, politics, and literature. The workers who flocked to study circles and reading clubs had no notion themselves of creating so grandiose a thing as a working class culture or proletarian world-view. But those revolutionary activists who believed in Proletarian Culture as the principal path toward socialism and who set out to organize workers' schools and cultural clubs were overwhelmed by the response. It must have seemed to them to prove their assumptions about the vital role of culture in the revolutionary movement.

But the former God-builders and Vperedists were not the only revolutionaries to be interested in the popular movement for education and culture. The Bolshevik faction perceived very early that the cultural enthusiasm among the workers might easily be converted into a political force. They created cultural organizations in order to mobilize and enlist the workers into the revolutionary movement. At first the Bolsheviks did not want to educate the workers as much as direct their energies into political channels. A Soviet scholar has suggested that "Creating . . . a network of workers' cultural-educational organizations was one of the canals which the Bolsheviks used for the formation of the political army of the revolution."[5]

There is no doubt that the Bolsheviks were leaders

in the cultural organization of the working class. As early
as March 6, 1917, the Petrograd Committee of the RSDRP resolved to establish regional and local organizations of
workers' cultural clubs.[6] They were not the only revolutionary party involved, however, as the spring of 1917 saw a
proliferation of similar cultural organizations under the
auspices of such institutions as the Petrograd Soviet, regional dumas, and factory and plant workers' committees.[7]

Nevertheless, the enthusiasm for cultural organization on the part of the Bolshevik faction was far more than
just a political tactic, a means of simply attracting workers
into the revolutionary movement. Lunacharsky's enthusiasm
for working class culture was soon reflected by more practical, political Bolsheviks. The May 7, 1917 issue of Pravda
announced that,

> The proletariat--that titan of all revolutions
> and builder of mankind's glorious future--
> must have its own powerful art, its own poets
> and painters. The full blossoming of prole-
> tarian art will be attained, of course, only
> in a socialist system. But now already . . .
> the spark of free art must flame up into a
> bright fire. This the moment demands; this
> the revolution demands. We call all poets,
> writers, and painters to gather together under
> the publication of "Priboi" in the "Circle of
> Proletarian Art."[8]

However, the Bolshevik faction never went as far as
Bogdanov had in their estimation of the power of cultural
revolution. As orthodox Marxists, they continued to stress
the economic preconditions of socialism, and as practical
activists, they focused their energies toward the seizure of
political power. Though the Bolsheviks understood the value

of harnessing the educational-cultural aspirations of the
working class, few leading Bolsheviks were willing to become active in organizing them. This lack of interest at
the leadership level of the Bolshevik faction allowed the
workers' cultural movement in 1917 to be taken over by the
millenarian Bolsheviks.

It was Lunacharsky who assumed the leadership of the
Proletarian Culture movement in Petrograd in 1917. Lunachar-
sky--along with all the former members of the Vpered Group
(excepting only Aleksinsky and Bogdanov)--had rejoined the
Bolshevik faction soon after Lenin's "April Theses" signified that Bolshevism was making a turn toward radicalism
once again. Nevertheless, Lunacharsky's political involvement in the faction was quite marginal. Though he was welcomed back into the Bolshevik faction with open arms, he was
never again allowed to ascend to its policy-making circles.
Lenin was personally very fond of Lunacharsky but questioned
his political judgement.

It was probably for this reason that Lunacharsky's
cultural activities were not just permitted but encouraged.
It gave him something to occupy his energies and keep him
out of political mischief. It also solved the problem of
who would be in charge of organizing the cultural movement;
that occupation appealed to few Bolsheviks. (After the Bolsheviks attained political power in October, they had a similar difficulty in filling the Commissariat of Enlightenment
with administrators, and this allowed Lunacharsky and his

comrades in the Proletarian Culture movement to take control over that institution.)

Lunacharsky had returned to Russia in the second "sealed train" to cross Germany after Lenin's. He arrived in Petrograd in May and immediately flung himself into revolutionary-cultural activity. He served as the head of the cultural-educational section of the Petrograd City Duma until he was arrested in July in connection with the July uprising. Then, following his release from prison in September, Lunacharsky was elected chairman of the Cultural-Educational Commission of the Petrograd Committee of the Bolshevik faction.[9] This commission had a significant membership; it included Kalinin, Lebedev-Poliansky, Kerzhentsev, and Menzhinsky—all of them former members of the Vpered Group.[10]

Lunacharsky wasted no time in beginning to organize Russia's multitude of cultural clubs and study circles into a hierarchical network. On September 10, he opened the first meeting of the Cultural-Educational Commission, and only days later he summoned the first Petrograd Conference of Proletarian Cultural-Educational Organizations. It was no simple Bolshevik gathering. It was composed of 208 delegates from the Petrograd Soviet, factory and plant committees, town and regional dumas, soldiers' committees, peasant organizations, the Socialist-Revolutionary Party, as well as delegates from the Bolsheviks' own cultural organizations.

The conference was convened from October 16 to 19—less than a week before the October Revolution.[11] The mili-

tant spirit of the working class cultural movement was revealed in its resolution that ". . . the cultural-educational movement of the proletariat must be suffused with the militant spirit of socialism and its goal must be to arm the
workers with knowledge, to organize its feelings with the
help of art, and to strengthen it in its titanic struggle
for a new social system."[12]

However, the spirit that was being mobilized under
the official auspices of the Bolshevik faction was being
channelled along quite unorthodox lines. As was signified
by the composition of the Bolshevik Cultural-Educational Commission, the revolutionary working class culture movement
was dominated by those former Vperedists who were dedicated
to Bogdanov's program of Proletarian Culture. Kalinin and
Lebedev-Poliansky, like Lunacharsky, had rejoined the Bolshevik faction immediately after they returned to Russia,
and both were active members of the Commission that Lunacharsky led.

If the Bolshevik leadership was glad to see these
former "Godly-otzovists" (as Lenin had once termed them),
they were soon to have a rude awakening. The former Bolshevik schismatics soon demonstrated the same independence of
thought that had caused their first break with Lenin. Not
two years would go by before Lenin suddenly realized that a
nationwide network of workers' organizations had sprung up--
all following policies that bore a strong resemblance to God-
building. The Bolsheviks ultimately found it necessary to

suppress the cultural movement that they had encouraged
Lunacharsky and his friends to promote during the summer of
1917.

Of course, the key figure in the growth of the independent revolutionary cultural movement and the cause of its
eventual clash with Bolshevism was the author of the Proletarian Culture program. Bogdanov had not rejoined the Bolshevik faction. After the February Revolution, he made his
way to Moscow. He was in Moscow at the same time that Lunacharsky was organizing the cultural-educational conferences
in Petrograd, and Bogdanov was involved in exactly the same
thing.

However, Bogdanov's cultural organization was an
independent movement from the very beginning; he would have
nothing to do with the Bolshevik faction or the Soviet Government. Bogdanov's organization was known simply as the
Proletkult, and its more modest members considered the cultural movement to be one of several independent aspects of
the struggle for socialism. Bogdanov, however, thought dif-
ferently; he had always placed culture over politics, and he
believed his movement to be the primary force of the proletarian revolution.

Bogdanov's first Moscow conference of cultural organizations was held in December, 1917, two months later than
the one Lunacharsky had convened in Petrograd. The Moscow
conference was composed of 288 delegates, and they were more
purely of working class origin than Lunacharsky's rather

eclectic assemblage had been. The Moscow conference received the greatest part of its delegates from factory committees and trade unions. This conference provided the foundation for the Moscow Proletkult which declared itself to be
"an independent mass class organization with full autonomy."[12]

As the chairman of the Moscow Proletkult, Bogdanov
sought to expand it into a national organization paralleling
the Commissariat of Enlightenment but remaining completely
independent of it. His old comrade, Lebedev-Poliansky, became the head of the Petrograd Proletkult when a branch was
established in the capital.

In his opening address to the First Congress of the
Proletkult in 1918, Lebedev-Poliansky gave a full expression
to the idea of complete political independence for the Proletkult. He argued that the Commissariat of Enlightenment
was an institution of the state and was hence obliged to concern itself with the needs of all the social classes in
Russia. The working class, he asserted, needed a cultural
organization dedicated entirely to proletarian needs and to
those of no other class. Such was to be the role of the
Proletkult.

Lebedev-Poliansky insisted that the Proletkult
would be strictly and uncompromisingly working class in membership and orientation and would hence be the most revolutionary mass organization in Soviet society. He also stressed that it was the nature of government organs to dominate--
they only issue directives and determine content. Bureau-

cratic interference, however, would only stifle the spontaneous development of working class culture.[13]

> Indeed, proletarian culture must be worked
> out in an independent process at the lowest
> levels among the broad mass of the workers.
> Only they can express their world-view in its
> full measure. The Proletkult therefore does
> not give directives; according to its very
> nature it must use only the best means to es-
> tablish the independence of the proletariat
> and strengthen and unify all that is involved
> in [working class] life naturally and without
> the issuance of directives. "The cultural
> independence of the proletariat"--that is the
> leading slogan that life itself advances.
> In coordianting our work with the Commis-
> sariat of Enlightenment, we do not have in
> mind the subjection of lower institutions to
> higher ones, but friendly, free cooperation.[14]

In the meantime, Lunacharsky had been appointed Commissar of Enlightenment when the new Soviet government was
formed. As a well known and popular Bolshevik, he could
hardly have been kept out of the government, despite his political unreliability. Not only was Lunacharsky already
deeply involved in cultural and educational work, but the
Commissariat of Enlightenment was insignificant in terms of
real political power. His appointment must have seemed a
safe one. Nevertheless, Lunacharsky immediately used his
influence to aid the Proletkult. He even defended its independence from government control. The official organ of the
Proletkult quoted the Commissar of Enlightenment as saying:

> As the party is a laboratory of the politi-
> cal line of the communist majority in power
> in the soviets . . . , just so the cultural-
> educational organizations of the proletariat
> are a laboratory for the realization of the
> revolutionary-cultural programs of the prole-
> tariat in the country and, of course, in the
> world.[15]

Later Lunacharsky stressed the full equality and
independence of the Proletkult even more explicitly when he
said that "From the very first I pointed out the full paral-
lelism: the party in the political realm, unions in the
economic realm, and the Proletkult in the cultural realm."[16]
It was, of course, not long before the party showed that it
was unwilling to share the leadership of the revolution with
either the unions or the Proletkult.

The Rebirth of God-building in the Program of the Proletkult.

The Proletkult grew rapidly during the first year
of the revolution. It quickly spread into a nationwide organization, and its structure paralleled the institutions of
the Commissariat of Enlightenment. It was headed by a central executive body with a hierarchy of regional, city, and
village organizations. The principal difference between the
Proletkult and the Commissariat of Enlightenment was that
the latter was an official state institution with a responsibility to educate all the citizens of the Soviet Union.
It therefore devoted most of its attention and energy to providing primary and secondary education. The Proletkult, on
the other hand, was not an arm of the state and admitted responsibility only to the working class; it devoted its attention exclusively to the cultural needs of the adult working
class.

Bogdanov had never been interested in primary education, at any rate. He took it for granted that a general,
elementary education was a prerequisite for proletarian

cultural development, but he was willing to leave that job to the professional teachers--even those of bourgeois origin. Bogdanov's idea of a proletarian university was a school for adult workers. His university would not even teach recent high school graduates but would rather admit only men and women who had already spent ten or more years earning their living as wage laborers.

As the self-proclaimed exclusive spokesman for the cultural needs of the working class, the Proletkult considered itself to be more revolutionary than the Commissariat of Enlightenment. Nevertheless, the Proletkult was heavily dependent upon financial grants from the Commissariat and could hardly have existed without them. So dependent was the Proletkult upon state aid that it could probably never have flourished if a believer in Proletarian Culture like Lunacharsky had not been Commissar of Enlightenment. Lunacharsky made sure that the Proletkult was well funded and gave it all the political protection he was capable of giving. Even after Lenin made it clear that he could not abide the existence of an independent revolutionary movement in the Soviet Union, Lunacharsky postponed the dissolution of the Proletkult as long as he could.

Lunacharsky's loyalties had always been divided in the personal politics of the Russian Social-Democratic movement. He had liked Martov very much and was uncertain which side to take in the party schism of 1903. He was again unsure of what to do in the Bolshevik schism of 1909, but in both cases Lunacharsky sided with Bogdanov. At the same time, he also felt personally close to Lenin, and he made a rapprochement with Lenin while he was still a member of the Vpered Group.

In his theoretical expressions, Lunacharsky consistently took the most extreme revolutionary positions, but in politics he usually followed the lead of his closest friends. Before 1917 Lunacharsky was primarily under Bogdanov's influence; after 1917 he followed Lenin. He vacillated only in that instance when Lenin and Bogdanov were in direct conflict; he protected Bogdanov's Proletkult as long possible but acquiesced to Lenin's demands in the end. (He was, of course, powerless to do otherwise than acquiesce.)

Lunacharsky had also been divided in his dedication to the cultural heritage of the West and his desire for violent revolution. He had actually spent the most tumultuous months of 1905 in Italy engrossed in studying that country's literature and art. He returned to Russia in 1905 only when summoned by the party. Furthermore, Lunacharsky had devoted most of his time from 1911 to 1917 to translating French poetry, writing plays, and producing several volumes of literary and artistic criticism. He was a lover of culture and was hostile to any radical demands that bourgeois culture be destroyed along with bourgeois political and economic institutions. He even resigned his position as Commissar of Enlightenment for a short time in November, 1917 when he heard a rumor that Bolshevik forces had destroyed the Kremlin in the seizure of Moscow.

Lunacharsky seems to have been eminently suited to head a Commissariat of Enlightenment in a large revolutionary state. His job was to minister to the cultural and educational needs of numerous classes and ethnic groups. He had to promote socialist culture while preserving the cultural treasures of the past. Lunacharsky sought to protect and nurture all Soviet artists and writers regardless of their social origin or political ideology. Advancing the cultural program and organization of his long-time comrade, Bogdanov, was only one aspect of Lunacharsky's professional activity. For Lunacharsky the Proletkult was only one aspect of the revolution.

Bogdanov was quite the opposite of Lunacharsky; he was a man of single purpose and supreme intellectual self-confidence. In his acquaintance with Bogdanov in Vologda in 1899, Berdiaev had considered him to be mildly insane; he saw Bogdanov to be the victim of an idee fixe.[17] Whether the gigantic conceptual task of systems-building is the cause or the result of insanity, Bogdanov may have suffered the same psychological disturbances as Saint-Simon, Fourier, and Comte. Bogdanov had taken upon himself the task of organizing all human knowledge into one logical system. He further believed that his "organizational science" would provide the foundation of the coming socialist paradise. Bogdanov pursued the political and cultural program that was based on his philosophical system with a single-minded passion.

The Proletarian Culture movement was the ultimate
goal toward which Bogdanov's entire intellectual life had
been directed. As he had made clear as early as 1911, he
considered Proletarian Culture to be no mere aspect or side-
light of the proletarian revolution. Rather, it was the
very essence of that revolution. In his own way Lunacharsky
was able to adapt the Proletkult into the system of Soviet
government as just one aspect of the struggle to build
socialism; he believed it to be parallel with and equal to
the Communist party and the trade unions. But such an expression never issued from Bogdanov's pen. (Nor, for that
matter, from the pen of that other single-minded revolutionary, Lenin. Neither Lenin nor Bogdanov could admit the
equality of a rival.) According to Bogdanov's theory of
society and revolution, culture was the source of revolutionary change, and all other aspects of the revolution were
subordinate to it.

The Proletkult began to publish its official organ,
Proletarskaia Kul'tura, in the summer of 1918. In the first
issue, Bogdanov asked that the working class direct its
greatest energy toward establishing its own independent culture. Indeed, he proposed that "cultural independence"
should be the first and foremost slogan of the working
class.[18] He further asserted that the lack of proletarian
culture was the only thing preventing the creation of socialism.

Bogdanov argued that all the preconditions for socialist revolution, according to Marx's analysis, had been
present in Europe in 1914. The reason why the workers of
Europe had willingly participated in the world war instead
of overthrowing the capitalist system was simply because
they lacked a unifying, spiritual class culture.

Once again he was implying that consciousness determines existence. Economic and social conditions in
Europe before the war had not been sufficient to prepare the
ground for socialism. The proletariat would not revolt
until it had created for itself an independent class culture
--a socialist culture.

Thus the dictatorship of the proletariat--as it
existed in Russia in 1918--did not mean the same thing to
Bogdanov as it did to Lenin and other politically oriented
Social-Democrats. In Bogdanov's understanding of the situation, very little had changed in 1917 in regard to the socialist revolution. The new Soviet Government was incapable
of creating socialism since it sought to do so through social,
political, and economic programs. The government was ignoring the only possible way to create socialism--to first
transform the spiritual consciousness of the Russian working
class.

Furthermore, Bogdanov argued, after the Bolsheviks
had attained political power, they had to deal with the
practical problems of administering a huge land, organizing
its economy, and waging a civil war. The Social-Democratic

government could no longer maintain the single-minded program it had pursued while an underground party; it now had
to mediate between the unions, the peasantry, and the still
necessary bourgeois technicians, managers, and entrepre-
neurs.

Thus the Proletkult, alone of all national organizations in Bogdanov's opinion, could claim to be exclusively
concerned with the needs of the proletariat. The Proletkult
was animated by the conviction that it was the true vanguard
of the working class. Despite the fact that the Social-Democratic party held political power and the dictatorship of
the proletariat was acknowledged to exist, the Proletkult
still maintained the aura of an underground revolutionary
party.

The Proletkult had its central committee and central
organ; it was composed of numerous local circles in a hierarchical organization which periodically sent delegates to a
national congress. It held that its program for Proletarian
Culture was the only valid course for Socialist revolutionaries to follow in Russia and the world. Far from simply
paralleling the Communist party and the trade unions, the
Proletkult believed itself to be superior to them.

It was thus inevitable that the Communist party and
the Proletkult should come into conflict. The party considered itself to be the sole representative of the working
class and the final arbiter of the intepetation of Marxism
in concrete social policies. The Communists considered it

inconceivable that another group could claim to speak for
the proletariat and to claim to have an alternative program
for building socialism--particularly when that group was
distinctly unorthodox in its understanding of Marxism.

The ultimate suppression of the Proletkult by the
Communist party in 1920 was a reenactment of the expulsion
of the otzovists and God-builders from the Bolshevik faction
a decade previously. The ideas involved were the same:
orthodox Marxists and political realists struggled against
philosophical innovators and visionary revolutionary extrem-
ists. Even the personnel were the same: Lenin a-
gainst Bogdanov and his friends. Just as Bogdanov's empiriomonism and Lunacharsky's religious socialism was transformed
into the Proletarian Culture ideology, so the Vpered Group
was reincarnated as the Proletkult.

The essential identity of the ideas and the people
in the two left Bolshevik movements--the Vpered Group and the
Proletkult--are revealed in the proceedings of the First
Congress of Proletarian Cultural-Educational Organizations.
This congress was convened in Moscow from September 15 to 20,
1918. The congress was attended by all the former Vperedists who had supported Bogdanov's program for Proletarian
Culture in 1911 with the exception only of Lunacharsky. Lunacharsky had been scheduled to address the congress but was
unable to attend. He and Lenin were named "Honorary Co-
Chairmen" of the Congress.

Bogdanov attended the Congress as a delegate from

the organizational bureau of the congress, but he assumed no
official position at the congress. He probably kept a low
profile in the official ranks of the Proletkult because he
had not rejoined the Bolshevik party (as all the other former Vperedists had done), and he knew he was persona non
grata with Lenin and the Bolshevik leadership.

However, all the other former Vperedists occupied
the highest official positions in the Proletkult organization. Lebedev-Poliansky was elected chairman of the congress
and subsequently became the chairman of the central committee
of the Proletkult. The two co-vice-chairmen of the central
committee were Kalinin and Mashirov-Samobytnik. Mashirov-
Samobytnik had not been an actual member of the Vpered Group,
but he had participated in Lunacharsky's Proletarian Culture
study circle in Paris in 1913. The central committee also
included Bogdanov, but the remaining eight official members
and eight candidate members were all newcomers to the Proletarian Culture movement. The composition of the editorial
board of the central organ, Proletarskaia Kul'tura, was
another matter entirely. It was an enclave of former Vperedists. Its five members were Bogdanov, Kalinin, Kerzhentsev,
Lebedev-Poliansky, and Mashirov-Samobytnik.[20]

Besides dominating the Proletkult's executive offices,
the former Vperedists also dominated the congress intellectually. Lebedev-Poliansky reported to the Congress on "Revolution and the Cultural Tasks of the Proletariat," Kalinin
spoke on "The Psychology of the Industrial Proletariat," and

Bogdanov actually delivered two reports to the convention:
"Science and the Proletariat" and "Art and the Proletariat."
Lunacharsky had been scheduled to deliver the latter address,
but he was unable to attend the congress. The only non-
Vperedists to read reports and present resolutions for the
approval of the delegates were Krupskaia and Ignatov. Krupskaia spoke on the ideals of the upbringing of socialist
youth, and Ignatov simply read the proposed constitution of
the Proletkult to the assembly.

In fact, the entire Proletariat Culture movement was
little more than an elaboration, continuation, and commentary on the essay, The Cultural Tasks of Our Time, that Bogdanov had written in 1911.

In his welcoming address to the congress, as presi-
dent of the organizational bureau (he had not yet been elected chairman of the congress), Lebedev-Poliansky reiterated
the two basic tenets of Bogdanov's idea of Proletarian Culture: that by tansforming culture the Proletkult would be
preparing the foundation of the new socialist society and
that it was independent from all other proletarian revolutionary organizations. Going beyond Lunacharsky's assertion
that the Proletkult paralleled the Communist party and the
trade unions, Lebedev-Poliansky claimed that the political
and economic movements were only subordinate elements in the
cultural struggle of the proletariat.

> The great struggle for this culture is given
> to the proletariat, and from the very first
> step it is necessary to decisively underline
> the fact that this struggle is a new indepen-

<u>dent</u> form of the struggle of the proletariat <u>with</u> the bourgeoisie.

The experience which we have obtained in these months of revolution demonstrates that our work upon the creation of proletarian culture cannot be confined within the organizational bounds of the political or economic struggle. This is patently obvious. Culture is something large and whole, and the political and economic struggle is just a part of that culture--although for many social-historical reasons it appeared much earlier. Now these three aspects of the workers' movement must pour together into one powerful stream to give us the power to transform the culture of the old, dying world . . .[20]

Furthermore, in his subsequent report to the Congress, "The Revolution and the Cultural Tasks of the Proletariat," Lebedev-Polainsky began by explicitly recognizing the creation of the program of Proletarian Culture by the <u>Vpered</u> Group.

The question of proletarian culture does not appear now for the first time; it was raised a long time ago. About ten years ago a literary group of Bolsheviks was formed which advanced the proposition that the proletariat must develop its struggle for its own culture . . . in order to further its political and economic struggle and in order to give greater ideological independence to all forms of proletarian struggle.

In analyzing the results of the 1905 Revolution, those comrades concluded that the propaganda and slogans of the revolution were not sufficiently inspired by socialist ideology . . .[21]

Following the same interpretations and arguments that Bogdanov had used in "The Contemporary Situation and the Tasks of the Party" and <u>The Cultural Tasks of Our Time</u>,--both statements of program for the <u>Vpered</u> Group--Lebedev-Poliansky insisted that the creation of a proletarian culture had to precede the socialist revolution and not follow it. After

all, he echoed Bogdanov, the bourgeoisie had elaborated
their world-view before and not after the French Revolution.
Their "Great Encyclopedia" was the crystallization and sys-
tematization of their world-view. The time had now arrived,
Lebedev-Poliansky announced, for the proletariat, under the
guidance of the Proletkult, to create its own world-view and
write its own encyclopedia.[22]

The chairman of the congress concluded his report
with yet another argument that Bogdanov had originated: the
world was at war because the proletariat lacked its own independent world-view. Since the workers had been instructed
in bourgeois schools, this argument ran, they naturally
acquired the cultural forms of thought of the capitalists.
And the workers would continue to be subjugated by the bourgeoisie as long as they did not develop their own class self-
consciousness.

This may have been a reverberation of the left Bolshevik dismay at the treaty of Brest-Litovsk. The world war
had not sparked a European working class revolution and
neither had the October Revolution. If the fact of a Russian
workers' revolution was not enough to rouse Europe, then the
assumptions upon which the revolutionaries were operating
had to be re-thought.

After all, the justification of a proletarian revolution in Russia in 1917 had not been based upon economic conditions. No one argued that Russia was ripe for socialism
according to Marx's prescription. Most Bolsheviks argued

that Europe was ripe for socialist revolution, and their
seizure of power in Russia would ignite a general European
working class revolt. Once it became obvious that the new
Soviet government would have to survive on its own, however,
the political principles of its leaders began to moderate.
This moderation enhanced the Proletkult's sense of being the
sole remaining representative of revolutionary socialism.
It also prompted them to explain the failure of European
revolution upon the lack of a class culture among the working class.

Lebedev-Poliansky insisted that the Proletkult was
the only movement capable of preparing the working class of
Russia and the world for the socialist revolution. Only by
first transforming their world-view could the proletariat
achieve the unity and capability for creating socialism. He
ended his address to the gathering: "Long live Proletarian
Culture, the greatest weapon for the victory of world-wide
socialism."[23]

The resolution that Lebedev-Poliansky proposed for
the approval of the congress was a neat summary of nearly
everything that Bogdanov had propounded during the last
decade. The congress approved it unanimously. (There were,
however, five abstentions.)

> The First All-Russian Congress of Cultural-
> Educational Organizations, recognizing:
> 1. that the cultural-educational movement
> among the proletariat must assume an indepen-
> dent position along with the political and
> economic movements,
> 2. that its task is the elaboration of
> a proletarian culture which, with the elimina-

tion of class divisions in society, will become universal,
    3. and that the building of this new cul-
ture must be based on social labor and comradely cooperation,
    resolves that:
    1. to attain the set goal, the proletariat
must command all the attainments of preceding
cultures and take from them all that bears the
mark of universality,
    2. it must approach this learning [of
the past] critically and rework it in the cru-
cible of its own class self-consciousness,
    3. proletarian culture must maintain the
character of revolutionary socialism in order
that the proletariat can arm itself with knowledge, organize its feelings by means of new
art, and reform its own day-to-day relationships
in a new, purely proletarian--that is collec-
tivist--spirit,
    4. in building the new culture the prole-
tariat must expend to the maximum its class
energy, its independence, and utilize as well
the help of the revolutionary socialist intelligentsia as far as that is possible,
    5. in laying down the foundations of this
new form of the workers' movement--the Pro-
letkult--and insisting upon its organizational
indpendence in order that a strictly proletarian culture shall develop in its entirety,
the congress suggests that government institutions, central and local, are obliged to
aid with all means this new movement in order
to more directly strengthen the victory of the
proletarian revolution, in order to defeat the
bourgeoisie not only materially, but spiritually, in order to more quickly erect the new
edifice of the coming socialist society.[24]

The other former Vperedists who addressed the Congress,

Bogdanov and Kalinin, concluded their reports as Lebedev-

Poliansky had done by offering grandiose, if rather vague,

resolutions for the delegates to approve. These resolutions

expressed the specific attitudes the Proletkult should main-

tain toward science, the proletarian university, the new en-

cyclopedia, education, workers' clubs, unions, worker coopera-

tives, children's upbringing, literature, theatre, music, and the representational arts. These specific proposals and resolutions were all couched in the same tone of moral righteousness; the leaders of the Proletkult believed themselves to be the true bearers of the culture of the future. They thought of themselves as the evangels of a new faith--a vanguard of uncompromising revolutionaries who would persevere in the struggle for the liberation of the working class and carry on the great revolutionary socialist tradition even within the new Soviet society.

In his closing speech to the congress, Lebedev-Poliansky made explicit the mood of evangelism that infused the Proletkult. He echoed the sentiments that Lunacharsky had expressed at the outset of the revolution when he compared the revolutionary movement to the "fighting church," and he thereby revealed the debt that Proletarian Culture owed to the spirit of God-building.

> You remember, of course, the biblical story of Simon. All his life he awaited the Messiah, and upon seeing Jesus he cried out, "Now free your slave!"
> Several of us Bolsheviks who ten years ago abroad raised the question of proletarian culture, thought to ourselves: How can we ever carry this banner through all the obstacles of reaction, down the path of heavy theoretical arguments and disagreements, and lay down the foundation stone? And now, closing the First All-Russian Conference of the Proletkult, I-- as one of those who held that banner--want to say with pride that we carried that banner through and unfurled it. On this day we hand it to you, into your hopeful hands.[25]

This religious enthusiasm became a distinguishing characteristic of the Proletarian Culture movement during the early Soviet period. The spokesmen of the Proletkult dwelt as much upon the glories of their ultimate socialist goal as they did on their role in promoting the socialist revolution. Echoing the attitudes of the God-builders, Mashirov-Samobytnik asserted that proletarian struggle and creativity would not simply end when the revolution came.

> Class struggle is a temporary phenomenon; there remains the constant struggle with nature. All techniques and sciences of the future must be directed toward the struggle with nature.[26]

Lunacharsky had expressed similar attitudes earlier in the summer of 1918 at a Proletkult conference held in Petrograd.

> . . . The proletariat has stood up as Man with a capital M. It is exactly like Prometheus who is opening up new paths. And this is why at every proletarian holiday and here in the Palace of Proletarian Culture, I feel as if I am at a peculiar divine worship for the sake of the future of mankind. We do all this solemnly; we do not know upon what world we are working. The future historian with a trembling hand will write down on great pages the chronicle of our times, and perhaps with tears of tender emotion he will write the history of the Proletkult--this first sprout of the free, great, superb workers' art.[28]

Bogdanov chose to view the future of the proletariat in metaphysical rather than religious terms. His image was rather manichean: mankind is the power of reason and light fighting against the dark forces of spontaneous and elemental anarchy. Bogdanov said that the collectivist poet ". . . will sense the whole universe as the realm of endeavor, the struggle of the forces of life with the forces of elemental anarchy, the forces of the striving for the unity of conscious-ness with the black forces of destruction and disorganization."28

It is impossible to know to what extent the great
numbers of working class members of Proletkult circles, clubs,
and study groups actually believed in Bogdanov's vision of
Proletarian Culture and its role in the socialist revolution
and unlimited potential to recreate the world. Certainly
the platform that was approved unanimously by the First All-
Russian Congress of the Proletkul't was not by any stretch
of the imagination a direct transcription of popular working
class attitudes toward culture. The ideas did not originate
on the floor of the conference, and the major resolutions on
cultural tasks, on science, and on art were not even amended
or elaborated upon by the delegates.

In fact, all the resolutions (except those offered
by Krupskaia in regard to the education of young people) were
written by Lebedev-Poliansky and Bogdanov and were approved
by the congress in their original form. Perhaps the fact
that the Proletkult was later so easily decapitated by the
Communist party and merged with the Commissariat of Enlightenment shows that the working class in Russia was hungry
only for basic education and cared little for the ideological vagaries of those who headed the organization that promised to give them that education.

Nevertheless, at higher cultural levels, the Proletkult showed a definite appeal. Artists and writers of proletarian origin (or at least of proletarian orientation)
were attracted to the Proletkult because of its idealism and

its utopian fervor. More than any other organization during the years of War Communism--the Soviet Union's "Heroic period"--the Proletkult embodied the idealism and the optimism for a better world that had been unleashed by the revolutions of 1917.

The most notable literary groupings that formed out of writers associating with the Proletkult were the "Smithy" in Moscow and the "Cosmist" in Petrograd. Two of the most popular writers associated with the Proletkult (and two of the most utopian) were Gastev and Gerasimov--writers who had been members of Lunacharsky's Proletarian Culture circle in Paris in 1913. The agressive millenarian mood of these writers dominated Soviet culture during the War Communism period; all other more moderate and conventional artists were put on the defensive. Only the Futurists were self confident enough to compete with the Proletkult as spokesmen for the great proletarian revolution.[29]

The poets of the Proletkult glorified the workers, their labor, and their unlimited powers of creativity (all themes redolent of God-building) in grandiose poetry laden with hyperbole and cosmic terminology. Proletarskaia Kul'-tura, the official organ of the Proletkult, was peppered with poems of millenarian expectation such as this:

The Iron Messiah

Here he is: the savior, ruler of the world.
Lord of titanic powers,
In the roar of countless steel machines,
In the glare of electric suns.

They thought he would appear in starry vestments,
In the halo of secretness,
But he came to us in bluish puffs of smoke,
From factories and plants of the workers' districts.

They thought he would appear in brilliance and glory,
Meek and tender,
But he, like burning lava,
Came exultantly and tumultuously.

Here he strides through bottomless seas,
Steely, inexorably, impetuously.
He is throwing sparks of rebellious ideas,
He spreads purifying flames.

Where sounds his powerful cry,
The bowels of the earth are revealed,
Mountains part before him in an instant,
The poles of the earth come nearer together.

Where he passes he leaves tracks
Of resounding iron lines.
He brings joy and light to all.
He plants flowers in the wilderness.

He brings a new sun to the world,
He destroys thrones and dungeons,
He calls the people to eternal brotherhood,
He wipes away all boundaries and borders.

His scarlet sign is a symbol of struggle,
The saving beacon for the oppressed.
With him we will be victorious over the yoke of fate,
We will attain a glorious paradise.[30]

The Suppression of the Proletkult.

The tremendous growth of the Proletkult organization,
the publication of its monthly journal, and its national conference soon attracted the attention of Lenin and other
policy makers in the Communist party. The existence of
80,000 working class members of local Proletkult study circles
and workers' clubs combined with its ideological deviation
from Marxism and above all its vehement insistence on its
total independence from either party or government made the

Proletkult a social movement that could not be ignored.[31]

Apparently, Lenin became interested in the Proletkult in May, 1920 when he happened to read the latest edition of Bogdanov's Short Course of Economic Science.[32] Back
in 1897, when Lenin had read it for the first time, he had
praised it highly. But with each new edition Bogdanov had
revised it to reflect the new developments in his philosophy
and revolutionary world-view. By the time of the tenth edition in 1919, it had very little orthodox scientific socialism in it at all. Bogdanov focused not upon material economic development but upon the development of the ideology of
economic classes. When he dealt with the socialist revolution, Bogdanov simply rephrased the ideas of cultural preparation for socialism that he had been preaching for the last
ten years.

Reading Bogdanov's heresies once again must have
brought back to Lenin uncomfortable memories of machism, otzovism, and God-building. He could hardly have forgotten
the years from 1905 to 1909 when Bogdanov held so influential
a position among the left Bolsheviks. Preparations were then
(spring, 1920) underway for the convocation of a second All-
Russian Conference of the Proletkult. A thriving counter-
ideology combined with a mass organization under the leadership of an old rival was not the sort of thing to be considered lightly by the man whose party claimed to be the true
vanguard of the working class. The radical socialist program
and utopian expectations of the Proletkult also must have

seemed particularly unsuitable to Lenin on the eve of the up-
coming dramatic policy reversals of the New Economic Policy.

In August, 1920, Lenin wrote to Pokrovsky to ascer-
tain the legal position of the Proletkult and to learn who
its leaders were, by whom they had been chosen, how much
money the Commissariat of Enlightenment granted it, and anything else important about the role, character, and operation
of the Proletkult.[33] Pokrovsky was at that time Lunacharsky's
assistant Commissar of Enlightenment. No doubt Lenin wrote
to Pokrovsky and not to Lunacharsky because he knew that the
latter was too close a friend of Bogdanov to be completely
dependable on this subject. Pokrovsky had been a philosophical opponent of Bogdanov since 1911.

Although the Proletkult was theoretically under the
"control" of the Commissariat of Enlightenment, Lenin might
well query, "How is this done in reality?"[34] Indeed, at the
end of August, 1920--at the same time that Pokrovsky was res-
ponding to Lenin's questions--Lunacharsky was announcing the
independence of the Proletkult in an official Commissariat
of Enlightenment publication:

> . . . The Proletkult is a completely indepen-
> dent cultural-educational organ of the working
> class. In its tasks it is one of the first
> and most important creators of the coming soc-
> ialist system . . . Local powers must not in
> any way interfere in the execution of the Pro-
> letkult's affairs. . . . I ask that local
> soviet institutions do not hold the local
> bureau [of the Proletkult] at arms length
> but to show them all cooperation in regard
> to supply, distribution of money, execution
> of directives, the allocation of accomodations,
> and in all similar areas.[35]

The Proletkult conference in the fall of 1920 was
held from October 5 to 12. Lenin told Lunacharsky on the
seventh of that month that in his address to the conference
he must inform the delegates that the Proletkult must become
fully subordinate to the Commissariat of Enlightenment. It
must have come as a surprise to Lenin, therefore, to read
in Izvestiia on the morning of October 8 that "Comrade Lunacharsky indicated that the Proletkult must be assured of a
special position of the fullest autonomy . . ."[36]

Finding it thus impossible to force the Commissar of
Enlightenment to suppress the Proletkult, Lenin took his case
to the Central Committee of the Communist party. And even
there he found some rather surprising support for the Proletkult. Bukharin would not agree to dismantle the Proletkult,
and Lenin had to be content with simply the organizational
subordination of the Proletkult to the Commissariat of Enlightenment.[37]

There then began a series of letters and official
orders from the Central Committee to the leaders of the Proletkult. The conclusion was that in December, 1920 all political and scientific educational efforts of the Proletkult
were taken over directly by the Commissariat of Enlightenment. The Proletkult was allowed independence only in the
realm of art and literature. Another stricture was the re-
moval of Bogdanov and Lebedev-Poliansky from the Presidium
of the Proletkult.

By late 1920 the Proletkult had already become di-

vided against itself. Bogdanov had not managed to convert
all the members of the organization to his way of thinking.
Just as there had been in the Vpered Group, there existed a
strong Bolshevik-oriented faction within the movement. It
was this faction that responded to the Central Committee's
letters and directives. Under such circumstances, Bogdanov
and Lebedev-Polainsky were discouraged from continuing their
struggle. The official journal, Proletarskaia Kul'tura, was
able to publish only two more issues after its two principal
editors resigned.

Lebedev-Poliansky went to work for his old friend,
Lunacharsky. He edited a number of educational journals,
helped to organize the Sverdlov Proletarian University, became a professor in the Communist Academy, and worked for the
Commissariat of People's Economy. After 1920, Lebedev-Poliansky avoided politics and devoted himself to literature.
He edited numerous collections and wrote several volumes of
literary criticism.

Bogdanov spent the next few years "clearing off his
desk." He published several collections of his past writings,
and he revised his Short Course of Economic Science yet one
more time. Like Lebedev-Polainsky, Bogdanov also abandoned
politics. He made no new attempt to create and lead an ideological movement. In 1924 he was invited to join the Workers'
Opposition but declined the honor. Instead, Bogdanov turned
his attention to science. He established a state institute
for blood transfusion where he experimented with this pioneer-

ing medical treatment. In 1928 Bogdanov died when he attempted to cure a patient ill with malaria by exchanging blood
with him.

As for the remaining Proletkult organization, it
lasted less than a year from the time that Bogdanov and Lebedev-Poliansky left it. On November 22, 1921, the Central
Committee passed a resolution that finally ended the Proletkult's effective existence. Over the course of 1922 all
local Proletkult clubs and circles were absorbed into the
Commissariat of Enlightenment.

It was surely no coincidence that the demise of the
Proletkult occurred simultaneously with the sudden about-
face in economic and political policies of the New Economic
Policy. The Soviet government suddenly realized that it
could not function without the aid of bourgeois specialists
and that its progress toward a socialist economy was facing
a crisis. The resurgence of bourgeois capitalist techniques
and business management was accompanied by a dampening of
revolutionary expectations and a revival of non-proletarian
art and literature. The Proletkult had dominated the cultural life of the period of War Communism. Following 1921
the revolutionary socialist idealists and utopians felt their
hopes slipping away; their artistic views fell out of popular
favor.

A renaissance of socialist idealism was not to occur
again until the late years of the decade. The idealists who
had first expressed their demands for socialist revolution

and their visions of socialist paradise at the beginning of
the twentieth century and who had lived to see their ideals
finally manifested in a huge national organization within a
revolutionary socialist state ultimately saw their dreams
fade. The now aging generation of Bogdanov, Lunacharsky,
and Lebedev-Poliansky had completed its work. When the new
socialist idealism of the first five year plan and the col-
lectivization campaign arose, it was championed by a new
revolutionary youth. A new generation of utopians had come
of age.

NOTES TO CHAPTER VIII

[1]N. A. Trifononv, "Soratniki (Lunacharskii i Gor'kii posle Oktiabria)," Russkaia Literatura, no. 1 (1968), pp. 25-26.

[2]Ibid., p. 25.

[3]Lunacharskii, Sochineniia, vol. 7, pp. 192-93.

[4]John Reed, Ten Days that Shook the World (New York: Signet, 1967), p. 39.

[5]V. V. Gorbunov, "Iz istorii kul'turno-prosvetitel'-noi deiatel'nosti petrogradskikh bol'shevikov v period pod-gotovkoi Oktiabria," Voprosy Istorii KPSS, no. 2 (1967), p. 26.

[6]Ibid.

[7]Ibid., p. 27.

[8]Ibid., p. 31.

[9]Sheila Fitzpatrick, The Commissariat of Enlightenment (Cambridge: Cambridge University Press, 1970), pp. 8-9.

[10]Gorbunov, p. 32.

[11]Ibid., pp. 32-33.

[12]Fitzpatrick, p. 91.

[13]P. I. Lebedev-Polianskii, ed., Protokoly pervoi vse-rossiiskoi konferentsii proletarskikh kul'turno-prosve-titel'nykh organizatsii (Moscow: "Proletarskaia Kul'tura," 1918), p. 21.

[14]Ibid.

[15]Organizatsionnoe biuro, "K sozyvu vse-rossiiskoi kon-ferentsii kul'turno-prosvetitel'nykh rabochikh organizatsii," Proletarskaia Kul'tura, no. 1 (1918), p. 27.

[16]Lunacharskii, Sochineniia, vol 7, p. 205.

[17]Dream and Reality, p. 130.

[18]"Ot redaktsii--Pod znamia 'Proletkul'ta,'" Prole-tarskaia Kul'tura, no. 1 (1918), p. 2.

[19]Konferentsiia, p. 55.

[20] Ibid., p. 6.

[21] Ibid., p. 17.

[22] Ibid., pp. 18-19.

[23] Ibid., p. 21.

[24] Ibid., p. 29.

[25] Ibid., p. 89.

[26] Ibid., p. 27.

[27] Lunacharskii, Sochineniia, vol. 7, p. 200.

[28] Konferentsiia, p. 74.

[29] Gleb Struve, Russian Literature under Lenin and Stalin, 1917-1953 (Norman: University of Oklahoma Press, 1971), p. 28.

[30] Vladimir Kirillov, Zheleznyi messiia," Proletarskaia Kul'tura, no. 2 (1918), p. 26.

[31] Gorbunov, p. 30.

[32] Fitzpatrick, p. 175.

[33] Gorbunov, p. 32.

[34] Ibid.

[35] Ibid.

[36] Ibid., p. 33.

[37] Fitzpatrick, p. 180.

AFTERWORD

LENIN'S MILLENIALISM

It has been the thesis of this work that the God-
builders were not religious deviants on the fringe of the
Russian Social-Democratic movement but were rather at its intellectual center. The God-builders differed from their
comrades only by being more introspective and philosophically fearless than other Marxist revolutionaries. They gave
explicit expression to the idealist, religious, and millenarian spirit that was inherent in the organization and program of Bolshevism.

The chief obstacle to appreciating the millenial motivations of the Bolshevik faction--and particularly of its
leader--is that the Bolsheviks did not display the personality traits that are usually associated with apocalyptic visions and utopian expectations. The religious chiliast who
believes that the world is about to come to an end and who
dreams of a paradise and reign of goodness that will follow
the apocalypse is usually identifiable by a total incompre-
hension of the real world. He either withdraws from reality
and commits his fantasies to paper, or he destroys himself
in a futile and violent attempt to hasten the apocalypse.

At first glance, Lenin would seem to be just the opposite of such a millenarian. After all, one can hardly

355

glance through the many, heavy volumes of Lenin's collected
works without being impressed with his material, practical
interests. Lenin is usually to be found assessing the material economic and political conditions within Russia and elaborating on the specific details of the Bolshevik faction's
program, strategy, tactics, or organization. Lenin's detailed grasp of the situation in Russia and his accurate understanding of his party's relation to it is impressive.

Lenin was also an eminently successful practical politician. He created a revolutionary organization uniquely
suited to the circumstances of revolutionary activity in
Russia. He understood the mood of the Russian workers as
well as the mood of his own faction; he knew when to call
for action and when to bide his time. He knew when to stand
resolutely upon principle and when to compromise.

Alone of all political leaders in Russia in 1917,
Lenin realized the possibility of assuming political power,
and he did not let the opportunity slip past him. Not only
did he know how to manipulate the unwilling Bolshevik leadership into initiating the October insurrection, he successfully directed the new Soviet government through war, civil
war, and foreign intervention. The party that Lenin organized then went on to build one of the most powerful nations
the world has seen.

Nevertheless, appearance can conceal as well as reveal. It is conceivable that a man possessing the patterns
of thought and action of a practical politician might simul-

taneously be motivated by a millenarian vision. The fact
that the revolution which Lenin so ardently desired and so
persistently struggled to create ultimately produced a stable
government and a viable economic system does not at all mean
the the revolution was necessarily "successful" in terms of
Lenin's own desires and expectations. It is entirely possible,
in other words, to see Lenin as a successful politician motivated by millenial ideals that he failed to achieve once in
power.

Another major obstacle to appreciating Lenin's millenialism is the fact that he espoused the world-view of
Marxism. Marx had sought to eliminate subjective human emo-
tions from the historical process. He saw socialism as arising from the development of objective, material forces. Thus
the ethical or religious motivations of revolutionaries are
irrelevant to the revolution in which they participate. A
consistent Marxist would not dwell upon his own subjective
idealism.

Logically, of course, a Marxist could both profess to
believe in materialism and determinism and yet be motivated
in his commitment to the revolutionary movement by feelings
of moral righteousness, by the desire to influence forcibly
the course of events, or by the expectation of a paradise on
earth. After all, the _desire_ for socialist revolution must
have its source in the personality of the revolutionary and
not in the theory of Marxism. Lenin was not a revolutionary
because he had read Marx's works; Marxism made sense to him

because he was a revolutionary.

Lenin was not attracted to Marxism by an intellectual need for scientific knowledge of economics. He was a Marxist because Marxism promised him something he desired very strongly--socialist revolution. Lenin gauged the Marxian validity of any practical political proposal by whether it contributed to or detracted from the revolutionary movement. His commitment to Marxism was sincere; Lenin did not merely manipulate Marx's theories to serve his own political ends. But Lenin was a convinced Marxist because he thought that Marxism was a revolutionary doctrine hostile to any other interpretation. No proposal, in Lenin's opinion, could possibly be true to Marxism if it did not further the revolutionary movement, and proposals were by definition Marxian if they did contribute to the struggle for socialism.

Indeed, revolution was the foremost goal of Lenin's life and the guiding principle of all his intellectual and political activity. All Lenin's political thought--on party organization, strategy, or tactics; on voluntarism, democracy, tolerance, cooperation--was dependent in one way or another upon Lenin's impatient desire for social revolution. Whatever promoted the revolution was, by Lenin's definition, the correct interpretation of Marxism. Similarly, whatever seemed to delay the revolution was a violation of the principles of Marxism as Lenin understood them.

It is in this stubborn and obsessive preoccupation with the necessity of immediate and violent destruction of

Russian society that Lenin's essential similarity with the
God-builders is most clearly to be seen. In What is to be
Done? Lenin had revealed the extent to which he did not share
Marx's sense of materialist determinism. He objected to
Bernstein's revision of Marxism only because Bernstein had
denied that violent revolution was a necessary path to socialism. Lenin actually denied that the working class could
make socialist revolution by itself and insisted that an
elite group of conscious revolutionaries had to assume the
leadership of the revolution. Thus Lenin's impatient desire
for revolution led him to assume a voluntarist and idealist
position. He denied material determinism, accepted the
validity of subjective ideals, and proposed that individual
will could and should influence the course of history.

In One Step Forward, Two Steps Back, Lenin further
revealed the extent to which he did not believe in the scientific validity of Marxism. In 1905 Lenin announced that he
would not be satisfied by a bourgeois revolution made by and
for the capitalists. Lenin wanted a "dictatorship of the
proletariat and peasantry." He envisaged an "uninterrupted
revolution" led by the Bolshevik faction and manned by the
proletariat that would initiate and carry through the bourgeois-democratic revolution and then transform it into the
socialist revolution. In the years of the 1905 Revolution,
Lenin was indistinguishable from an idealist in questions of
philosophy. Though he himself did not discourse upon philo-

sophical themes, Lenin's political program embodied the
idealism that the God-builders were developing in their revision of the philosophical foundation of scientific socialism.

When it came, the conflict between the God-builders
and Lenin that led to the schism of 1909 had everything to
do with political tactics and nothing to do with ideology.
Lenin perceived that the times were not ripe for armed insurrection, and he believed that the God-builders' continued
agitation for immediate social revolution was likely to destroy the Social-Democratic movement. He only then began to
use the left Bolsheviks' unorthodox and revisionist philosophy (that had previously seemed unimportant to him) as a
means of discrediting them in the eyes of other Social-Democrats.

And even when Lenin did attack the philosophy of the
millenarian Bolsheviks, he did so on the basis of revolutionary tactics and not on the grounds of technical philosophy.
Lenin emphasized that such a philosophy was typical of reactionaries and not revolutionaries. Indeed, there is not a
single line in Materialism and Empiriocriticism that deals
directly with the problems of ontology, epistemology, and
causality that the God-builders had raised in their philosophical speculations. Lenin was content simply to show that
their world-view was not consonant with Marx's scientific
socialism and that it had nothing to contribute to the revolutionary movement.

In Days with Lenin, Gorky related an exchange between Lenin and Bogdanov that illustrates Lenin's attitude toward philosophy. The meeting took place at Gorky's villa on Capri before the schism in the Bolshevik faction had become official.

> A. A. Bogdanov . . . had to listen to these biting words: "Schopenhaur said that 'clear thinking means clear speaking,' and I think he never said a truer word. You don't explain yourself clearly, Comrade Bogdanov. Explain to me in a few words what your 'substitution' will give to the working class, and why Machism is more revolutionary than Marxism?"[1]

Lenin was a politician and not a theoretician. He had no interest whatsoever in the intellectual quest for truth that had inspired the God-builders to revise the philosophical foundations of revolutionary socialism. All Lenin cared about was the mechanics of the actual revolutionary movement. He had long since found Marxism to be a philosophy that adequately supported the movement, and he was content to accept that philosophy without reservation. (Lenin was also practical enough a politician to ignore the principles of Marxism whenever he felt the observance of them would not contribute to the struggle for socialism.)

An essential element of Lenin's preoccupation with the idea of revolution was his conviction that there was no other political process through which progress toward an ideal social system could occur. Lenin never seriously considered the possibility of gradual reform. At different times, Lenin advocated cooperation with moderate political parties and even participation in the parliamentary system. But he always explicitly insisted that such tactics not be used as a means of reform but be clearly recognized as means of furthering the revolutionary movement. Lenin wanted to support the Kadets in 1905 "as a rope supports a hanged man." And when he advocated Social-Democratic participation in the Duma after 1907, Lenin did not want the delegates to attend the Duma in order to advance progressive legislation but to use the Duma as a forum for revolutionary socialist propaganda.

Part of Lenin's objection to the idea of peaceful, gradual reform was that he did not trust the political regime in Russia to deal fairly with the reformers. Whenever he saw a reform in the system whose object seemed to be the betterment of the working class, Lenin interpreted it as a mere fraud--an attempt by the government to dull the popular impetus toward revolution by offering deceptive reforms. Lenin interpreted reforms to be means of increasing the oppression of the working class and not liberating it.

In regard to certain reforms giving factory workers the rights of organization and representation, Lenin argued that they were no more than devices for the police to use to control and limit the working class movement.

> . . . The proletariat will remain in prison
> as hitherto, without light, without air, and
> without the elbow-room it needs for the strug-
> gle to attain its complete emancipation. In
> this prison the government is now cutting a
> tiny aperture instead of a window, and in such
> a manner that this aperture is of more use
> to the gendarmes and spies who guard the pri-
> soners than it is to the prisoners themselves.[2]

Reforms, Lenin asserted, ". . . are always insincere, always half-hearted, often spurious and illusory, and usually hedged around with more or less subtly hidden traps."[3]

Closely connected with his aversion to the idea of gradual reform was Lenin's extreme antipathy toward the liberal middle classes--the social class that was the chief advocate of the notion that reform within the limits of the existing legal system was the proper political strategy. In Lenin's opinion, the liberals were spineless, unprincipled, and consistently took the side of the old regime whenever working class unrest seemed to threaten social stability.

If Lenin revealed the attributes of a practical realist in regard to matters of political strategy, in his attitudes toward the bourgeoisie, he betrayed a zealous and fanatical dedication to the cause of socialist revolution. Just as militant evangelizers of a religious faith reserve special scorn for complacent co-believers, so Lenin was particularly hostile to those members of his own social class and cultural milieu who had not been converted to the socialist revolutionary movement. Lenin despised middle class liberals and always singled them out for special vituperation.

It was for this reason that Lenin was so insistent that the Social-Democrats should take the leadership of the 1905 Revolution and that they should not fear to alienate the liberals by proposing radical programs. Lenin believed the liberals were fundamentally incapable of making a revolution, and he therefore asserted that the real bourgeois-democratic revolution could occur in Russia only after the bourgeoisie had succumbed to its own cowardice and abandoned the revolution to the proletariat.[4]

When, in his proposed platform for the Fourth Congress of the RSDRP, Lenin spoke of cooperating with the bourgeois parties in the revolution, the parties to which he was referring were the Socialist-Revolutionary Party, the Peasant Union, and certain trade unions. Lenin rejected out of hand any sort of cooperation with middle class liberal professionals.[5]

There were two elements in Lenin's detestation of the middle class. He first of all seems to have found them morally reprehensible simply because they did not choose to support the revolutionary struggle for socialism. (At least the terms in which Lenin excoriated the liberals were laden with moral judgement: rotten, despicable, base, servile, cowardly, etc.)

But Lenin also hated the liberals because they were his political opponents; they were the class that sought to transform Russia by a means fundamentally opposed to revolution. In their desire to achieve progress through gradual, legal means, the middle class was the real political opponent of the revolutionaries. It was they (and not the autocracy) who offered the only viable alternative to revolution. Thus it was a result of his fervent dedication to violent revolution that Lenin passionately resisted both the method of reform and the social class that promoted that method.

As in all other questions of program, strategy, and
tactics for achieving socialism, Lenin rejected all non-revolutionary approaches for no reason other than that they were
not revolutionary. In 1905 he outlined the reformist view
of change that he so despised:

> "We must choose"--this is the argument the
> opportunists have always used to justify them-
> selves, and they are using it now. Big things
> cannot be achieved at one stroke. We must
> fight for small but achievable things . . .
> We must not be utopians and strive after big
> things. We must be practical politicians;
> we must join in the demand for small things,
> and these small things will facilitate the
> fight for the big ones. We regard the small
> things as the surest stage in the struggle for
> big things.
>   This is how all the opportunists, all the
> reformists, argue; unlike the revolutionaries.[6]

But when it came to proving that such a concept of
gradual piecemeal change was invalid as a means of achieving
socialism, Lenin did not challenge it by appealing to either
facts or logic. Instead, he resorted to the familiar argument that he used against any proposal that he opposed. Reform, Lenin argued, is wrong simply because it is not revolutionary.

> To what conclusion does this argument inevi-
> tably lead? To the conclusion that we need
> no revolutionary programme, no revolutionary
> party, and no revolutionary tactics. We do
> not need a revolutionary Social-Democratic
> Party. What we need is a party of democratic
> and socialist reforms.[7]

Consequently,

> By supporting such a reform, by including it
> among our slogans, we dim the revolutionary
> consciousness of the proletariat and weaken
> its independence and fighting capacity.[8]

Once again, Lenin's arguments make it apparent that his dedication to the principle of revolution was not based upon material political calculations but upon the faith that revolution has some unique property that made it the only possible means of progress toward the ideal society.

During the period of reaction between the two revolutions, Lenin--like the political realist he was--counselled moderation and reconstruction of the Social-Democratic movement. But when Russia's next revolutionary situation arose in the winter of 1917, Lenin's maximalist temperament was reawakened. As he had in 1905, Lenin insisted that the proletariat should not permit the bourgeoisie to take control of the revolution. In an early "Telegram to Bolsheviks Leaving for Russia," Lenin demanded that the Bolsheviks should refuse to support the provisional government, begin to arm the proletariat, and neither seek nor permit rapprochement with any other revolutionary or political party.[9]

Lenin continued to advocate this policy in his "Letters from Afar." In the first of those letters, he argued that since the provisional government was composed of members of the bourgeoisie it must not be joined or cooperated with. Instead, the Bolsheviks must begin "the transition from the first stage of the revolution to the second."[10] In the fifth letter, Lenin clarified the meaning of this: he wanted the Bolsheviks and the proletariat to take charge of the revolution and ensure that it would not remain at the stage of a democratic republic but would continue to develop directly into socialism.[11]

Not merely a fellow Marxist but a fellow Bolshevik
--Lev Kamenev--objected that socialist revolution was unthinkable at the present time since the bourgeois revolution
was not yet complete. Once again, Lenin's insistence upon
immediate socialist revolution had nothing to do with a
simple desire to apply Marxism to Russian reality and everything to do with his inner revolutionary impulse. At this
point Lenin's voluntarism led him to distort Marx's thought
more than interpret it.

Indeed, Lenin's exegesis of Marxism in support of
his own revolutionary program was murky and dodged the real
issue in a maze of verbiage. Lenin first quoted Kamenev's
attack upon his own policies.

> "As for Comrade Lenin's general scheme," writes
> Comrade Kamenev, "it appears to us unaccept-
> able inasmuch as it proceeds from the assump-
> tion that the bourgeois-democratic revolution
> is <u>completed</u>, and builds on the immediate trans-
> formation of this revolution into a socialist
> revolution."[12]

Lenin responded by pointing out that,

> . . . There are two big mistakes here.
>   First. The question of "completion" of the
> bourgeois-democratic revolution is <u>stated</u>
> wrongly. The question is put in an abstract,
> simple, so to speak one-color way, which does
> <u>not</u> correspond to the objective reality. To
> <u>put</u> the question <u>this</u> way, to ask <u>now</u> "whether
> the bourgeois-democratic revolution <u>is</u> com-
> pleted" and to say <u>no more</u>, is to prevent one-
> self from seeing the exceedingly complex real-
> ity which is at least two-colored. This is
> in theory. In practice, it means surrender-
> ing helplessly to <u>petty-bourgeois revolution-
> ism</u>.[13]

What was really at issue, of course, was simply the question of whether or not the Bolsheviks should attempt to assume political power and lead the proletariat in continuing and deepening the revolution. Marx's views on the economic stages of historical development were really irrelevant. To follow Marx's theories too slavishly, Lenin obviously thought, could be counter-revolutionary. Lenin chose to follow what he took to be the spirit of Marxism and not necessarily the letter.

State and Revolution, written a few months later, sought to prove that Lenin's demand for immediate, violent revolution by the working class was entirely consistent with Marxism. It was--like What is to be Done?--an elaborate expression of the idea that "without a revolutionary theory, a revolutionary party is unthinkable." That is, Lenin took the necessity of a revolutionary party as an article of faith, and then he looked to Marxism for the revolutionary theory on which it could be based.

As he had always done throughout his polemical career, Lenin did not argue that his political opponents within the Social-Democratic movement were making mistakes of fact or logic in their application of Marxist theory to Russian reality. Instead, he accused them simply of interpreting Marxism in a manner that tended to discourage the demand for immediate revolution. He condemned the "opportunists" for "blunting the revolutionary edge" of Marxism. "They omit, obscure, or distort the revolutionary side of their theory, its revolutionary soul."[14]

In State and Revolution, Lenin did not analyze the social, economic, and political situation in Russia in the summer of 1917 and attempt to prove that the time was ripe for proletarian revolution. Instead, he pored through all the works of Marx and Engels in which they referred to the revolutionary destruction of the state and tried to discover in them a theoretical foundation for the destruction of Russia's political and social system.

State and Revolution also revealed Lenin's temperamental revulsion toward the notion of reform and gradual progress. It is significant that in the entire work Lenin offered no appraisal of the prospects for social progress under the Provisional Government; he did not try to prove that the Provisional Government was incapable of bettering Russia through democratic means. Instead, Lenin took as an article of faith that bourgeois, liberal, democratic means were fundamentally incapable of producing socialism.

Lenin simply did not believe that a new socialist society could be built upon the political and social foundation that had arisen in February, 1917. He rejected any sort of government that was not controlled by the working class, and he did not believe that the working class could attain power by any means other than violent revolution. Consequently, he wanted to continue the revolutionary destruction of the old regime until the slate had been wiped clean and a totally new society could be constructed from the ground up. Lenin's principal theme was that, "It is clear that the liberation of the oppressed class is impossible not only without violent revolution, but also without the destruction of the apparatus of state power . . ."[15]

Lenin's point was that the socialist revolution had to be made in a quick, conscious act and not simply be allowed to develop. There was to be nothing gradual or evolutionary about the transfer of power from the bourgeoisie to the proletariat. Lenin took great pains to demonstrate that the bourgeois state would not gradually "wither away" into communism. ". . . Engels speaks . . . of the proletariat revolution 'abolishing' the bourgeois state, while the words about the state withering away refer to the remnants of the proletarian state after the socialist revolution."[16]

Lenin emphasized in State and Revolution that he was not a "utopian," that he did not offer any fantastic visions of the future of socialism in Russia. Despite his disclaimers, however, he betrayed an extremely optimistic notion of what political and social organization would be like after the proletariat destroyed the autocratic state. Lenin envisioned a society in which administrative functions were so simplified and systematized that any literate person would be able to perform them. It would be necessary only to "supervise and record, know the four rules of arithmatic, and issue appropriate receipts."[17]

Lenin saw the post-revolutionary society as a real community in which "the whole of society will have become a

single office and a single factory with equality of labor
and pay."[18] The administration of this community would be
spontaneous and voluntary. All members of the society would
be disinterested yet dedicated and public-spirited citizens.
Abuse of governing institutions (or any sort of "excess"
whatsoever) would be dealt with immediately by independent
public initiative.

> . . . No special machine, no special apparatus
> of suppression is needed, for this [stopping
> of excesses]; this will be done by the armed
> people themselves, as simply as any crowd of
> civilized people, even in modern society, in-
> terferes to put a stop to a scuffle or to pre-
> vent a woman from being assaulted.[19]

And all this is only what Lenin thought the first
stage of communist society would be like immediately after
the revolution. In the higher stage, there would be no state
of any kind.[20]

It is a measure of Lenin's millenarian conception
of change that he both envisioned an ideal society in the
near future and could propose no way of achieving it other
than by a virtually magical act of destruction. Apart from
razing Russia's political and social institutions to the
ground, Lenin did not have a positive program for political
construction. He did not suggest what specific changes were
necessary or what new institutions should be created.

Lenin took advantage of the notion that "one must not
build utopias" in order to avoid the necessity of making concrete plans for that time when the working class revolution
had completed its destruction of the old regime. Indeed,

Lenin seemed to want revolution simply for the sake of destruction (that was the whole point of <u>State and Revolution</u>)
as if the elimination of the evil, bourgeois world were sufficient to allow the working class to spontaneously create
the new world of socialism.

In is this apocalyptic conception of revolution that
reveals the similarity in spirit between Lenin and a religious millenarian. Lenin looked upon Russian society as a
prophet might view a city that has turned its back on God.
He treated his contemporary world as something so irredem-
iably evil that it could not be moderated or transformed,
and he considered society's evilness so inherently corrupting that it could not be compromised with or dealt with
other than with fire and brimstone. Lenin's summons to revolution had the same significance as the Christian chiliastic
Day of Judgement: once the evil of the world is destroyed
in a universal cataclysm, goodness will automatically be
allowed to flourish. Thus Lenin felt it unnecessary to offer
any plans for the future. His idea of revolution was founded
upon the faith that good would naturally and inevitably follow the elimination of evil.

Lenin's considerable political acumen--knowing when
the Bolsheviks could successfully assume power, convincing
his party leadership to actually stage an insurrection, and
directing the young Soviet government during its infancy--
might seem to argue against any apocalyptic, visionary qualities in his personality. There is no denying that Lenin was

a political realist with a fine sense of the balance of
power in Russia in 1917.

Nevertheless, if Lenin had been no more than a political realist and successful strategist, there is no reason
why he should not have excercised his organizational and
leadership skills in the legal political arena. Lenin's
qualities as a politician are really irrelevant to the question of his millenarian personality. A man of Lenin's political acumen would have risen to the heights of Russia's
political arena whether he was a monarchist, an Octobrist,
a Kadet, or a Socialist-Revolutionary. The point, of course,
is not how good his political judgement was, but rather the
goals toward which Lenin excercised that judgement.

Lenin passionately and single-mindedly dedicated his
life to the violent overthrow of the existing government in
Russia in the belief that socialist society would inevitably
arise from such a destructive revolution. Lenin concerned
himself with party organization, strategy, and tactics because he was politically talented. But the fact of his political effectiveness in the real world should not conceal the
fact that Lenin's vision of the nature of the world and the
means of transforming it were in fact identical with the
beliefs of the millenarian Bolsheviks.

Both Lenin and the God-builders believed that human
thought and will were independent of material causality.
They believed that compromise with the status quo was impossible, and that the revolution was the necessary prelude to

the almost magical birth of an ideal new world. These Bolsheviks differed only in their realms of endeavor. Gorky
wrote revolutionary novels. Lunacharsky wrote essays on religious socialism. Bogdanov build a system of philosophy.
Lenin organized a revolutionary party.

The God-builders were artists and philosophers whose
contribution to the revolution was literary and theoretical.
Lenin's interests and genius lay in political organization;
he combined the personality of a lawyer with the spirit of a
chiliast. His life work was to embody the millenarian conception of revolution in a practical, organizational form.

NOTES TO THE AFTERWORD

[1]M. Gorky, Days with Lenin (London: Martin Lawrence, Ltd., n.d.), p. 26.

[2]V. I. Lenin, "An Era of Reforms," CW, vol. 6, p. 515.

[3]Ibid., p. 506.

[4]Two Tactics, p. 100.

[5]V. I. Lenin, "A Tactical Program for the Unity Congress," CW, vol. 10, p. 158.

[6]V. I. Lenin, "Once Again About the Duma Cabinet," CW, vol. 11, p. 69.

[7]Ibid., pp. 69-70.

[8]Ibid., p. 72.

[9]V. I. Lenin, "Telegram to Bolsheviks Leaving for Russia," CW, vol. 24, p. 299.

[10]V. I. Lenin, "First Letter from Afar," CW, vol. 23, p. 306.

[11]V. I. Lenin, "Fifth Letter from Afar," CW, vol. 23, p. 341.

[12]V. I. Lenin, "Letters on Tactics," CW, vol. 24, p. 50.

[13]Ibid.

[14]V. I. Lenin, State and Revolution, CW, vol. 25, p. 390.

[15]Ibid., p. 393.

[16]Ibid., pp. 401-2.

[17]Ibid., p. 478.

[18]Ibid., p. 479.

[19]Ibid., p. 469.

[20]Ibid., p. 479.

REFERENCES

REFERENCES

Akademiia Nauk SSSR, Institut Mirovoi Literatury. Letopis'
zhizni i tvorchestva A. M. Gor'kogo. 7 vols. Moscow:
Akademiia Nauk SSSR, 1958.

Baron, Samuel H. Plekhanov, The Father of Russian Marxism.
Stanford: Stanford University Press, 1963.

Berdiaev, Nicolas. Dream and Reality. New York: MacMillan
Company, 1951.

_____. "Subjectivism and Objectivism." Russian Philosophy,
pp. 149-156. Edited by J. M. Eadie, J. P. Scanlan,
and M. B. Zeldin. Chicago: Quadrangle Books, 1965.
Vol. 3.

_____. Sub specie aeternitatis: opyty filosofskie, sots-
ial'nye i literaturnye. St. Petersburg: Izdanie
M. V. Pirozhkova, 1907.

Bogdanov, A. Empiriomonism. 2nd ed. 3 vols. St. Petersburg:
S. Dorovatovskago i A. Charushnikova, 1905.

_____. Filosofiia zhivogo opyta. St. Petersburg: Izdanie
M. I. Semenova, n.d.

_____. Inzhener Menni. 3rd ed. Petrograd: Tovarishchestvo
Khudozhestvennoi Pechati, 1908.

_____. Iz psikhologii obshchestva. 2nd ed. St. Petersburg:
Elektropechatnia tovarishchestva "Delo," 1906.

_____. Krasnaia zvezda. St. Petersburg: Tovarishchestvo
Khudozhestvennoi Pechati, 1908.

_____. Kul'turnye zadachi nashego vremeni. Moscow: Iz-
danie S. Dorovatovskago i A. Charushnikova, 1911.

_____. Nauka ob obshchestvennoi soznanii. Moscow: Knigo-
Izdatel'stvo Pisatelei v Moskve, n.d.

_____. Novyi mir. Moscow: Izdanie S. Dorovatovskago i A.
Charushnikova, 1905.

_____. O proletarskoi kul'ture. Leningrad, Moscow: Iz-
datel'skoe Tovarishchestvo "Kniga," 1924.

_____. Osnovy istoricheskago vzgliada na prirodu. St. Petersburg: Izdanie Spb. Aktsionern. Obshchestva Pech. Dela "Izdatel'," 1899.

_____. Prikliucheniia odnoi filosofskoi shkoly. St. Petersburg: Izdatel'skoe tovarishchestvo "Znanie," 1908.

_____. "Proletariat v bor'be za sotsializm." Vpered, no. 1 (1910), pp. 1-8.

_____. "Sotsializm v nastoiashchem." Vpered, no. 2 (1911), pp. 59-71.

_____. Sovremennoe polozhenie i zadachi partii. Paris: Izdanie Gruppy "Vpered," 1910.

Britikov, A. F. Russkii sovetskii fantasticheskii roman. Leningrad: Izdanie "Nauka," 1970.

Deiateli revoliutsionnogo dvizheniia v Rossii. Moscow: Izdatel'stvo Vsesoiuznogo Obshchestva Politicheskikh Katorzhan i Ssyl'no-poselentsev, 1931. Vol. 5.

Elwood, Ralph Carter, ed. Resolutions and Decisions of the Communist Party of the Soviet Union. Toronto: University of Toronto Press, 1974.

Fitzpatrick, Sheila. The Commissariat of Enlightenment. Cambridge: Cambridge University Press, 1970.

Galerka i Riadovoi. Nashi nedorazumeniia. Geneva: Izdanie Avtorov, 1904.

Gorbunov, V. V. "Iz istorii kul'turno-posvetitel'noi deiatel'-nosti petrogradskikh bol'shevikov v period podgotov-koi Oktiabria." Voprosy Istorii KPSS, no. 2, 1967, pp. 25-35.

Gorky, M. The Confession. New York: Frederick A. Stokes, 1916.

_____. Days with Lenin. London: Martin Lawrence, Ltd., n.d.

_____. Seven Plays of Maksim Gorky. New Haven: Yale University Press, 1945.

Institut Marksizma-Leninizma pri TsK KPSS. Istoriia Communisticheskoi Partii Sovetskogo Soiuza. Moscow: Gosudarstvennoe Izdatel'stvo Politicheskoi Literatury, 1966.

_____. Tretii S"ezd RSDRP, Protokoly. Moscow: Gosudarstvennoe Izdatel'stvo Politicheskoi Literatury, 1959.

Kirillov, Vladimir. "Zheleznyi messiia." Proletarskaia Kul'-
    tura, no. 2, 1918, p. 26.

[Lebedev]-Polianskii, V. [P. I.]. "Pod znamia 'Proletkul'ta.'"
    Proletarskaia Kul'tura, no. 1, 1918, pp. 3-7.

Lebedev-Polianskii, P. I., ed. Protokoly pervoi vserossiiskoi
    konferentsii proletarskikh kul'turno-prosvetitel'nykh
    organizatsii. Moscow: "Proletarskaia Kul'tura," 1918.

Lenin, V. I. Collected Works. 45 vols. Moscow: Progress Pub-
    lishers, 1960-1970.

Liadov, M. N. Iz zhizni partii v 1903-1907 godakh. Moscow:
    Gosudarstvennoe Izdatel'stvo Politicheskoi Literatury,
    1956.

Literaturnyi raspad. 2nd ed. 2 vols. St. Petersburg: Izdat-
    el'stvo "T-va Izdatel'skoe Biuro," 1908.

Livshits, S. Partiinye universitety podpol'ia. Moscow: Iz-
    datel'stvo Vsesoiuznogo Obshchestva Politkatorzhan
    i Ssyl'no-poselentsev, 1929.

Lunacharskii, A. V. "Buduscshee religii." Obrazovanie, no. 10,
    1907, pp. 1-25.

    _____. Etiudy kriticheskie i polemicheskie. Moscow: Iz-
    danie Zhurnala "Pravda," 1905.

    _____. Otkliki zhizni. St. Petersburg: Izdatel'stvo O. N.
    Popovoi, 1906.

    _____. Religiia i sotsializm. 2 vols. St. Petersburg:
    Izd. Shipovnik, 1908.

    _____. Sobranie sochinenii: kritika, estetika, kniga-
    vvedenie. Moscow: "Khudozhestvennaia Literatura,"
    1967. 7 vols.

    _____. Velikii perevorot. St. Petersburg: Izdatel'stvo
    Z. I. Grzhebina, 1919.

Novgorodtsev, P. I., ed. Problemy idealizma. Moscow: Izdanie
    Moskovskago Psikhologicheskago Obshchestva, 1902.

Ocherki po filosofii marksizma. St. Petersburg: n.p., 1908.

Ocherki realisticheskago mirovozreniia. St. Petersburg: S.
    Dorovatovskago i A. Charushnikova, 1905.

Organizatsionnoe biuro. "K sozyvu vserossiiskoi konferentsii
    kul'turno-prosvetitel'nykh rabochikh organizatsii."
    Proletarskaia Kul'tura, no. 1, 1918, pp. 24-31.

Ostroukhova, K. "Gruppa 'Vpered.'" Proletarskaia Revoliuts-
    iia, no. 1, 1925, pp. 198-220.

_____. "Otzovisty i ul'timatisty." Proletarskaia Revo-
    liutsiia, no. 6, 1924, pp. 14-32.

Otchet pervoi sotsial-demokraticheskoi propagandistsko-agi-
    tatorskoi shkoly dlia rabochikh. Paris: "Soiuz,"
    1910.

Otchet vtoroi sotsial-demokraticheskoi propagandistsko-agi-
    tatorskoi shkoly dlia rabochikh. Paris: Izdanie
    Gruppy "Vpered," 1911.

Protokoly sovershcheniia rasshirennoi redaktsii "Proletarii."
    N.p.: Partizdat, 1934.

Reed, John, Ten Days that Shook the World. New York: Signet,
    1967.

Struve, Gleb. Russian Literature under Lenin and Stalin,
    1917-1953. Norman: University of Oklahoma Press,
    1971.

Trifonov, N. A. "A. V. Lunacharskii i M. Gor'kii." In
    M. Gor'kii i ego sovremenniki. Ed. K. D. Muratova.
    Leningrad: "Nauka," 1968, pp. 118-151.

_____. "Soratniki (Lunacharskii i Gor'kii posle oktiabria)."
    Russkaia Literatura, no. 1, 1968, pp. 23-48.

V. I. Lenin i A. M. Gor'kii: pis'ma, vospominaniia, doku-
    menty. Moscow: "Nauka," 1969.

Voitynskii, n. "O gruppe 'Vpered' (1909-1917)." Proletarskaia
    Revoliutsiia, no. 12, 1929, pp. 59-119.

Vol'skii, Stanislav A. Filosofiia bor'by. Moscow: Knigaiz-
    datel'stvo "Slovo," 1909.

_____. "O proletarskoi kul'ture." Vpered, no. 2, 1911,
    pp. 71-82.

Wolfe, Bertram D. The Bridge and the Abyss. New York:
    Praeger, 1967.